Teacher's Resource Book

MATH*thematics*

Book 2

The STEM Project

McDougal Littell
A HOUGHTON MIFFLIN COMPANY
Evanston, Illinois • Boston • Dallas

McDougal Littell: www.mcdougallittell.com
Middle School Mathematics: www.mlmath.com

Acknowledgments

Writers

The authors of *Middle Grades Math Thematics, Books 1–3,* wish to thank the following writers for their contributions to the Teacher's Resource Books for the *Math Thematics* program: **Mary Buck, Roslyn Denny, Jean Howard, Sallie Morse, Patrick Runkel, Thomas Sanders-Garrett, Christine Tuckerman.**

Photography

Front Cover Doug Milner/Uniphoto Picture Agency (t); Joe McBride/Tony Stone Images (b); **5-1** Doug Milner/Uniphoto Picture Agency; **6-1** Joe McBride/Tony Stone Images; **Back Cover** Joe McBride/Tony Stone Images.

The STEM Project

Middle Grades Math Thematics is based on the field-test version of the STEM Project curriculum. The STEM Project was supported in part by the

 NATIONAL SCIENCE FOUNDATION

under Grant No. ESI-9150114. Opinions expressed in *Middle Grades Math Thematics* are those of the authors and not necessarily those of the National Science Foundation.

ISBN: 0-395-89471-9
1 2 3 4 5 6 7 8 9 10–B–03 02 01 00 99 98

About the Teacher's Resource Book

This Resource Book contains all of the teaching support that you need to teach *Math Thematics*, Book 2, Modules 5 and 6. This teaching support includes the following material:

Spanish Glossary

A Spanish translation of the Glossary from the pupil textbook in blackline master form. The Spanish Glossary is located at the beginning of the Teacher's Resource Book for Modules 1 and 2.

Teaching Commentary

Planning the Module Contains a Module Overview and charts showing Module Objectives, Topic Spiraling, Topic Integration, Materials needed, and Teacher Support Materials. Also included are a Guide for Assigning Homework for regular and block schedules, Classroom Ideas, and a Home Involvement Math Gazette. For more information on the Guide for Assigning Homework and pacing, see pages vii-viii.

Teaching Suggestions Complete and comprehensive teaching suggestions for each section of the module. These include a Section Planner, a Section Overview, Materials List, Section Objectives, Assessment Options, Classroom Examples, Closure Questions, a Section Quiz, and notes on Customizing Instruction. Each page features a two-page pupil edition reduced facsimile for easy visual reference to the pupil textbook.

Blackline Masters

Labsheets Blackline masters used in conjunction with various Exploration questions to present data and extend the scope of the Exploration. Answers are provided at point of use in the annotated Teacher's Edition.

Extended Exploration Solution Guide
A comprehensive discussion of the Extended Exploration in the pupil textbook, including how to assess student responses and performance.

Alternate Extended Exploration
An extended exploration that can be substituted for the one in the pupil textbook, including teaching notes and assessment procedures.

Warm-Up Exercises and Quick Quizzes
A page featuring the Warm-Up Exercises from the annotated Teacher's Edition and the Section Quizzes from the Teaching Suggestions of this Resource Book. Each page is printed in large easy-to-read type and can be used to create an overhead visual or used as a hand-out. Answers for the exercises and the quiz are provided at the bottom of each page.

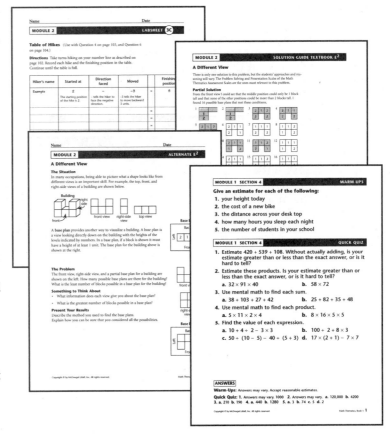

Practice and Applications One to two pages of additional practice for each section of the module. Answers are provided in the Answer section of this Resource Book.

Study Guide Two to three pages of Study Guide for each section of the module. These Study Guide pages feature key concepts, worked-out examples, exercises, and spiral review. They can be used for review and reteaching. Answers are provided in the Answer section of this Resource Book.

Technology Activity A technology activity related to the technology page of each module. Answers are provided in the Answer section of this Resource Book.

Assessment Assessment options include a mid-module quiz and two module tests, Forms A and B. Answers are provided in the Answer section of this Resource Book.

Standardized Assessment A page of standardized multiple-choice questions for each module. Answers are provided in the Answer section of this Resource Book.

Module Performance Assessment A Performance Assessment task for each module. Answers are provided in the Answer section of this Resource Book.

Answers Complete answers to all blackline masters.

Cumulative Test with Answers A cumulative test on both the modules of this Resource Book. Answers to the test follow immediately.

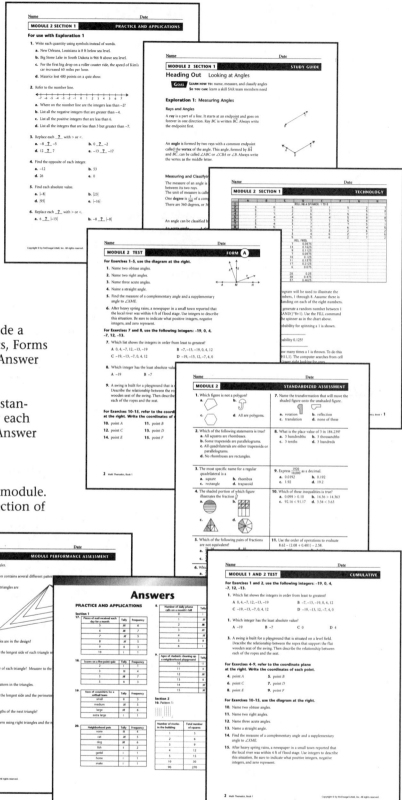

Table of Contents

Pacing and Assigning Homework

Pacing Chart

The Pacing Chart below shows the number of days allotted for each of the three courses: a Core Course, an Extended Course, and a Block Scheduling Course. The Core and Extended Courses require 140 days, and the Block Scheduling Course, 70 days. The time frames include the Module Projects, the Extended Explorations (E^2), and time for review and assessment.

Module	1	2	3	4	5	6	7	8
Core Course	18	16	21	19	17	18	17	14
Extended Course	18	16	21	19	17	18	17	14
Block Scheduling	9	8	11	10	8	9	8	7

Core Course

The Core Course is intended for students who enter with typical, or about average, mathematical skills. The daily assignment provides students with about 20–30 minutes of homework a night taken from appropriate Practice and Application (PA) exercises. Exercises range from straightforward skill practice, to applications that require reasoning, problem solving, and making connections across mathematical strands. The assignments include all the exercises suggested for use as embedded assessment. Each section's Spiral Review (SR) is included, as are all Reflecting on the Section (ROS) problems. Because of all the elements to be covered, assignments for the one-day sections may take more time. Also, sometimes a lengthy Reflecting on the Section problem (or other essential exercise) may cause an assignment to run longer. These problems have been denoted with a star (*). In such cases, teachers may want to spread the assignment out over more than one day, or may wish to provide class time for students to complete the work.

Extended Course

The Extended Course is designed for students who enter with strong or above average mathematical skills. Daily assignments cover all the essential material in the Core Course, including the embedded assessment exercises, the Spiral Review (SR), and the Reflecting on the Section (ROS) problems. Assignments also contain more difficult problems, including all the Challenge (Chal) and Extension (Ext) exercises. As in the Core Course, each assignment is designed to be completed in about 20–30 minutes. Some Extension or Reflecting on the Section problems may cause assignments to run long. These longer problems are denoted by a star (*).

Block Scheduling Course

The Block Scheduling course is intended for schools that use longer periods, typically 90-minute classes, for instruction. The course covers all eight modules. The assignments range from straightforward application of the material to exercises involving higher-order thinking skills. Daily assignments are designed to provide about 40–50 minutes of homework, and to cover all the essential material in the Core Course, including the embedded assessment exercises, the Spiral Review (SR), and Reflecting on the Section (ROS).

Guide for Assigning Homework

The Guide for Assigning Homework appears on each module's opening pages. The first chart suggests Core and Extended Assignments. The second chart offers assignments and pacing for Block Scheduling.

Regular Scheduling (45 min class period)

Section/ P&A Pages	Core Assignment	Extended Assignment	exercises to note		
			Additional Practice/Review	Open-ended Problems	Special Problems
1 pp. 465–470	**Day 1:** 1–3, 5–8, SR 23–25	1–3, Chal 4, 5–8, SR 23–25	EP, p. 470		
	Day 2: 9–11, 14–17	9–11, 14–17	PA 12, 13, 18–20		
	Day 3: 21, *ROS 22, SR 26–32	21, *ROS 22, SR 26–32, Ext 33		ROS 22; Mod Proj 3; St Sk, p. 470	Mod Proj 1–3
2 pp. 480–484	**Day 1:** 1–9, SR 25–32	1–9, SR 25–32	EP, p. 483		
	Day 2: 10–14, 18–20, ROS 24	10–14, 18–20, Chal 23, ROS 24	PA 15–17, 21, 22	Std Test, p. 483; E^2, p. 484	PA 19; E^2, p. 484

Additional Practice/Review
Each section contains additional support and practice for the objectives:
- **Extra Skill Practice (EP)** A page for each section, including exercises for each day and a set of Standardized Testing or Study Skills exercises.
- **Practice and Application (PA)** Exercises beyond the 20–30 minute homework period, covering the same skills and concepts as the Core Assignment.
- **Toolbox (TB)** Teaching and practice for pre-book skills applied in this section or in upcoming sections.

Open-ended Problems
Included in this category are exercises where students generate examples, create designs, or use original ideas. The Extended Exploration (E^2) from each module appears here. It is designed to provide a rich problem solving experience, with multiple approaches or solutions. The listing may include Reflecting on the Section (ROS), Career Connection (Career), Module Project (Mod Proj), Study Skills (St Sk), or Standardized Testing (Std Test) exercises, as well as other Practice and Application (PA) exercises where appropriate.

Special Problems Exercises in this category require extra time or additional materials, such as a calculator or a newspaper. All Extended Exploration (E^2) and Module Project (Mod Proj) activities are listed, as well as many Practice and Application (PA) exercises labeled Research, Create Your Own, or Home Involvement. (The E^2 and the final Module Project questions are listed with the sections they follow.) Although Special Problems are not included in the Core Assignment, they are accessible to all students. Teachers may allot class time or extra days for students to complete them.

Block Scheduling (90 min class period)

	Day 1	Day 2	Day 3	Day 4	Day 5	Day 6	
Teach	Sec 1 Expl 1–2	Sec 1 Expl 3; Sec 2 Expl 1	Sec 2 Expl 2; Sec 3 Expl 1	Sec 3 Expl 2–3	Sec 4	Sec 5	Allow 2 days review/assess/projects
Apply/ Assess (P&A)	Sec 1: 1–3, 5–11, 14–17, SR 23–25	Sec 1: 21, *ROS 22, SR 26–32 Sec 2: 1–9, SR 25–32	Sec 2: 10–14, 18–20, *ROS 24 Sec 3: 1–8, SR 23–26	Sec 3: 9–13, 17–20, ROS 22, SR 27–32	Sec 4: 1–6, 10–14, ROS 16, SR 17–26	Sec 5: 1–4, 6–8, 10–12, 16–18, ROS 20, SR 21–29	
Yearly Pacing	**Mod 7:** 8 days		**Mods 1–7:** 63 days		**Remaining:** 7 days	**Total:** 70 days	

MIDDLE GRADES

MATHThematics

MODULE 5

Recreation

- **Planning and Teaching Suggestions, p. 5-8**
- **Labsheets, p. 5-43**
- **Extended Explorations, p. 5-49**
- **Blackline Masters, p. 5-52**

RECREATION

Module Overview

Students will examine the mathematics related to recreational activities, such as running, riding roller coasters, bungee jumping, movie viewing, and playing basketball. Skills are developed in the areas of proportion, percents, collecting and analyzing data, and determining the probability of events.

Module Objectives

Section	Objectives	NCTM Standards
1	◆ Use a proportion and mental math to write a rate as a unit rate. ◆ Recognize and write rates. ◆ Find the mean, median, mode, and range of a data set and choose the best average. ◆ Make and interpret a stem-and-leaf plot. ◆ Interpret a histogram.	1, 2, 3, 4, 10
2	◆ Use cross products to solve proportions. ◆ Use proportions to solve problems. ◆ Make and interpret a scatter plot. ◆ Sketch a fitted line to make predictions. ◆ Interpret a box-and-whisker plot.	1, 2, 3, 4, 9, 10
3	◆ Estimate percents using common fraction/percent equivalents or a percent bar model. ◆ Find a percent using a proportion. ◆ Estimate a percent of a number. ◆ Use a proportion to find a percent of a number. ◆ Use a proportion to find the whole amount when a part and a percent are given.	1, 2, 3, 4, 7
4	◆ Write ratios in fraction, decimal, and percent forms. ◆ Use mental math or "nice" fractions to write ratios as percents. ◆ Use mental math or "nice" fractions to estimate percents. ◆ Use experimental probabilities represented as percents to make predictions. ◆ Use a tree diagram or an area model to find probabilities in a multistage experiment.	1, 2, 3, 4, 5, 7, 11

Topic Spiraling

Section	Connections to Prior and Future Concepts
1	Section 1 uses data to discuss ratio, rate, unit rate, proportions, mean, median, mode, range, and stem-and-leaf plots. These topics are introduced in Modules 3 and 6 of Book 1. Histograms are introduced as an extension of bar graphs in Module 1, and are revisited in Module 8 of Book 3.
2	Section 2 reviews solving proportions using cross products from Module 6 of Book 1. The topic is applied to percent in Section 3 and to similar figures in Module 6. Scatter plots with fitted lines are used to represent and make predictions from data. These topics are introduced in Module 6 of Book 1, and reviewed in Modules 1 and 8 of Book 3. Box-and-whisker plots are interpreted for the first time. These plots are made in Module 7.
3	Section 3 elaborates on the meaning of percent explored in Module 1. Percents are estimated using "nice" fractions and percent bars. Proportions are used to find a percent of a number. Percent concepts and these first two cases of percent are covered in Modules 3, 4, 6, and 8 of Book 1. Section 3 introduces finding a whole when a part and a percent are given. Module 7 covers percents greater than 100%, percent of change, and using equations to find percents.
4	Section 4 extends work begun in Modules 3 and 4 of Book 1 to include three decimal places when converting among fraction, decimal, and percent forms of ratios. Probability and tree diagrams from Modules 1 and 3 of Book 2 are applied. Probabilities expressed as percents are used to make predictions. Tree diagrams and area models are used to find probabilities in multistage experiments. Further work with geometric probability is found in Module 6.

Integration

Mathematical Connections	1	2	3	4
algebra (including patterns and functions)	314, 321, 322, 324	329–330, 336–338, 341, 343	352, 355, 356	371
data analysis, probability, discrete math	315–325	331–343	350–357	361–373
Interdisciplinary Connections and Applications				
social studies and geography	321, 323	343		
reading and language arts	312			
science	321, 322, 323	326, 329, 337–338		
health, physical education, and sports	313–319, 321, 323	331, 332, 343		358–366, 368–369, 371
recreation		327–329, 334–335, 339, 340	344, 350, 354	
buildings, communication, jobs, money, surveys	322	338–339, 342	353, 356	355, 373

Guide for Assigning Homework

Regular Scheduling (45 min class period)

Section/ P&A Pages	Core Assignment	Extended Assignment	Additional Practice/Review	Open-ended Problems	Special Problems
			exercises to note		
1 pp. 321–326	**Day 1:** 1–12, SR 19–21	1–12, Chal 13, SR 19–21	EP, p. 325		
	Day 2: 14–16	14–16	TB, p. 595		
	Day 3: 17, ROS 18, SR 22–30	17, ROS 18, SR 22–30		St Sk, p. 325; E^2, p. 326	E^2, p. 326
2 pp. 337–343	**Day 1:** 1–11, SR 19–21	1–11, SR 19–21	EP, p. 343		
	Day 2: 12, 14, 15, SR 22–24	12, Chal 13, 14, 15, SR 22–24			
	Day 3: 16, 17, ROS 18, SR 25–27	16, 17, ROS 18, SR 25–27		PA 16d; Mod Proj 1–2; Std Test, p. 343	Mod Proj 1–2
3 pp. 353–357	**Day 1:** 1–7, SR 27–32	1–7, SR 27–32	EP, p. 357		
	Day 2: 8–14, SR 33–35	8–14, SR 33–35			
	Day 3: 15–21, 23, 25, ROS 26	15, 17, 20, 21, Chal 22, 23, 25, ROS 26, *Ext 36–38, Chal 39	PA 24	PA 24, ROS 26	Mod Proj 3–6
4 pp. 368–373	**Day 1:** 1–12	1–12	EP, p. 372		
	Day 2: 13, 14, 16, 17, SR 26–29	13, 14, Chal 15, 16, 17, SR 26–29			
	Day 3: 18–23, ROS 25	18–23, Chal 24, ROS 25	Career 30–31		Mod Proj 7–11
Review/ Assess	Review and Assess (PE), Quick Quizzes (TRB), Mid-Module Quiz (TRB), Module Tests— Forms A and B (TRB), Standardized Assessment (TRB)				Allow 5 days
Enrich/ Assess	E^2 (PE) and Alternate E^2 (TRB), Module Project (PE), Module Performance Assessment (TRB)				
Yearly Pacing	**Mod 5:** 17 days	**Mods 1–5:** 91 days	**Remaining:** 49 days		**Total:** 140 days

Key: PA = Practice & Application; ROS = Reflecting on the Section; SR = Spiral Review; TB = Toolbox; EP = Extra Skill Practice; Ext = Extension; *more time

Block Scheduling (90 min class period)

	Day 1	Day 2	Day 3	Day 4	Day 5	Day 6	
Teach	Sec 1 Expl 1–2	Sec 1 Expl 3; Sec 2 Expl 1	Sec 2 Expl 2–3	Sec 3 Expl 1–2	Sec 3 Expl 3; Sec 4 Expl 1	Sec 4 Expl 2–3	Allow 2 days review/assess/projects
Apply/ Assess (P&A)	Sec 1: 1–12, 14–16, SR 19–21	Sec 1: 17, ROS 18, SR 22–30 Sec 2: 1–11, SR 19–21	Sec 2: 12, 14–17, ROS 18, SR 22–27	Sec 3: 1–14, SR 27–35	Sec 3: 15–21, 23, 25, ROS 26 Sec 4: 1–12	Sec 4: 13, 14, 16–23, *ROS 25, SR 26–29	
Yearly Pacing	**Mod 5:** 8 days		**Mods 1–5:** 46 days		**Remaining:** 24 days	**Total:** 70 days	

Materials List

Section	Materials
1	No materials required
2	Labsheets 2A and 2B, rubber band, 50 pennies, large and small paper clips, tape, lined paper, metric ruler, small plastic bag, uncooked spaghetti
3	Labsheet 3A, frequency table from *Setting the Stage*
4	Large paper cup, cotton ball, masking tape, ruler, results from Questions 6–7, graph paper; for Review and Assessment: Review and Assessment Labsheet

Support Materials in this Resource Book

Section	Practice	Study Guide	Assessment	Enrichment
1	Section 1	Section 1	Quick Quiz	Alternate Extended Exploration
2	Section 2	Section 2	Quick Quiz	Technology Activity
3	Section 3	Section 3	Quick Quiz Mid-Module Quiz	
4	Section 4	Section 4	Quick Quiz	
Review/ Assess	Sections 1–4		Module Tests Forms A and B Standardized Assessment Module Performance Assessment	

Classroom Ideas

Bulletin Boards:
- pictures and articles of teenagers participating in recreational activities
- brochures from theme parks with maps
- pictures of and articles on favorite athletes with season statistics

Student Work Displays:
- free-throw activity results
- zoo tours from the E^2
- data displays from the Module Project

Interest Center:
- games involving probability

Visitors/Field Trips:
- statistician, marathon runner
- athletic event

Technology:
- Module 5 Technology Activity in TRB for PE p. 333
- computer graphing software

The Math Gazette
Recreation

MODULE 5

Sneak Preview!

Over the next three weeks in our mathematics class, we will be developing proportion and percent skills, collecting and analyzing data, and determining probability of events while completing a thematic unit on Recreation. Some of the topics we will be discussing are:

✗ use of free time

✗ walking rates

✗ visits to zoos and amusement parks

✗ movie ratings

✗ sports activities

Ask Your Student

How can you estimate distances using your running rate? (Sec. 1)

How are audience approval ratings for movies determined? (Sec. 3)

How can an athlete's performance be predicted using statistics? (Sec. 4)

Connections

Literature:
Students will read an excerpt from *Zanboomer*, by R. R. Knudson. In the story, a high school student, Zan Hagen, takes up cross-country running. In the excerpt, her coach helps her train for a three mile race. Your students might enjoy reading this book or others about young people training for sports events.

Science:
Students use rates to determine the amounts of food necessary for animals in a zoo. Your student

may be interested in finding other rates and statistics that are used in the study of animals by veterinarians, biologists, and zoologists. Students also explore the relationship between weight and the stretch of a rubber band to model bungee jumping.

Physical Education:
Running rates and basketball statistics are used to study percents and ratios. Your student may want to explore the statistics related to his or her other leisure time activities.

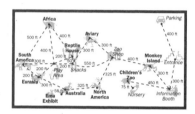

E² Project

Following Section 1, students will have approximately one week to complete the E² project, *What's for Lunch?* Students will use a map showing the paths in a zoo and a table showing feeding times for the animals to create possible tours for zoo visitors.

Recreation

Section Title	Mathematics Your Student Will Be Learning	Activities
1: Run for Your Life	◆ using ratios, rates, and unit rates ◆ solving proportions ◆ choosing the best average ◆ analyzing data using stem-and-leaf plots and histograms	◆ use visual displays to represent and analyze data ◆ use a map to design tours for feeding times at a zoo
2: Just for Fun	◆ solving proportions by finding cross products ◆ making scatter plots and drawing fitted lines ◆ using box-and-whisker plots to analyze and compare data	◆ investigate how the stretch of a rubber band increases as weight is added ◆ use graphing technology to make scatter plots ◆ create survey questions and conduct a survey using a random sample
3: You Be the Critic	◆ estimating percents ◆ using a proportion to find what percent one number is of another ◆ using a proportion to find a part of the whole amount or to find the whole amount when the percent is known	◆ conduct a survey to determine students' ratings of movies or television shows ◆ combine data and compare the results for the survey they conducted in Section 2
4: Make Every Shot Count	◆ writing fractions as decimals or percents ◆ using percents to make predictions ◆ using tree diagrams to find theoretical probabilities of multistage events	◆ simulate shooting free throws to determine an average ◆ shade a 10 x 10 grid to find the probability of a multistage event ◆ choose a visual display for the results of the survey in Sections 2 and 3

Activities to do at Home

◆ Plan a trip or family vacation using highway maps or flight information. Make a map to show possible routes, including stops, travel times, or distances. (After Sec. 1)

◆ Look for rates, ratios, and percents around your home. You might want to explore gas and electric meters, food labels, the mail, newspapers, magazines, or television. (After Sec. 3)

◆ Look at the games you have at home and use experimental or theoretical probability to study the game, comparing theoretical and experimental probabilities of dice rolls, spinners, and so on. (After Sec. 4)

Related Topics

You may want to discuss these related topics with your student:

 Participation in individual and team sports

 Entertainment

 Travel

MODULE 5

Section ① Ratios and Data Displays

Section Planner

DAYS FOR MODULE 5

1 2 3 **4 5 6 7 8 9 10 11 12**

SECTION 1

First Day
Setting the Stage, *p. 312*
Exploration 1, *pp. 313–314*

Second Day
Exploration 2, *pp. 315–317*

Third Day
Exploration 3, *pp. 318–319*
Key Concepts, *pp. 319–320*

Block Schedule

Day 1
Setting the Stage, Exploration 1,
Exploration 2

Day 2
Exploration 3, Key Concepts
(Day 2 continues in Sec. 2.)

RESOURCE ORGANIZER

Teaching Resources
• Practice and Applications, Sec. 1
• Study Guide, Sec. 1
• Warm-Up, Sec. 1
• Quick Quiz, Sec. 1

Section Overview

In Section 1, students will explore running times to learn about the relationship between a ratio and a rate. Unit rates are defined, and students will use unit rates to compare rates. They will also learn how a proportion can help them find a unit rate. Students will examine a table of data listing running times to find the mean, median, and mode of the data. They will learn that when data values are spread over a wide range, a stem-and-leaf plot or a histogram may describe the data more effectively than an average value. Students will discuss the significance of clusters and gaps in a data set. They will identify the median and the mode in a stem-and-leaf plot. They will learn the significance of frequencies and intervals in a histogram. They will also recognize that data values are not apparent in a histogram.

It is assumed that students understand mean, median, and mode. Students who require review of these topics may do so on page 595 of the Toolbox exercises.

SECTION OBJECTIVES

Exploration 1
• use a proportion and mental math to write a rate as a unit rate
• recognize and write rates

Exploration 2
• find the mean, median, mode, and range of a data set and choose the best average
• make and interpret a stem-and-leaf plot

Exploration 3
• interpret a histogram

ASSESSMENT OPTIONS

Checkpoint Questions
• Question 9 on p. 314
• Question 18 on p. 317

Embedded Assessment
• For a list of embedded assessment exercises see p. 5-13.

Performance Task/Portfolio
★Exercise 13 on p. 322 (challenge)
• Exercise 14 on p. 322 (writing)
• Exercise 16 on p. 323
• Exercise 18 on p. 324 (visual thinking)
★Extended Exploration on p. 326

★= a problem solving task that can be assessed using the Assessment Scales

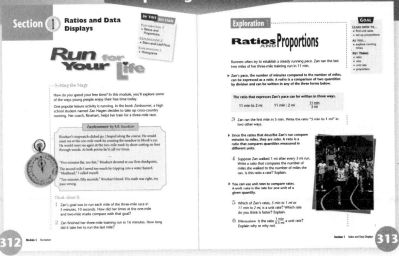

Setting the Stage

MOTIVATE

You may want to read the excerpt on page 312 out loud or have a student read it out loud. Some students will have experience in track or cross country or running for conditioning, and may be able to share how they have used rates and other mathematics in their running experiences. Point out that Zan's mile pace is very fast for high school, and that she would be a championship-level athlete. In fact, if she could run at her shorter-distance rate of 5 minutes 10 seconds the whole 26 mile length of a marathon, she would shatter the women's world record!

Exploration 1

PLAN

Classroom Management

Exploration 1 can be completed in small groups or individually. You may wish to address the discussion-oriented *Questions 6* and *7* as a whole class to explore a wider variety of responses. You will want to pay special attention to the key terms in this Exploration to make sure students understand and can differentiate them. You may want to have students note the key terms in their journals. Make sure that students note the connection between equivalent fractions and using proportions with rates and ratios. Frequently use all three forms of expressing a ratio so that students will be able to set up proportions correctly when solving problems.

GUIDE

Developing Math Concepts

For *Questions 3–5*, make sure that students build the important habit of labeling the unit of measure for each quantity. *Question 4* leads students to identify that a ratio may compare two quantities that share the same units (miles to miles), while a rate compares two quantities with different units (minutes to miles).

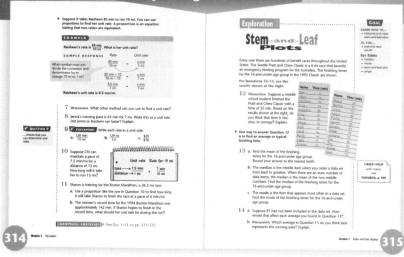

Exploration 1 continued

Developing Math Concepts In the *Example* on page 314, point out to students that when solving proportions, the numerators have the same unit of measure and the denominators have the same unit of measure.

Classroom Examples
Suppose it takes Juan 87 min to run 12 mi. What is Juan's unit rate?

Answer:

Rate		Unit rate
$\dfrac{87 \text{ min}}{12 \text{ mi}}$	$=$	$\dfrac{x \text{ min}}{1 \text{ mi}}$
$\dfrac{87 \text{ min} \div 12}{12 \text{ mi} \div 12}$	$=$	$\dfrac{x \text{ min}}{1 \text{ mi}}$
$\dfrac{7.25 \text{ min}}{1 \text{ mi}}$	$=$	$\dfrac{x \text{ min}}{1 \text{ mi}}$

Juan's unit rate is 7.25 min/mi.

Common Error For *Question 8*, students who do not label rates may have difficulties knowing "which number goes where" as they try to compare Jenna's and Raisheen's rates.

Checkpoint As students find unit rates for *Question 9*, make certain they can follow the procedure shown in the *Example* on page 314 and can verbally explain the process.

▌ HOMEWORK EXERCISES ▶

See the Suggested Assignment for Day 1 on page 5-13. For Exercise Notes, see page 5-13.

Exploration 2

PLAN

Classroom Management If students are familiar with the concepts of mean, median, and mode, and with stem-and-leaf plots, have students perform Exploration 2 in small groups. Because *Questions 12, 14(b), 17,* and *19* contain many subjective items, you may want to address these questions as a whole class. If students are unfamiliar with the concepts, you may perform the entire Exploration as a whole class, making sure that students can differentiate among the three types of averages discussed. You may want students to use calculators to find the means in *Questions 13(a)* and *14(a)*.

Customizing Instruction

Alternative Approach For *Question 8*, record distances and times for a pace of 9 min/1 mi in a table. Students will be able to see the pattern 9 min/1 mi, 18 min/2 mi, 27 min/3 mi, ..., 63 min/7 mi, ... Explain that the table describes many different equivalent fractions for this rate, including the solution. Some students may then be able to write a rule to find times for other distances (9 × number of miles = number of minutes).

Technology You can help students familiar with a graphing calculator make a table of distances and times and then graph the results with a scatter plot or line plot. A computer spreadsheet display of a scatter plot and line graph created from a table of the distances and times will provide a good visual representation of ratio and proportion for the class. Make sure that students understand how the points are plotted using the two axes. Ask students what pattern they notice about the points plotted (they lie along a line), and how this might help them decide if another fraction is equivalent to the ones represented (the point representing it will also lie on this line).

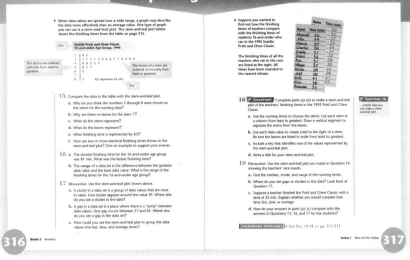

Exploration 2 continued

GUIDE

Developing Math Concepts In *Question 15*, point out to students that because all of the data values from the table on page 315 are given by the stem-and-leaf plot on page 316, you can calculate the mean from the plot. Because the stem-and-leaf plot shown orders the data, it is especially easy to find the median and mode of the data from the plot. For *Question 17*, explain that observing clusters and gaps in data helps give you a mental picture of the data and helps you interpret the data for others.

Checkpoint For *Question 18*, make certain students understand how to complete all parts correctly on their own and that they have recorded the correct plot. When recording the leaves from the original data set, it may be easier for students first to write the leaves for each stem in the order they occur in the data instead of in numerical order. Then they can go back and order the leaves. Have students space the leaves equally, and watch for common errors such as writing a stem more than once, skipping stems when there is no leaf, or placing commas between each leaf.

Classroom Examples
Find the least data value, greatest data value, range, median, and mode using the stem-and-leaf plot below.

Average Speeds of Indianapolis 500 Winners from 1973–1997 (All times are rounded to the nearest mi/h.)

```
13 | 4 9
14 | 3 5 6 8 9 9
15 | 3 4 7 9 9 9
16 | 1 1 1 2 2 2 4 8
17 | 1 6
18 | 6
```

17 | 6 represents 176 mi/h.

Answer: least: 134; greatest: 186; range = 186 – 134 = 52; median: 159; modes: 159, 161, and 162

HOMEWORK EXERCISES

See the Suggested Assignment for Day 2 on page 5-13. For Exercise Notes, see page 5-13.

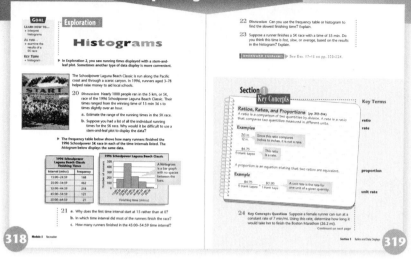

Exploration 3

PLAN

Classroom Management

Exploration 3 is brief, and contains some subtle content, so it is best performed as a whole class. Throughout the Exploration, you will want to help students identify and describe the similarities and differences in both form and use between histograms and stem-and-leaf plots. This should include that if a stem-and-leaf plot is turned 90° counterclockwise, it can be viewed as similar to a histogram, but with the stems representing the intervals.

GUIDE

Developing Math Concepts

For *Question 20*, make sure that students understand that they *could* make a stem-and-leaf plot if they knew each time, but that a frequency table and histogram are much more efficient ways of picturing this much data.

Developing Math Concepts

For the histogram shown on page 318, stress that a bar graph compares numbers of items in categories, while a histogram compares numbers of items in intervals. For this reason, the bars in a bar graph don't touch, but those in a histogram do. For *Question 22*, point out that because you cannot find the slowest or fastest times from the histogram, you can only estimate the range. You can, however, find the *largest possible* range by finding the difference between the farthest right-hand boundary of any bar and the farthest left-hand boundary of any bar.

HOMEWORK EXERCISES

See the Suggested Assignment for Day 3 on page 5-13. For Exercise Notes, see page 5-13.

CLOSE

Closure Question What are some ways to represent data? How do these ways compare?

Sample Response: Give the range, the mean, the median, and the mode, or draw a histogram or a stem-and-leaf plot. The range, the mean, the median, and the mode are numbers, whereas the histogram and the stem-and-leaf plot are a visual representation.

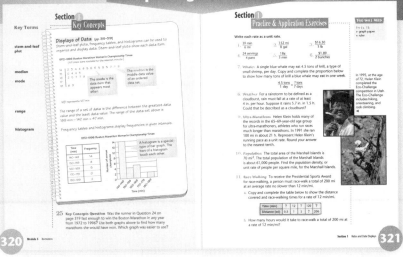

SUGGESTED ASSIGNMENT

Core Course
Day 1: Exs. 1–12, 19–21
Day 2: Exs. 14–16
Day 3: Exs. 17, 18, 22–30

Extended Course
Day 1: Exs. 1–13, 19–21
Day 2: Exs. 14–16
Day 3: Exs. 17, 18, 22–30

Block Schedule
Day 1: Exs. 1–12, 14–16, 19–21
Day 2: Exs. 17, 18, 22–30;
Sec. 2, Exs. 1–11, 19–21

EMBEDDED ASSESSMENT

These section objectives are
tested by the exercises listed.

**Use a proportion and
mental math to write a
rate as a unit rate.**
Exercises 2, 4, 6, 8, 10

Recognize and write rates.
Exercises 8, 9, 10, 12

**Find the mean, median,
mode, and range of a data
set and choose the best
average.**
Exercises 15, 16b, 16c

**Make and interpret a
stem-and-leaf plot.**
Exercises 14, 16a

Interpret a histogram.
Exercise 17

Practice & Application

EXERCISE NOTES

Developing Math Concepts
For *Ex. 8*, remind students to support their answers with mathematical reasoning. For *Exs. 8–10*,
stress to students that always
labeling the units when working
with rates and proportions will
ensure accuracy and correct interpretation. Some students may use
tables and patterns to help them
solve these exercises. Help them
make a connection between these
tables and proportions. For *Ex.
11(b)*, students will need to convert their answers from minutes
to hours.

Customizing Instruction

Home Involvement Those helping students at home
will find the Key Concepts on pages 319 and 320 a
handy reference to the key ideas, terms, and skills of
Section 1.

Absent Students For students who were absent for
all or part of this section, the blackline Study Guide for
Section 1 may be used to present the ideas, concepts,
and skills of Section 1.

Extra Help For students who need additional practice, the blackline Practice and Applications for Section
1 provides additional exercises that may be used to
confirm the skills of Section 1. The Extra Skill Practice
on page 325 also provides additional exercises.

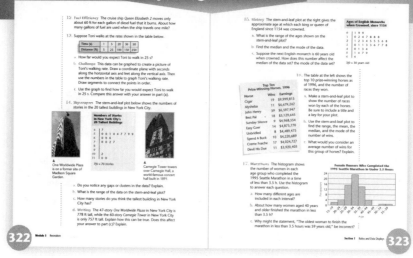

Practice & Application

Writing For *Ex. 14(d)*, encourage students to support their explanations with realistic mathematical examples.

Common Error For *Ex. 17(a)*, some students may subtract ages shown in an interval and answer 4 when the answer should be 5. Remind them, for example, that the ages 15, 16, 17, 18, and 19 must all be included in the interval 15–19. Each interval covers 5 years, since the length of an interval is the difference in the minimum ages represented by successive bars.

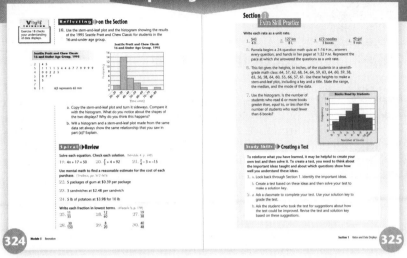

Closing the Section

While examining running paces, students have learned how to use proportions to find the unit rate equivalent to a given rate. Proportions will recur frequently in future applications, including in the next section, where cross products will be addressed. Creating and interpreting stem-and-leaf plots increases students' abilities to work with the averages mean, median, and mode. The *Reflecting on the Section* exercise on page 324 ties together the use of stem-and-leaf plots and the use of histograms. This exercise allows students to compare and contrast these two types of data displays, including examining the relationship between stems and intervals.

QUICK QUIZ ON THIS SECTION

1. Write $\dfrac{\$14.50}{3 \text{ lb}}$ as a unit rate.

2. At 65 mi/h, how long will it take to drive 442 mi?

3. Find the range, the median, and the mode.

   Point Spreads of 20 Super Bowls

   ```
   0 | 3 4 4 5 7 9
   1 | 0 0 2 4 6 7 7 9
   2 | 1 2 5 8 9
   3 | 6
   ```

   1 | 2 represents 12 points.

4. Use the histogram to find how many students scored between 70 and 89.

   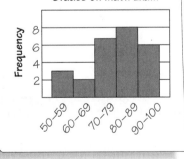

   Grades on Math Exam

For answers, see Quick Quiz blackline on p. 5-52

Section ② Proportions and Plots

Section Planner

DAYS FOR MODULE 5

1 2 3 **4 5 6** 7 **8 9 10 11 12**

SECTION 2

First Day
Setting the Stage, *p. 327*
Exploration 1, *pp. 328–330*

Second Day
Exploration 2, *pp. 331–332*

Third Day
Exploration 3, *pp. 334–335*
Key Concepts, *p. 336*

Block Schedule

Day 2 continued
Setting the Stage, Exploration 1,
Exploration 2

Day 3
Exploration 3, Key Concepts

RESOURCE ORGANIZER

Teaching Resources
• Practice and Applications, Sec. 2
• Study Guide, Sec. 2
• Technology Activity, Sec. 2
• Mid-Module Quiz
• Warm-Up, Sec. 2
• Quick Quiz, Sec. 2

Section Overview

In Section 2, students will begin by reviewing equivalent ratios. In Section 1, they learned how to use proportions to find unit rates. In this section, students will compare the cross products in a proportion to determine whether two ratios are equivalent. They will also use cross multiplication and division to solve an equation for the missing number in a proportion. Having learned the cross product property of proportions, students will model real-life problems with proportions, which they will then solve and check.

Students will also interpret and draw scatter plots. They will model a line of fit for a scatter plot. The technology page describes how students can use spreadsheet software or other graphing technology to make scatter plots. In Exploration 3, students will learn how they can use a box-and-whisker plot to analyze a set of data. They will then practice drawing box-and-whisker plots, and will investigate the use of these plots to compare two or more sets of data.

SECTION OBJECTIVES

Exploration 1
• use cross products to solve proportions
• use proportions to solve problems

Exploration 2
• make and interpret a scatter plot
• sketch a fitted line to make predictions

Exploration 3
• interpret a box-and-whisker plot

ASSESSMENT OPTIONS

Checkpoint Questions
• Question 13 on p. 330
• Question 19 on p. 332
• Question 26 on p. 335

Embedded Assessment
• For a list of embedded assessment exercises see p. 5-22.

Performance Task/Portfolio
★Exercises 14–15 on p. 339
• Exercise 16 on p. 340 (automobile racing)
• Exercise 18 on p. 341 (visual thinking)
• Module Project on p. 342
• Standardized Testing on p. 343

★= a problem solving task that can be assessed using the Assessment Scales

SECTION 2 MATERIALS

Exploration 2
◆ Labsheet 2A
◆ rubber band
◆ 50 pennies
◆ large paper clip
◆ small paper clip
◆ tape
◆ lined paper

◆ metric ruler
◆ small plastic (sandwich) bag
◆ strand of uncooked spaghetti

Exploration 3
◆ Labsheet 2B

Practice and Application Exercises
◆ graph paper
◆ ruler

Module Project on p. 342
◆ clipboard or other writing surface

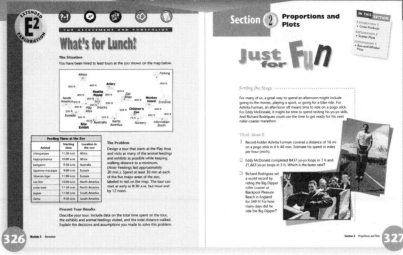

Setting the Stage

MOTIVATE

Students are naturally fascinated by the things that people will do to get in the record books. Students continue their study of rates and proportions using some fascinating record data. Have groups or individual students read page 327 and answer *Questions 1–3*. Have the class explain and discuss the methods they used to solve the problems. You may want to have students look in record books to find more feats they find amazing. Then students can suggest units and proportions they want to use to picture these records in new ways.

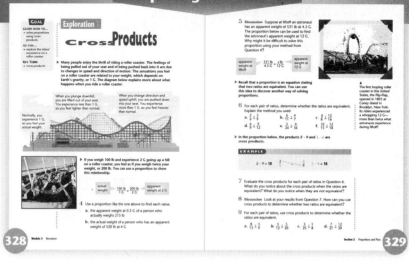

Exploration 1

PLAN

Classroom Management
Students can complete most of Exploration 1 individually, though for *Questions 5* and *8*, you may want them to discuss their explanations with at least 2 other students. For *Questions 10* and *12*, bring together the whole class so that you can ensure that all students understand how to write fractions with a common denominator and how to solve a simple equation by dividing both sides by the same number.

GUIDE

Developing Math Concepts In the Example on page 329, ask students how they know that the ratios $\frac{2}{6}$ and $\frac{3}{9}$ are equivalent (both ratios are equal to $\frac{1}{3}$ when rewritten in simplest form). In *Question 10(a)*, make sure that students understand that when they rewrite two ratios with a common denominator they are just multiplying each of the ratios by 1. To make the denominators equal, multiply $\frac{4}{6}$ by 1 in the form of $\frac{9}{9}$, and multiply $\frac{6}{9}$ by 1 in the form of $\frac{6}{6}$. Then the denominators are 6 • 9 and 9 • 6, which are the same. For *Question 12*, point out to students that

they can write the equation as $531 \cdot 12 = 4.5x$ or as $4.5x = 531 \cdot 12$. Some students may feel more confident solving an equation with x on the left side.

Customizing Instruction

Visual Learners Represent equivalent ratios using tiles or sketches to show that equivalent ratios are made of the same "building blocks," for example, that the ratios $\frac{4}{6}$ and $\frac{6}{9}$ are both made of groups in the ratio $\frac{2}{3}$. If two ratios are not equivalent, they cannot be divided into the same basic ratio groups.

Technology As the purpose in this Exploration is to understand cross products rather than on calculation skills, allow students to use a calculator. Encourage students to use estimation and number sense whenever they use a calculator to ensure that their results are reasonable.

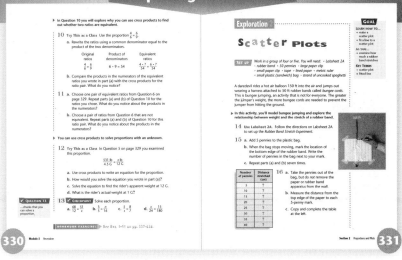

Exploration I continued

Classroom Examples

Use cross products to show that the two fractions below are equivalent.

Answer:

$$9 \cdot 20 = 180$$
$$\frac{9}{12} = \frac{15}{20}$$
$$15 \cdot 12 = 180$$

Since both cross products are equal, the two fractions are equivalent.

Checkpoint Prior to *Question 13*, have a few students verbalize how to solve a proportion. Some students may choose to solve parts *(b)* and *(d)* by rewriting the ratios with a common denominator. Check that students are able to solve proportions using cross products. This will help them avoid confusion when a variable is in the denominator. Remind students to check their solutions by multiplying to make sure the cross products are equal.

HOMEWORK EXERCISES

See the Suggested Assignment for Day 1 on page 5-22. For Exercise Notes, see page 5-22.

Exploration 2

PLAN

Classroom Management

Students perform Exploration 2 in groups of 4 or 5. Each group member should have a task, such as apparatus constructor (1 or 2 students), penny handler, reader, and recorder. Each group will need the supplies on the list, a portion of wall or other surface where they can attach the rubber band apparatus, and a copy of Labsheet 2A to construct a plot of the data. Since *Question 17* asks students to plot the data points from all groups, you will need to coordinate the exchange of data among the groups. This also dictates that all of the rubber bands should be the same size, and should preferably be new. You may want to experiment with different sizes of rubber bands ahead of time to make sure that the amount of stretch is sufficient and appropriate to the Exploration.

Students will need close monitoring as they set up and complete the activity. The bottom of the rubber band should be even with the top edge of the paper. For *Question 18*, students can mark and then connect two points along the spaghetti. You can also use a transparent ruler or a piece of string and a straightedge in lieu of spaghetti. Because groups work at different speeds, in-group discussion may work best for *Questions 18(c)* and *20*, though you can have groups compare their insights as a class when all groups have completed Exploration 2.

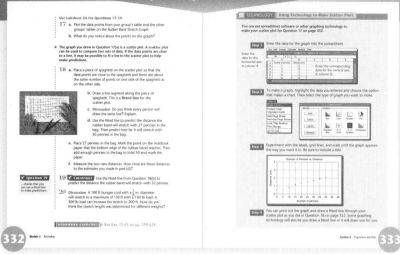

Exploration 2 continued

GUIDE

Developing Math Concepts

For *Question 17*, point out that the axes of a scatter plot are determined in the same manner as for other graphs, with a horizontal scale for one of the measures and a vertical scale for the other.

Common Error

For *Question 17*, if students expect all the points to lie along a line, they may tend to adapt their data measurements so that the data fit a line. Emphasize that a scatter plot records actual measurements, not predictions, and that these measurements should be as accurate as possible.

Classroom Examples

The results from the Rubber Band Stretch Experiment for one group are graphed in the scatter plot below. Draw a fitted line on the graph.

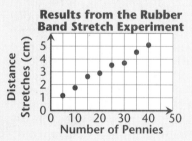

Results from the Rubber Band Stretch Experiment

Sample Answer: A fitted line should be drawn so that about half of the data values are above the line and the other half are below the line.

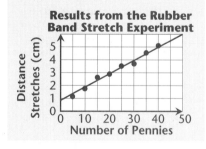

Results from the Rubber Band Stretch Experiment

Developing Math Concepts

For *Question 18*, stress that finding the fitted line is an estimate, so predictions may vary somewhat. Also, *about* half of the points lie on either side of the line, so students should not count points. Students are trying to estimate the central tendency of scatter plot data that varies. At this level, "eyeballing" is probably the best strategy.

Checkpoint

For *Question 19*, all students should make and justify their own predictions to the other group members. This will ensure that students are interpreting the graph properly, and that they are able to make reasonable estimates.

▌ HOMEWORK EXERCISES ▶

See the Suggested Assignment for Day 2 on page 5-22. For Exercise Notes, see page 5-22.

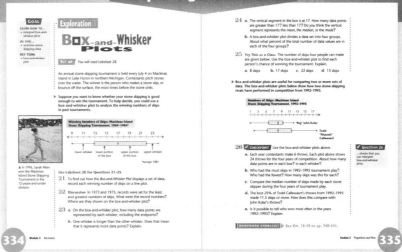

Exploration 3

PLAN

Classroom Management
Exploration 3 is best performed
in small groups to encourage
interaction and interchange
about box-and-whisker plots.
Each student will need Labsheet
2B, though students in a group
could share labsheets. *Question
25* is highlighted for whole-class
discussion.

GUIDE

Developing Math Concepts For
Question 21, you could also have
students represent the data with a
stem-and-leaf plot. For *Question
22*, you may want to have the students find the range of the data.
For *Question 23(b)*, you may
want to introduce the term *outliers*
for data points that lie far to the
right or left of most other data
points. Explain that outliers can
"stretch" one or both whiskers.

Common Error For *Question
24(a)*, some students may think
that the median is represented by
the middle of the box. Point out
that the median is the middle of
the data set, and may or may not
lie near the middle of the box.

Developing Math Concepts
For *Question 24(b)*, you may want
to introduce the terms *quartile*,
lower quartile, and *upper quartile*.
These terms may help students
remember that each graph division represents a quarter, or 25%,
of the data. Ask students what portion of the data values are represented by the box (half, or 50%).
For *Question 25*, encourage students to connect the values 25%,
50%, and 75% with the endpoints
and inside mark of the box as they
discuss the chances of winning.

Classroom Examples
**The box-and-whisker plot
below is from data on the number of students in each class
that participate in extra-curricular activities. Use the plot to
find the least and greatest values, median, and range of the
data.**

**Students Who Participate in
Extra-Curricular Activities**

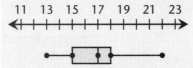

Answer: least: 13; greatest: 22;
median: 17; range: 9

Checkpoint *Question 26* asks
several questions to check students'
interpretation of box-and-whisker
plots. You may want to have students answer each question in sentence form to help you evaluate
their level of understanding. For
part *(e)*, encourage students to
make up specific examples to help
them explore the possibilities.

▐ HOMEWORK EXERCISES ▶

See the Suggested Assignment
for Day 3 on page 5-22. For
Exercise Notes, see page 5-22.

CLOSE

Closure Question Describe
how you can use cross products.
Sample Response: Cross products
can be used to solve a proportion.
You can use the fact that in a true
proportion the cross products are
equal to find an equivalent equation that can then be solved using
division.

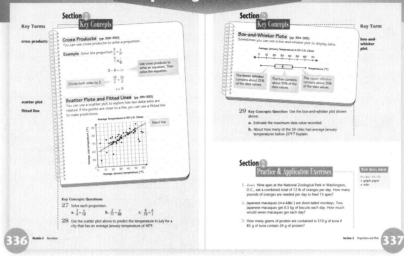

SUGGESTED ASSIGNMENT

Core Course
Day 1: Exs. 1–11, 19–21
Day 2: Exs. 12, 14, 15, 22–24
Day 3: Exs. 16–18, 25–27

Extended Course
Day 1: Exs. 1–11, 19–21
Day 2: Exs. 12–15, 22–24
Day 3: Exs. 16–18, 25–27

Block Schedule
Day 2: Sec. 1, Exs. 17, 18,
          22–30;
          Exs. 1–11, 19–21
Day 3: Exs. 12, 14–18, 22–27

EMBEDDED ASSESSMENT

These section objectives are
tested by the exercises listed.

**Use cross products to solve
proportions.**
  Exercises 8, 10

**Use proportions to solve
problems.**
  Exercises 2, 4, 6

**Make and interpret a scatter
plot.**
  Exercises 12, 14a, 15a

**Sketch a fitted line to
make predictions.**
  Exercises 12, 14b–c, 15b–c

**Interpret a box-and-
whisker plot.**
  Exercises 16, 17

Practice & Application

EXERCISE NOTES

Developing Math Concepts
For *Exs. 1–6*, encourage students
always to write the units when
they write proportions to solve
problems. Students who are
unsure about writing proportions
can look back to the situations
described at the bottom of page
328 and the top of page 329.

Customizing Instruction

Home Involvement Those helping students at home
will find the Key Concepts on pages 336 and 337 a
handy reference to the key ideas, terms, and skills of
Section 2.

Absent Students For students who were absent for
all or part of this section, the blackline Study Guide for
Section 2 may be used to present the ideas, concepts,
and skills of Section 2.

Extra Help For students who need additional practice, the blackline Practice and Applications for Section
2 provides additional exercises that may be used to
confirm the skills of Section 2. The Extra Skill Practice
on page 343 also provides additional exercises.

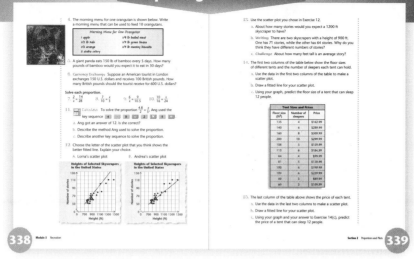

Practice & Application

Developing Math Concepts

For *Ex. 13*, students should realize that not only must about half the points lie on either side of the fitted line, but that the fitted line needs to be as close as possible to as many of the points as possible. This ensures that the direction of the fitted line reflects the trend shown by the points. This makes the fitted line useful for estimating and predicting values. For *Exs. 14* and *15*, students may vary in which measure they choose for the horizontal axis and which they choose for the vertical axis. Though the graphs may be oriented differently, emphasize that the fitted lines predict the same values.

Technology

For *Exs. 14* and *15*, you may want to have students verify their scatter plots using a graphing calculator or computer software, if all students have access. Make sure that students realize which axis is being used for which measure so they can properly interpret the plot.

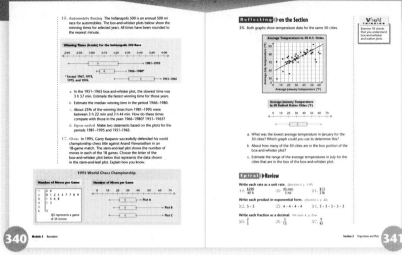

Practice & Application

Research In *Ex. 16*, you may wish to have students research the Indianapolis 500. Topics could include a history of the race, winning times for years before 1951, and why the years 1967, 1973, 1975 and 1976 are excluded from the data in the box-and-whisker plot. As an extension, you may wish to have students create box-and-whisker plots for the fifteen year intervals from 1936–1950 and 1921–1935 and compare the data with the plots shown on page 340.

Background In *Ex. 17*, you may wish to have a student or students familiar with chess give a short report to the class. The report could explain what the pieces are, how they move, and what the object of the game is.

Common Error In *Ex. 18(a)* students may use the fitted line rather than the data points to answer the question. Remind students that the points on the scatter plot are the actual data.

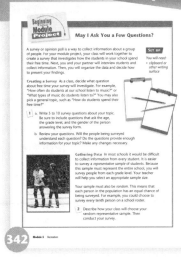

Beginning the Module Project

Read page 342 as a class and discuss the idea of a survey. Brainstorm possible topics to investigate about free time, such as music, sports, movies, clubs and social activities, nature, art, books, and so on. As students suggest survey questions, have them constantly evaluate whether or not their questions are clear, specific, and will give them useful, unambiguous data. Encourage student input on what sort of sample will be representative of the school as a whole. Students may need additional examples of random samples for clarification. Help students anticipate problems they might encounter, and suggest strategies they might use to solve these problems.

Closing the Section

Students have continued working with ratios and rates in Section 2, culminating in using cross products to solve proportions. They have recorded, displayed, and interpreted data, adding scatter plots and box-and-whisker plots to the stem-and-leaf plots and histograms they used to display data in Section 1. In the *Reflecting on the Section* exercise on page 341, students examine the same data set displayed both with a scatter plot and a box-and-whisker plot. This will help them compare the strengths and limitations of different data displays for different data sets. You may wish to encourage students to locate data of interest to them or generate data from activities they have chosen. Then the class can discuss what types of data displays might be best for their data, and how these displays will communicate the most relevant information to others.

QUICK QUIZ ON THIS SECTION

1. If there are 8 slices in one pizza, how many are there in 13 pizzas?

2. Solve the proportion $\frac{9}{15} = \frac{x}{70}$.

3. Make a scatter plot of the data in the table below.

Winning Distances for Men's Olympic Discus

Year	Distance (ft)
1900	118
1920	147
1936	166
1960	194
1980	219

4. Use your scatter plot in Question 3 to estimate the winning time for the year 2000.

5. The box-and-whisker plot shows data for a frog-jumping contest. What was the range of jumps? What was the median jump?

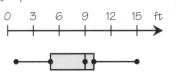

For answers, see Quick Quiz blackline on p. 5-53.

Section ③ Percent

Section Planner

DAYS FOR MODULE 5

1 2 3 4 5 6 **7 8 9 10 11 12**

SECTION 3

First Day
Setting the Stage, *p. 344*
Exploration 1, *pp. 345–347*

Second Day
Exploration 2, *pp. 348–349*

Third Day
Exploration 3, *pp. 350–351*
Key Concepts, *p. 352*

Block Schedule

Day 4
Setting the Stage, Exploration 1,
Exploration 2

Day 5
Exploration 3, Key Concepts
(Day 5 continues in Sec. 4.)

RESOURCE ORGANIZER

Teaching Resources
• Practice and Applications, Sec. 3
• Study Guide, Sec. 3
• Warm-Up, Sec. 3
• Quick Quiz, Sec. 3

Section Overview

Continuing the theme of leisure-time activities, Section 3 introduces its lesson on estimating percent with a discussion of movie ratings. Students will work with "nice" fractions to estimate percent equivalents of fractions. They will also use percent bar models, which will indicate halves, thirds, fourths, and fifths, to estimate percents. Students will continue to use these bar models to set up a proportion so that they can find the exact percent equivalent for a ratio. They will discuss when rounding to the nearest whole percent may not give the best estimate of a ratio.

In Exploration 3, students will find a part of a number two ways. First they will use a percent bar to estimate the part. Then they will find the exact part by solving a proportion. Students will also solve proportions to find a missing whole when they are given a part.

The Toolbox exercises on page 588 review modeling percent. Some students may benefit from the summary and exercises on this page.

SECTION OBJECTIVES

Exploration 1
• estimate percents using common fraction/percent equivalents or a percent bar model

Exploration 2
• find a percent using a proportion

Exploration 3
• estimate a percent of a number
• use a proportion to find a percent of a number
• use a proportion to find the whole when a part and a percent are given

ASSESSMENT OPTIONS

Checkpoint Questions
• Question 8 on p. 347
• Question 13 on p. 349
• Question 22 on p. 350
• Question 27 on p. 351

Embedded Assessment
• For a list of embedded assessment exercises see p. 5-31.

Performance Task/Portfolio
• Exercise 25 on p. 355
• Exercise 26 on p. 355 (research)
• Exercises 36–39 on p. 356 (extension)
★ Module Project on p. 356
★ Standardized Testing on p. 357

★ = a problem solving task that can be assessed using the Assessment Scales

SECTION 3 MATERIALS

Exploration 1
♦ Labsheet 3A
♦ frequency table from Questions 1 and 2

Exploration 2
♦ frequency table from Questions 1 and 2

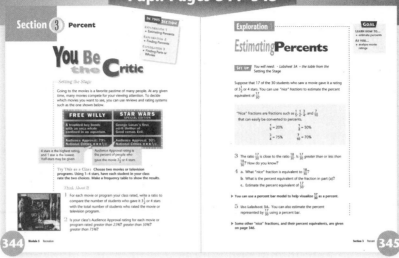

Setting the Stage

MOTIVATE

Complete the Setting the Stage section as a whole class. Students will use Audience Approval ratings of movies or television shows throughout Section 3 to build their knowledge of percents. Prior to having students choose movies or shows to rate, make a list of possible ratings, including half-star ratings. You may want to use voting to decide what movies or shows to rate, but choose ones that nearly everyone has seen. Make a category NS for students who have not seen a movie or show. Keep a tally as a class, but have each student record the data and frequency table for use in Explorations 1 and 2. You can have students answer *Questions 1* and *2* individually, but compare results and methods as a class.

Exploration I

PLAN

Classroom Management
All students will need their frequency tables from the Setting the Stage on page 344, as well as a copy of Labsheet 3A. Exploration 1 is best performed in a small group, but with all students recording and explaining in their own words. For *Questions 6–8*, as using "nice" fractions to estimate other fractions is somewhat of an art, be prepared to spend some time with extra examples. *Question 9* is highlighted for the whole class. You will want to have several examples ready to present to the class to illustrate parts *(b)* and *(c)*.

Managing Time Students may need extra time to practice using the fraction-decimal-percent relationships in the Student Resource on page 346. You may wish to spend a day reviewing how to convert between fractions, decimals and percents. The Extra Skill Practice exercises and performance task on page 357 can be helpful in doing this.

MODULE 5 ◆ SECTION 3

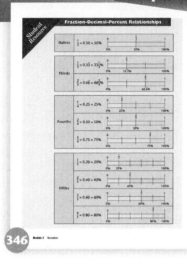

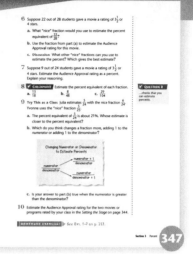

Exploration I continued

GUIDE

Developing Math Concepts
For *Question 6*, students will be examining changing either the numerator or the denominator or changing both. Show how by changing both by the same (and relatively *small*) amount, students can get a good estimate $\left(\text{as with } \frac{19}{25} \text{ or } \frac{24}{30}\right)$. At any rate, students should look for "nice" fractions that involve as small a change as possible.

Classroom Examples
Use a "nice" fraction to estimate $\frac{11}{45}$.

Answer: Subtract one from the denominator, since $\frac{11}{45}$ is close to $\frac{11}{44}$. Then $\frac{11}{45} \approx \frac{11}{44}$, or $\frac{1}{4}$.

Checkpoint For *Question 8*, check students' understanding by having them verbalize how they made their estimates.

Developing Math Concepts
For *Question 9*, help students understand the general guideline that changing the numerator or denominator by a fixed amount will cause less change if the larger of the two quantities is changed. As an example, you could show how adding 1 to the *denominator* of $\frac{5}{24}$ causes the smaller change, while adding 1 to the *numerator* of $\frac{24}{5}$ causes the smaller change.

HOMEWORK EXERCISES

See the Suggested Assignment for Day 1 on page 5-31. For Exercise Notes, see page 5-31.

Customizing Instruction

Technology For practice in finding "nice" fraction estimators, have students use calculators to find decimal values of fractions. This will give them instantaneous feedback. Students could come up with fractions they want to estimate as percents and then compare the values of several of their "nice" estimators to the actual value. When students find a close estimate, have them observe in what way they changed the original fraction.

Visual Learners Create a bulletin board with several examples of "nice" and/or simple fractions and their equivalent decimals and percents. You might want to use percent bars, 10-by-10 grids, circle graphs, or a combination of these. You can also add some visual examples of estimating percents. For example, compare visual representations of the fraction $\frac{6}{21}$ (about 28.57%) with the "nice" estimates $\frac{5}{20}$ (25%), $\frac{6}{20}$ (30%), and $\frac{7}{21} \left(33\frac{1}{3}\%\right)$.

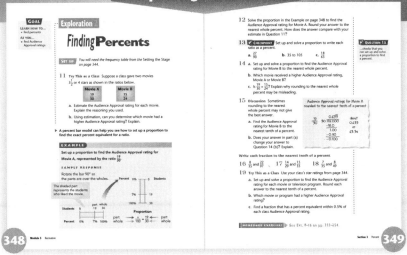

Exploration 2

PLAN

Classroom Management
Address *Question 11* and the
Example on page 348 as a whole
class. For the Example, you may
refer students to the Student
Resource on page 346 to provide
benchmarks for setting up percent bar models. You can also
refer them to Labsheet 3A.
Questions 12–18 can be completed as individuals or in small
groups. For *Question 19*, students will again need their frequency tables from the Setting
the Stage on page 344.

GUIDE

Developing Math Concepts
For *Question 11*, make sure stu-
dents examine both $\frac{18}{30}$ and $\frac{20}{30}$ as
estimates for $\frac{19}{30}$, and both $\frac{15}{25}$
and $\frac{16}{24}$ as estimates for $\frac{15}{24}$ so
that they can compare the dif-
ferent possibilities for part *(b)*.
For the Example on page 348,
you can show on the bar model
that the percent equivalent for
$\frac{19}{30}$ falls between those of $\frac{18}{30}$
(60%) and $\frac{20}{30}\left(66\frac{2}{3}\%\right)$.

Classroom Examples
**Use a percent bar model to set
up a proportion to find the
Audience Approval rating for
Movie C, represented by the
ratio $\frac{10}{25}$.**
Answer:

Students
Part Whole
0   10   25

0%   x%   100%
Percent

0% 0
x% 10
100% 25
Percent / Students

$$\text{Part} \to \frac{x}{100} = \frac{10}{25} \leftarrow \text{Part}$$
$$\text{Whole} \to \qquad\qquad \leftarrow \text{Whole}$$

Checkpoint For *Question 13*,
make sure students can demonstrate and explain the methods
they used to find an equivalent
percent.

Developing Math Concepts
For *Question 19(c)*, expect a lot
of trial and error from students.
Use a calculator to evaluate student suggestions quickly. For
most class sizes, adding 1 to
both the numerator and denominator will not be close enough
to meet the target. Some students may find that multiplying
by $\frac{10}{10}$, $\frac{100}{100}$, and so on, can get
them very close if they just
tweak the resulting numerator,
denominator, or both. Other
students may want just to pick a
denominator, such as 100, and
see if any of the possible numerators get them close enough.

HOMEWORK EXERCISES

See the Suggested Assignment
for Day 2 on page 5-31. For
Exercise Notes, see page 5-31.

MODULE 5 ◆ SECTION 3

5-29

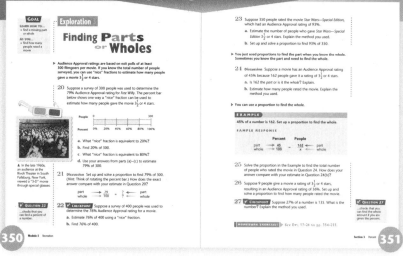

Exploration 3

PLAN

Classroom Management In Exploration 3, students will investigate finding the whole or part given the percent. As many will find this more difficult than finding the percent, expect students to need a lot of guidance. Students can complete Exploration 3 in small groups, though you may want to have the class as a whole discuss *Questions 21* and *24*. If students had difficulty with the previous Exploration, you may want to perform Exploration 3 as a whole class.

GUIDE

Developing Math Concepts
For *Question 20*, make sure that students realize that each interval along the percent bar represents 60, since $300 \div 5 = 60$.

Checkpoint *Question 22* checks both estimation and calculation. Make certain students are completing the estimation first, as some may do the calculation and then round for the estimate.

Developing Math Concepts
For *Question 23*, some students will begin connecting multiplication with finding the percent of a number. When students read the word "of," they should be expecting to multiply. At this level, however, setting up proportions will help ensure that students can work a wide variety of problems.

Classroom Examples
Suppose 72% of a number is 180. Set up and solve a proportion to find the whole.

Answer:

$$\begin{array}{cc} \text{Percent} & \text{Number} \end{array}$$

$$\begin{array}{l} \text{Part} \rightarrow \frac{72}{100} = \frac{180}{x} \leftarrow \text{Part} \\ \text{Whole} \rightarrow \qquad\qquad \leftarrow \text{Whole} \end{array}$$

$$72 \cdot x = 180 \cdot 100$$
$$72x = 18{,}000$$
$$\frac{72x}{72} = \frac{18{,}000}{72}$$
$$x = 250$$

Common Error For *Question 26*, some students still may not be sure "which number goes where" when setting up a proportion involving percents. Remind them that a percent is just a way to write a ratio with a denominator of 100.

Checkpoint For *Question 27*, make sure that students can set up a proportion and can explain their work. Encourage students to check their work. By reading "of" as multiplication, they can easily check their work by multiplying $\frac{27}{100}$ times their result to make sure that it equals 135.

HOMEWORK EXERCISES

See the Suggested Assignment for Day 3 on page 5-31. For Exercise Notes, see page 5-31.

CLOSE

Closure Question Explain how to estimate and how to find the exact value of the percent equivalent for a fraction.

Sample Response: To estimate the percent equivalent, change the numerator or denominator of the fraction slightly so that the result is equivalent to a "nice" fraction whose percent equivalent is known. For the exact percent equivalent, set up and solve the proportion that equates the fraction to $\frac{x}{100}$.

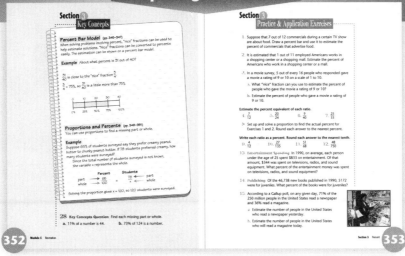

SUGGESTED ASSIGNMENT

Core Course
Day 1: Exs. 1–7, 27–32
Day 2: Exs. 8–14, 33–35
Day 3: Exs. 15–21, 23, 25, 26

Extended Course
Day 1: Exs. 1–7, 27–32
Day 2: Exs. 8–14, 33–35
Day 3: Exs. 15, 17, 20–23, 25,
      26, 36–39

Block Schedule
Day 4: Exs. 1–14, 27–35
Day 5: Exs. 15–21, 23, 25, 26;
      Sec. 4, Exs. 1–12

EMBEDDED ASSESSMENT

These section objectives are
tested by the exercises listed.

**Estimate percents using
common fraction/percent
equivalents or a percent
bar model.**

Exercises 1, 2, 4, 6

**Find a percent using a
proportion.**

Exercises 8, 10, 12, 14

**Estimate a percent of a
number.**

Exercises 15, 16

**Use a proportion to find a
percent of a number.**

Exercises 21, 25

**Use a proportion to find
the whole when a part
and a percent are given.**

Exercises 17, 20, 23

Practice & Application

EXERCISE NOTES

Developing Math Concepts
For *Exs. 2* and *4–7*, have students explain their work to
ensure that they are estimating
instead of rounding. For *Ex. 13*
and following exercises, make
sure students check their work.
Encourage them to use estimation to see that their calculations
are reasonable. Moreover, help
students learn to reread problems after finding a solution to
make sure that the answer is logical in the total context of the
problem. For example, if a student had found an answer of
59% for *Ex. 13*, this should seem
illogical upon rereading because
344 is very obviously less than
half of 833, so any answer must
be less than 50%.

Customizing Instruction

Home Involvement Those helping students at home
will find the Key Concepts on page 352 a handy reference to the key ideas, terms, and skills of Section 3.

Absent Students For students who were absent for
all or part of this section, the blackline Study Guide for
Section 3 may be used to present the ideas, concepts,
and skills of Section 3.

Extra Help For students who need additional practice, the blackline Practice and Applications for Section
3 provides additional exercises that may be used to
confirm the skills of Section 3. The Extra Skill Practice
on page 357 also provides additional exercises.

Practice & Application

Challenge For *Ex. 22(a)*, give students concrete numerical examples of how the median could be 0 in this case. Make sure they understand that every 0 is a data value and must be considered in any calculation of the different averages. Ask students what a box-and-whisker plot of this data might look like (it would have no lower whisker, and the left edge of the box would represent both the lower quartile and the median, so there would be no separate bar for the median in the box).

Consumer Economics For *Ex. 23*, you can tell students that one easy way to figure a tip of 15% at a restaurant is to take the total bill, and to it add half the total bill. Then a 15% tip is just one tenth of the sum. Ask students an easy way to find a tip of 20% (divide the total bill by 5; alternately, double the bill and then tip one tenth of this amount).

Closing the Section

Audience Approval ratings of movies and shows provide a context for estimating and finding percents in Section 3. Finding "nice" fractions to estimate other fractions develops students' number sense, and boosts confidence in dealing with fractions. Percent bar models especially help visual learners have a model for proportions involving percents, while looking at proportions involving percent as equating parts and wholes gives all students a model to approach a variety of problems involving percent. Percent problems also provide training in reading questions carefully, and in learning the importance of checking for logical sense. The *Reflecting on the Section* exercise on page 355 gives students a chance to apply their skills using percents to an important topic for this age (and any other)—discount pricing.

Working on the Module Project

Students previously created a survey and set out to gather data. Encourage students in each partner team to submit to class only data that is clear, complete, and legible. The class will need to tally the combined results on the board or other surface where all students can see and record the results. To analyze the data properly, urge students to keep careful track of all appropriate categories. They should realize that some categories (such as female and age 12) overlap, while other categories (such as grade 7 and grade 8) do not. So, combining some categories will give the overall results, while combining others may count some students more than once.

QUICK QUIZ ON THIS SECTION

1. Of 42 people surveyed, 27 rated a certain movie as 1 or 2 on a scale of 1 to 10. Use a "nice" fraction to estimate the percent of viewers giving this movie these "thumbs down" ratings.

2. Estimate the percent equivalent of $\frac{59}{81}$.

3. Write $\frac{42}{135}$ as a percent rounded to the nearest tenth.

4. 35% of what number is 63?

5. Suppose 75% of 6-year-olds weigh under 46 lb. How many 6-year-olds would you expect to weigh under 46 lb in a class of 32 age-six first-graders?

For answers, see Quick Quiz blackline on p. 5-54.

Section 4 — Percent and Probability

Section Planner

DAYS FOR MODULE 5

1 2 3 4 5 6 7 8 9 **10 11 12**

SECTION 4

First Day
Setting the Stage, p. 358
Exploration 1, pp. 359–360

Second Day
Exploration 2, pp. 361–362

Third Day
Exploration 3, pp. 363–365
Key Concepts, pp. 366–367

Block Schedule

Day 5 continued
Setting the Stage, Exploration 1, Exploration 2

Day 6
Exploration 3, Key Concepts

RESOURCE ORGANIZER

Teaching Resources
• Practice and Applications, Sec. 4
• Study Guide, Sec. 4
• Module Tests Forms A and B
• Standardized Assessment
• Module Performance Assessment
• Warm-Up, Sec. 4
• Quick Quiz, Sec. 4

Section Overview

In Section 4, students will use free throw statistics from a basketball tour to investigate how a fraction can be written as a decimal or a percent. Students will discuss the relationship between the decimal and percent forms of a ratio, and will describe how to convert between decimals and percents. They will use mental math to write fractions as percents using both equivalent fractions and "nice" fractions. Once students have gathered a table of data values expressed as ratios, they will use nice fractions and mental math to estimate percents for the ratios. Students will also consider their data values as experimental probabilities, which they will then use to make predictions. They will extend their study of experimental probability to finding theoretical probabilities. Students will draw tree diagrams to model multi-stage experiments. From the tree diagrams, they will be able to find the theoretical probability of each outcome. Students will also model multi-stage experiments by shading grids.

The Practice and Application Exercises include applications in sports, jewelry, and pharmacology.

SECTION OBJECTIVES

Exploration 1
• write ratios in fraction, decimal, and percent forms
• use mental math or "nice" fractions to write ratios as percents

Exploration 2
• use mental math or "nice" fractions to estimate percents
• use experimental probabilities represented as percents to make predictions

Exploration 3
• use a tree diagram or an area model to find the probabilities in a multi-stage experiment

ASSESSMENT OPTIONS

Checkpoint Questions
• Question 7 on p. 360
• Questions 10, 12 on p. 362
• Question 21 on p. 365

Embedded Assessment
• For a list of embedded assessment exercises see p. 5-39.

Performance Task/Portfolio
★Exercise 16 on p. 369
• Exercises 22–24 on p. 370
• Exercise 25 on p. 371 (journal)
• Exercises 30–31 on p. 371 (career)
★Module Project on p. 373

★= a problem solving task that can be assessed using the Assessment Scales

SECTION 4 MATERIALS

Exploration 1
◆ large paper cup
◆ cotton ball
◆ masking tape
◆ ruler

Exploration 2
◆ results from Questions 6–7

Exploration 3
◆ graph paper

Review and Assessment on pp. 374–375
◆ Review and Assessment Labsheet

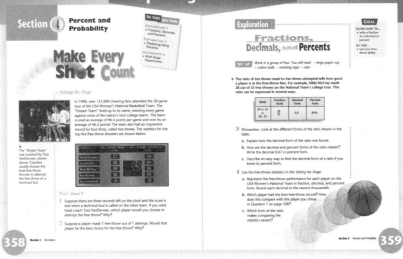

Setting the Stage

MOTIVATE

Women's basketball has been rapidly gaining attention and popularity in the United States, including professionally. As with most other sports, keeping statistics on the teams and players provides an interesting way to analyze the games. As a class, read page 358 and discuss the questions. Free-throw shooting provides an opportunity to connect ratios, decimals, and percents. Some students will have an idea of what their free-throw shooting percents might be for comparison to the statistics shown. *Questions 1* and *2* also foreshadow the concept of using statistical percents as experimental probabilities for predicting future results.

Exploration 1

PLAN

Classroom Management
Students can complete Exploration 1 in groups of about four students. You may want to review *Question 3* as a class to ensure that all students make the connections among ratios, decimals, and percents. Also review the *Example* on page 360, emphasizing the importance of using mental math. For *Question 6*, the groups of students will use a cotton ball and paper cup to simulate shooting free throws so they can collect data to analyze for *Question 7*. Prepare materials for each group or have materials set out for a member of each group to retrieve. Students will need plenty of floor space and time for this activity. As each student shoots, have another student to record the data for them and one to retrieve the cotton ball. Students can rotate these roles. Students will need their results from this experiment again for Exploration 2.

GUIDE

Developing Math Concepts For *Question 3*, you may want to make a percent bar model connecting the quantities from 0% to 100% with the decimals from 0.0 to 1.0 to make sure that students are making this connection.

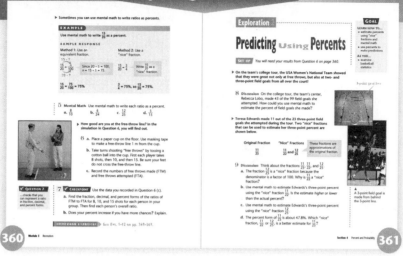

Exploration I continued

Checkpoint For *Question 7(a)*, have students reveal when they are able to find percent forms using "nice" fractions and when they have to divide or use a proportion to find a decimal or percent. Part *(b)* evaluates whether or not students really understand that a percent expresses a ratio of two quantities, and does not depend upon the particular size of either of the quantities.

Classroom Examples

Use mental math to write $\dfrac{5}{25}$ as a percent.

Answer:

Method 1: Use an equivalent fraction.

$$\frac{5}{25} = \frac{n}{100}$$

Since $25 \cdot 4 = 100$, $n = 5 \cdot 4 = 20$.

$$\frac{5}{25} = \frac{20}{100} = 20\%$$

Method 2: Use a "nice" fraction.

$$\frac{5}{25} = \frac{1}{5}$$

$$\frac{1}{5} = 20\%, \text{ so } \frac{5}{25} = 20\%.$$

▶ HOMEWORK EXERCISES

See the Suggested Assignment for Day 1 on page 5-39. For Exercise Notes, see page 5-40.

Exploration 2

PLAN

Classroom Management
Exploration 2 can be performed in the same groups as formed for Exploration 1. You may want to address the Example on page 362 as a whole class. For *Question 13*, students will need their results from the experiment in Exploration 1.

GUIDE

Developing Math Concepts
For *Question 9(a)*, stress that a fraction may be nice because its denominator is a factor of 100 or because it simplifies to a fraction whose denominator is a factor of 100 or to another "nice" fraction, such as $\dfrac{1}{3}$.

Customizing Instruction

Alternative Approach If you have access to a gymnasium with several baskets, you may want to have students follow *Question 6* using a real ball at the free-throw line. (You may want to mark a line closer than the free-throw line to give students a better chance to make baskets.) If you know a student or teacher who is a very good free-throw shooter, you may want to have that person shoot for the class, and have students record and analyze the data.

Career Information Women's professional basketball is taking off with the American Basketball League (ABL) and the Women's National Basketball Association (WNBA). You may want to have students research women's professional teams and their players through newspapers, magazines, or the internet. Have students give examples of some of the types of statistics that are recorded for the teams and players, especially those statistics that are given as percents.

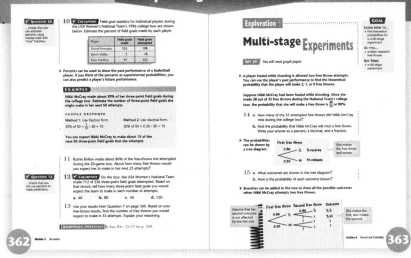

Exploration 2 continued

Checkpoint For *Question 10*, ask students to verbalize their thinking to observe how they are making their estimates.

Developing Math Concepts
For the Example on page 362, again connect the word "of" to multiplication. Ask students what proportion they could set up to solve this problem $\left(\frac{30}{100} = \frac{x}{50}\right)$, stressing the relationship of the parts to the wholes.

Checkpoint For *Question 12*, check that students are remembering to write the fraction $\frac{112}{336}$ as the "nice" fraction $\frac{1}{3}$. Students who do so should then see that they can predict the number of free throws made by multiplying one third times the number of attempts. Some students may also set up a proportion (perhaps using a bar model) to solve using cross products.

Classroom Examples
During the 1996–1997 American Basketball League season, Shannon Johnson of the Columbus Quest had a 3-point field goal percentage of 48%, the highest in the league. Estimate the number of 3-point field goals she might make in her next 50 attempts.

Answer:
Method 1: Estimate using fraction form.
$$48\% \text{ of } 50 = \frac{48}{100} \cdot 50$$
$$= \frac{24}{50} \cdot 50$$
$$= 24$$

Method 2: Estimate using decimal form.
$$48\% \text{ of } 50 = 0.48 \cdot 50$$
$$= 24$$

You can expect Shannon Johnson to make about 24 of her next 50 three-point field goal attempts.

HOMEWORK EXERCISES

See the Suggested Assignment for Day 2 on page 5-39. For Exercise Notes, see page 5-40.

Exploration 3

PLAN

Classroom Management
Many students may find exploring probabilities with grids and tree diagrams to be difficult. Unless you are sure you have capable students among all groups of three or four students, you may want to perform Exploration 3 as a whole class. Encourage broad participation to make sure students aren't being left behind. For *Question 16*, you may want to be prepared with additional experiments that you can simulate with a binary tree diagram, such as two-section spinners with unequal sections. *Question 20* is specifically marked for whole-class participation so that students connect using grids and tree diagrams with multiplying probabilities.

MODULE 5 ◆ SECTION 4

5-37

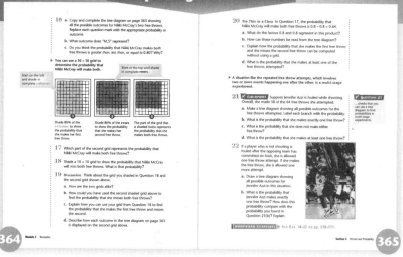

Exploration 3 continued

GUIDE

Developing Math Concepts

For *Questions 14–16*, you may
want at first to write out possibilities along the branches of a
tree diagram so that students
don't get distracted by abbrevia-
tions. You can write out the outcomes using the words "then"
or "followed by," such as
"scores, then misses" or "a miss,
followed by a miss." For
Questions 18–19, it may help
students if they always follow a
specific order for shading, for
example, always shade columns
for the first experiment and
rows for the second. Then they
can more easily distinguish outcomes such as SM and MS.

Checkpoint For *Question 21*,
students will have to demonstrate their ability first to find
the probabilities in an individual experiment and then to use
this information to create a tree
diagram to find probabilities in
a multi-stage experiment.
Students may have trouble find-
ing a "nice" fraction for $\frac{58}{64}$. You
may want to allow students to
use calculators to find the decimal probabilities, or to use the
estimate 0.90 for the probability
of making a free throw.

HOMEWORK EXERCISES

See the Suggested Assignment
for Day 3 on page 5-39. For
Exercise Notes, see page 5-40.

CLOSE

Closure Question Explain how
you can use percents to predict
future outcomes.

Sample Response: Use past performance to write the ratio of
desired outcomes to total outcomes. Convert this to a percent.
Multiply this percent by the total
number of future outcomes to
find the predicted number of
desired outcomes.

Customizing Instruction

Alternative Approach Another representation of
shading columns and rows can be shown using an
overhead base ten set. Place 8 "longs" vertically to
show 80% of the "flat" is covered. Place 8 "longs"
horizontally to show 80% of the "flat" is covered.
Students can see the area that is covered twice is
darker, giving a visual representation of the probability
that Nikki will make both free throws. Verbalize what is
being done: "Placing the first set of "longs" on the
"flat" represents the 80% probability of making the
first shot. Placing the second set of "longs" on the

"flat" represents the 80% probability of making the
second shot. Where they overlap represents 80% of
80%, or 0.8 × 0.8, which is 0.64, or 64%." You may
want to demonstrate additional examples under the
instruction of students or have students demonstrate
examples.

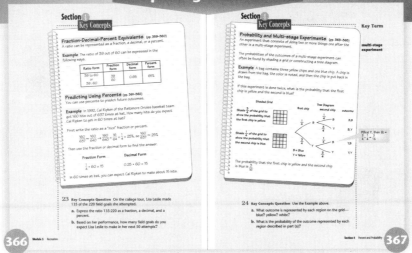

SUGGESTED ASSIGNMENT

Core Course
Day 1: Exs. 1–12
Day 2: Exs. 13, 14, 16, 17, 26–29
Day 3: Exs. 18–23, 25

Extended Course
Day 1: Exs. 1–12
Day 2: Exs. 13–17, 26–29
Day 3: Exs. 18–22, 24, 25

Block Schedule
Day 5: Sec. 3, Exs. 15–21, 23, 25, 26;
Exs. 1–12
Day 6: Exs. 13, 14, 16–23, 25–29

EMBEDDED ASSESSMENT

These section objectives are tested by the exercises listed.

Write ratios in fraction, decimal, and percent forms.
Exercises 1, 2, 4, 6

Use mental math or "nice" fractions to write ratios as percents.
Exercises 8, 10, 12

Use mental math or "nice" fractions to estimate percents.
Exercises 13, 17

Use experimental probabilities represented as percents to make predictions.
Exercises 14, 16

Use a tree diagram or an area model to find probabilities in a multistage experiment.
Exercises 18, 20, 22, 23

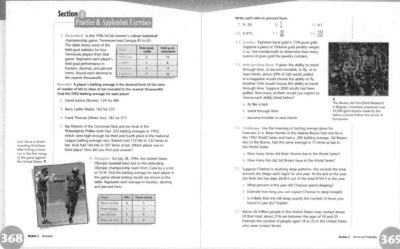

Practice & Application

EXERCISE NOTES

Background Information For *Ex. 5*, you may want to point out that the last person in the American League or National League to have a 0.400 season batting average was Ted Williams in 1941.

Extension For *Ex. 13*, you may want to have students write and solve a proportion to find out how many karats are in pure gold bars.

$$\left(\frac{18}{x} = \frac{75}{100} \; ; \; x = 24\right)$$

Customizing Instruction

Home Involvement Those helping students at home will find the Key Concepts on pages 366–367 a handy reference to the key ideas, terms, and skills of Section 4.

Absent Students For students who were absent for all or part of this section, the blackline Study Guide for Section 4 may be used to present the ideas, concepts, and skills of Section 4.

Extra Help For students who need additional practice, the blackline Practice and Applications for Section 4 provides additional exercises that may be used to confirm the skills of Section 4. The Extra Skill Practice on page 372 also provides additional exercises.

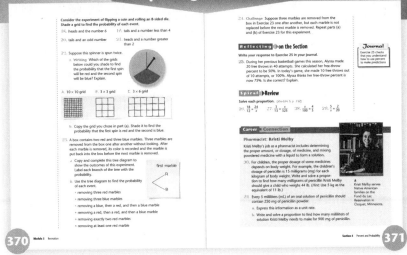

Practice & Application

Common Error For *Exs. 18–20*, some students may first try to shade a 10-by-10 grid and then become confused when trying to model rolling the 8-sided die. Point out that for a two-stage experiment, the number of possible outcomes of one experiment must divide evenly into the number of rows, and the number of possible outcomes of the other experiment must divide evenly into the number of columns. So, a 10-by-10 grid is useful when there are 2, 5, or 10 possible outcomes of each experiment.

Developing Math Concepts For *Ex. 23*, students should begin connecting that for a multi-stage experiment having two possible outcomes, such as the experiment in this exercise or repeatedly flipping a coin, the total number of outcomes is 2 multiplied by itself as many times as there are stages in the experiment.

Challenge For *Ex. 24*, you may want to give students the hint that they can still use the tree diagram from *Ex. 23*, but they must be very careful in assigning the probabilities for each branch. At the first branching they can still enter the probabilities 0.4 for red and 0.6 for blue, but after that, they must calculate new probabilities based on the remaining marbles.

MODULE 5 ♦ SECTION 4

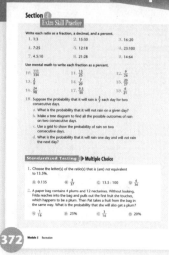

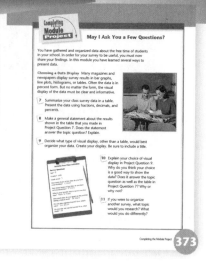

372   Module 5   Recreation

Completing the Module Project   373

Closing the Section

Throughout Section 4, students have been using data about free-throw shooting in basketball, including data from a simulation they have conducted. This has provided them the opportunity to increase their estimation skills and to work with equivalent ratios, fractions, decimals, and percents. Students have also begun using experimental data to predict future results based on past results and to make inferences about groups of different sizes. Through tree diagrams, students have listed the outcomes of multi-stage experiments, and have begun multiplying to find the probabilities of independent events.

QUICK QUIZ ON THIS SECTION

1. What is the batting average of a hitter who hit 62 times in 200 at-bats?

2. If a batter has hit .280 over the past three months, about how many hits would you expect her to get in her next 25 times at bat?

3. Write 10 : 85 in percent form rounded to the nearest tenth of a percent.

4. Consider the experiment of spinning the two spinners shown below and recording the two colors. Shade a grid to show the probability of getting two reds.

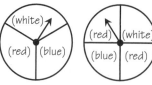

5. Use a tree diagram to show the probability of getting red and blue in either order with the two spinners above.

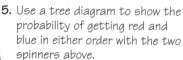

For answers, see Quick Quiz blackline on p. 5-55.

Completing the Module Project

Students will be summarizing and presenting the data collected from their surveys. Before students prepare their final displays, you may want to have teams compare their tables of classroom data to make sure everyone is working from clear and accurate information. You may want to have students bring in examples of displays of survey data that they have seen in newspapers or magazines. Have students discuss and list what makes each display clear and informative. Remind students that their visual display of the data should be clear enough for an outside viewer to interpret correctly without having to ask questions. Encourage student participation in evaluating what makes each display effective or ineffective.

MODULE 5 ◆ SECTION 4

Name _____ Date _____

Rubber Band Stretch Experiment

(Use with Question 14 on page 331.)

Directions

First

Hook the rubber band onto both paper clips. Then attach the plastic bag to the small paper clip.

Next

Tape the notebook paper to the wall. The lines on the paper should be vertical. Be sure the paper is level.

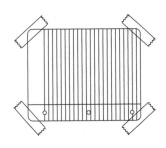

Then

Tape the large paper clip to the wall just above the notebook paper. The bottom of the rubber band should reach the top edge of the paper.

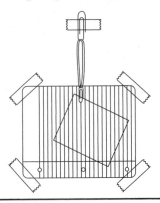

Rubber Band Stretch Graph

(Use with Questions 17–19 on page 332.)

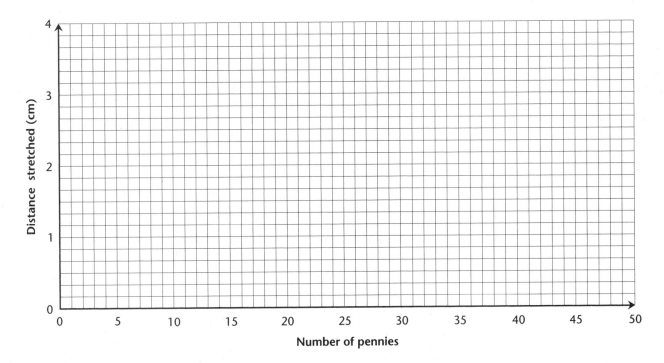

Math Thematics, Book 2 **5-43**

MODULE 5   **LABSHEET** (2B)

Box-and-Whisker Plot   (Use with Questions 21–25 on pages 334–335.)

Directions Plot the winning number of skips for each year from 1969–1984 (except 1981) on the line plot below the box-and-whisker plot. The first three values in the table have been plotted for you.

Mackinac Island Stone Skipping Tournament 1969–1984

Year	Winning number of skips	Year	Winning number of skips
1969	15 ✔	1977	24
1970	13 ✔	1978	18
1971	13 ✔	1979	17
1972	10	1980	15
1973	9	1981	(not available)
1974	19	1982	22
1975	24	1983	15
1976	23	1984	20

Mackinac Island Stone Skipping Tournament 1969–1984*

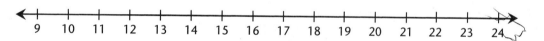

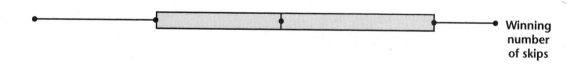

Winning number of skips

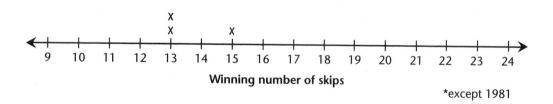

Winning number of skips

*except 1981

Name _____ Date _____

Estimating Percents (Use with Question 5 on page 345.)

Directions Complete the exercises below to learn how to use a percent bar model to estimate the percent rating represented by the fraction $\frac{17}{30}$.

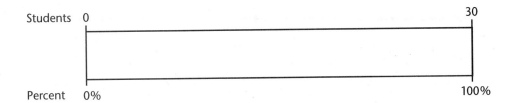

Students   0   30

Percent   0%   100%

a. Use vertical segments to divide the bar into five sections of equal size.

b. What "nice" fractions do the vertical segments you drew in part (a) represent?

c. Below the bar, write the percent that each vertical segment represents.

d. Across the top of the bar, write the number of students represented by each vertical segment.

e. Draw a segment for 17 students about where you think it should be located on the percent bar model. Shade the bar from 0 to 17.

f. Estimate the percent equivalent of $\frac{17}{30}$.

Name _____   Date _____

Bridge Length Graph (Use with Exercise 15 on page 375.)

Directions

• Plot the lengths of the bridges on the coordinate plane below.

• Draw a fitted line along the points on the graph.

Name of the Bridge	Location	Length (ft)	Length (m)
Golden Gate	California, U.S.A.	4200	1280
Forth Road	Queensferry, Scotland	3300	1006
Longview	Washington, U.S.A.	1200	366
Howrah	Calcutta, India	1500	457
Sydney Harbor	Sydney, Australia	1670	509
Zdákov	Czech Republic	1244	380
Tatara	Ehime, Japan	2920	890
Skarnsundet Bridge	Trondheim, Norway	1739	530
Dartford	Dartford, England	1476	450
Graf Spee	Germany	839	256
Amizade	Foz do Iguassu, Brazil	951	290
Fiumarella	Catanzaro, Italy	758	231

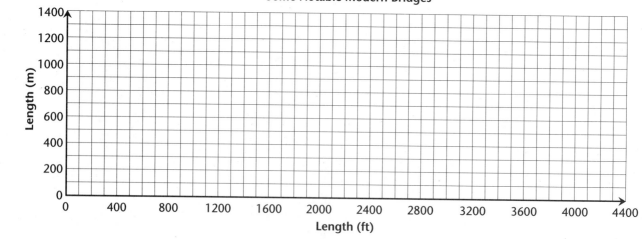

Some Notable Modern Bridges

a. About how many meters long is a 500-foot bridge?

b. About how many feet are in a meter?

Name _____ **Problem** _____

TEACHER ASSESSMENT SCALES

☆ *The star indicates that you excelled in some way.*

?→! Problem Solving

❶————❷————❸————❹————❺————☆→

❶ You did not understand the problem well enough to get started or you did not show any work.

❸ You understood the problem well enough to make a plan and to work toward a solution.

❺ You made a plan, you used it to solve the problem, and you verified your solution.

x² Mathematical Language

❶————❷————❸————❹————❺————☆→

❶ You did not use any mathematical vocabulary or symbols, or you did not use them correctly, or your use was not appropriate.

❸ You used appropriate mathematical language, but the way it was used was not always correct or other terms and symbols were needed.

❺ You used mathematical language that was correct and appropriate to make your meaning clear.

Representations

❶————❷————❸————❹————❺————☆→

❶ You did not use any representations such as equations, tables, graphs, or diagrams to help solve the problem or explain your solution.

❸ You made appropriate representations to help solve the problem or help you explain your solution, but they were not always correct or other representations were needed.

❺ You used appropriate and correct representations to solve the problem or explain your solution.

Connections

❶————❷————❸————❹————❺————☆→

❶ You attempted or solved the problem and then stopped.

❸ You found patterns and used them to extend the solution to other cases, or you recognized that this problem relates to other problems, mathematical ideas, or applications.

❺ You extended the ideas in the solution to the general case, or you showed how this problem relates to other problems, mathematical ideas, or applications.

Presentation

❶————❷————❸————❹————❺————☆→

❶ The presentation of your solution and reasoning is unclear to others.

❸ The presentation of your solution and reasoning is clear in most places, but others may have trouble understanding parts of it.

❺ The presentation of your solution and reasoning is clear and can be understood by others.

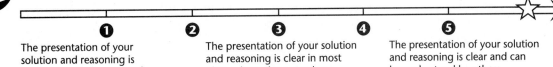

<u>Content Used:</u> _____   **Computational Errors:**   Yes ☐   No ☐

<u>Notes on Errors:</u> _____

_____

Name _____ **Problem** _____

▬▬ *If your score is in the shaded area, explain why on the back of this sheet and stop.*

☆ *The star indicates that you excelled in some way.*

  ### Problem Solving

① **②** **③** **④** **⑤** ☆→

① I did not understand the problem well enough to get started or I did not show any work.

③ I understood the problem well enough to make a plan and to work toward a solution.

⑤ I made a plan, I used it to solve the problem, and I verified my solution.

  ### Mathematical Language

① **②** **③** **④** **⑤** ☆→

① I did not use any mathematical vocabulary or symbols, or I did not use them correctly, or my use was not appropriate.

③ I used appropriate mathematical language, but the way it was used was not always correct or other terms and symbols were needed.

⑤ I used mathematical language that was correct and appropriate to make my meaning clear.

  ### Representations

① **②** **③** **④** **⑤** ☆→

① I did not use any representations such as equations, tables, graphs, or diagrams to help solve the problem or explain my solution.

③ I made appropriate representations to help solve the problem or help me explain my solution, but they were not always correct or other representations were needed.

⑤ I used appropriate and correct representations to solve the problem or explain my solution.

  ### Connections

① **②** **③** **④** **⑤** ☆→

① I attempted or solved the problem and then stopped.

③ I found patterns and used them to extend the solution to other cases, or I recognized that this problem relates to other problems, mathematical ideas, or applications.

⑤ I extended the ideas in the solution to the general case, or I showed how this problem relates to other problems, mathematical ideas, or applications.

 ### Presentation

① **②** **③** **④** **⑤** ☆→

① The presentation of my solution and reasoning is unclear to others.

③ The presentation of my solution and reasoning is clear in most places, but others may have trouble understanding parts of it.

⑤ The presentation of my solution and reasoning is clear and can be understood by others.

What's for Lunch? (E² on textbook page 326)

The Problem Solving, Representations, and Presentation Scales of the *Math Thematics* Assessment Scales should be used to assess student work. This E² has several solutions (possible tours). Students may visit as few as two animal feedings or up to five. When evaluating students' tours, check that all conditions have been met, the amount of time is included, and all assumptions are clearly stated.

The sample response below shows part of a student's solution.

Partial Solution

I wanted to visit many of the exhibits that included an animal feeding and also see a variety of animals. I noticed that the macaques would be fed at 9 A.M. in Eurasia and Eurasia is close to the play area, so I planned to go there first. South America has a llama feeding at 9:30 A.M. , so I went there next. In Africa they feed the hippopotamus at 10:00 A.M. and it is pretty close to South America, so I planned to go there next. Since the next feedings weren't until 11 A.M. I decided the zoo visitors might like to see some of the other exhibits. I decided that Australia and the Lemur Exhibit would be interesting. I saw a polar bear being fed once at the Baltimore Zoo and decided that it would a fun one to watch. The polar bear feeding is at 11:30, so I could be done by noon.

The table and map below show the route I chose, the areas visited, the amount of time, and the distance traveled on this tour. To determine the walking rate, I timed my parents as they walked along the sidewalk outside my house. Our house is about 50 feet across and they were able to walk this distance 6 times in one minute. This gave me a rate of 300 ft/min. In the table, all times were rounded to the next minute.

Area	Distance traveled to reach this area	Time to travel to this area	Start time	Animal to be fed	Animal feeding time	End time	Total distance traveled
Play Area	0	0	8:45 A.M.	none		8:50 A.M.	0
Eurasia	200 ft	1 min	8:51 A.M.	macaques	9:00–9:20 A.M.	9:21 A.M.	200 ft
South America	200 ft	1 min	9:22 A.M.	llama	9:30–9:50 A.M.	9:53 A.M.	400 ft
Africa	500 ft	2 min	9:55 A.M.	hippopotamus	10:00–10:20 A.M.	10:25 A.M.	900 ft
Australia	900 ft	3 min	10:28 A.M.	none		10:58 A.M.	1800 ft
Lemur Exhibit	50 ft	1 min	10:59 A.M.	none		11:20 A.M.	1850 ft
North America	375 ft	2 min	11:22 A.M.	polar bear	11:30–11:50 A.M.	noon	2225 ft

I realized that I could have included a feeding of the tiger in Eurasia or the jaguar in South America. I don't know if adding another feeding would have made this a better tour. I asked my friends and family and they thought they'd like to see the lemurs since they didn't know what they were, rather than see the tiger or jaguar fed.

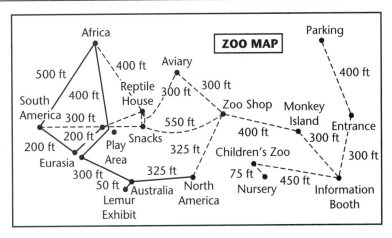

MODULE 5 ALTERNATE E²

Cube Houses

The Situation

Of all rectangular prisms, cubes have the greatest volume for a given surface area. Suppose an architectural company has designed a multi-purpose cube room. Five rooms are linked together by common walls to create a house. There are only two conditions on the construction of these houses:

- a house cannot be more than three cubes high, and
- the rooms of a house must be joined along a face of the cubes.

You will need:

- centimeter cubes (optional)

The Problem

These new houses are to be built in one area of town. The new home owners want every house to have a different floor plan. For example, Plans A and C below are the same, but Plan B is different. How many different house plans are possible?

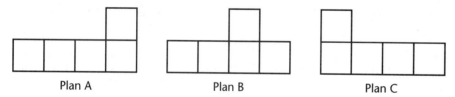

Plan A   Plan B   Plan C

Something to Think About

- How can you show that a house has two stories?
- How can you organize your work to be sure you have found every possible plan?

Present Your Results

Write a report to the architects that tells how many plans are possible. Be sure to describe the possible plans for perspective buyers.

Cube Houses

The Problem Solving, Representations, Connections, and Presentation Scales of the *Math Thematics* Assessment Scales should be used to assess student work. For the Connections Scale, students may extend the problem using a different number of cubes, look at the surface area of the houses, or try to find a pattern for the number of houses possible.

The sample response below shows part of a student's solution. This solution made use of a 2-dimensional viewpoint. Students may make 3-dimensional drawings of the houses or physical models.

Partial Solution

I decided to draw all 1-story houses first, then all 2-story houses, and finally all 3-story houses. In this way I would get all possibilities. My drawings are shown below. An empty square represents a single cube (one story). A square with a "2" represents two stories. A square with a "3" represents three stories.

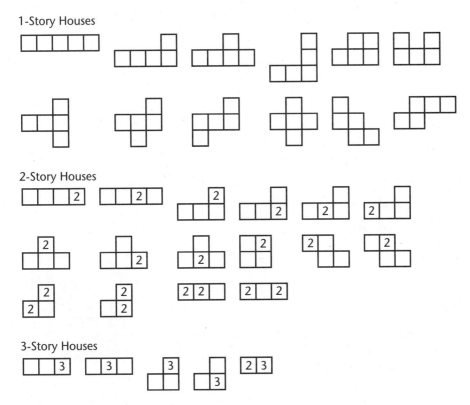

1-Story Houses

2-Story Houses

3-Story Houses

There are 12 possible 1-story houses, 16 different 2-story houses, and five 3-story houses. This makes a total of 33 different house plans using 5 cubes.

Divide.

1. $45 \div 9$ **2.** $93 \div 6$ **3.** $22.8 \div 4$

Find the mean.

4. 1, 3, 6, 2, 3   **5.** 2.7, 3.4, 1.9, 4.6, 2.7, 3.9

MODULE 5 SECTION 1   **QUICK QUIZ**

1. Write $\dfrac{\$14.50}{3\ lb}$ as a unit rate.

2. At 65 mi/h, how long will it take to drive 442 mi?

3. Find the range, median, and the mode.

Point Spreads of First 20 Super Bowls

```
0 | 3 4 4 5 7 9
1 | 0 0 2 4 6 7 7 9
2 | 1 2 5 8 9
3 | 6
```

1 | 2 represents 12 points.

4. Use the histogram to find how many students scored between 70 and 89.

Student Grades on Math Exam

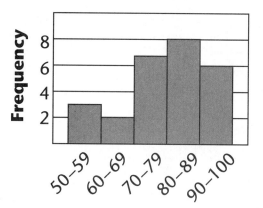

ANSWERS

Warm-Ups: 1. 5 **2.** 15.5 **3.** 5.7 **4.** 3 **5.** 3.2

Quick Quiz: 1. about $4.83/lb **2.** 6.8 h or 6 h 48 min **3.** range: 33 points; median: 15 points; modes: 4, 10, and 17 points **4.** 15 students

Complete each proportion.

1. $\dfrac{2}{1} = \dfrac{6}{?}$

2. $\dfrac{?}{8} = \dfrac{3}{1}$

3. $\dfrac{125}{30} = \dfrac{?}{6}$

Write in lowest terms.

4. $\dfrac{39}{52}$

5. $\dfrac{21}{49}$

MODULE 5 SECTION 2   **QUICK QUIZ**

1. If there are 8 slices in one pizza, how many slices are there in 13 pizzas?

2. Solve the proportion $\dfrac{9}{15} = \dfrac{x}{70}$.

3. Make a scatter plot of the data at the right.

Winning Distances for Men's Olympic Discus

Year	Distance (ft)
1900	118
1920	147
1936	166
1960	194
1980	219

4. Use your scatter plot in Question 3 to estimate the winning time for the year 2000.

5. The box-and-whisker plot shows data for a frog-jumping contest. What was the range of jumps? What was the median jump?

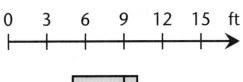

ANSWERS

Warm-Ups: 1. 3   **2.** 24   **3.** 25   **4.** $\frac{3}{4}$ **5.** $\frac{3}{7}$

Quick Quiz: 1. 104   **2.** 42   **3.**   **4.** about 235 ft
5. range: about 14 ft; median: about 9 ft

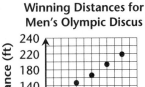

Winning Distances for Men's Olympic Discus

Convert each fraction to a percent.

1. $\dfrac{1}{4}$ **2.** $\dfrac{1}{10}$ **3.** $\dfrac{1}{2}$

Solve each proportion.

4. $\dfrac{x}{100} = \dfrac{14}{40}$ **5.** $\dfrac{32}{100} = \dfrac{50}{x}$

1. Of 42 people surveyed, 27 rated a certain movie as 1 or 2 on a scale of 1 to 10. Use a "nice" fraction to estimate the percent of viewers giving this movie these "thumbs down" ratings.

2. Estimate the percent equivalent of $\dfrac{59}{81}$.

3. Write $\dfrac{42}{135}$ as a percent rounded to the nearest tenth.

4. 35% of what number is 63?

5. Suppose 75% of 6-year-olds weigh under 46 lb. How many 6-year-olds would you expect to weigh under 46 lb in a class of 32 age-six first-graders?

ANSWERS

Warm-Ups: 1. 25% **2.** 10% **3.** 50% **4.** 35 **5.** 156.25

Quick Quiz: 1. Sample Response: 67% $\left(\text{from } \dfrac{28}{42} \text{ or } \dfrac{30}{45}\right)$; 63% $\left(\text{from } \dfrac{25}{40}\right)$; 60% $\left(\text{from } \dfrac{27}{45}\right)$

2. Sample Response: about 75% $\left(\text{from } \dfrac{60}{80}\right)$ **3.** 31.1% **4.** 180 **5.** about 24

Write the fraction as a decimal. Round answers to the nearest thousandth.

1. $\dfrac{3}{7}$ **2.** $\dfrac{11}{51}$ **3.** $\dfrac{67}{102}$

Find the probability of each outcome when you roll a six-sided die.

4. 2   **5.** an even number

1. What is the batting average of a hitter who hit 62 times in 200 at-bats?

2. If a batter has hit .280 over the past three months, about how many hits would you expect her to get in her next 25 times at bat?

3. Write 10 : 85 in percent form rounded to the nearest tenth of a percent.

4. Consider the experiment of spinning the two spinners shown and recording the two colors. Shade a grid to show the probability of getting two reds.

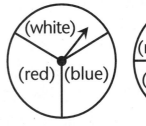

5. Use a tree diagram to show the probability of getting red and blue in either order with the two spinners above.

ANSWERS

Warm-Ups: 1. 0.429 **2.** 0.216 **3.** 0.657 **4.** $\dfrac{1}{6}$ **5.** $\dfrac{1}{2}$

Quick Quiz: 1. .310 **2.** about 7 **3.** 11.8% **4.** P(2 reds) $= \dfrac{2}{12} = \dfrac{1}{6}$

5. P(red and blue) $= \dfrac{1}{12} + \dfrac{1}{6} = \dfrac{1}{4}$

1st spin red

2nd spin red

MODULE 5 SECTION 1   **PRACTICE AND APPLICATIONS**

For use with Exploration 1

1. Write each rate as a unit rate.

a. $\dfrac{68 \text{ min}}{8 \text{ mi}}$ **b.** $\dfrac{138 \text{ mi}}{6 \text{ gal}}$ **c.** $\dfrac{\$8.40}{3 \text{ lb}}$

d. $\dfrac{48 \text{ servings}}{6 \text{ pans}}$ **e.** $\dfrac{\$.28}{4 \text{ min}}$ **f.** $\dfrac{\$2.67}{3 \text{ bunches}}$

g. $\dfrac{32 \text{ min}}{5 \text{ mi}}$ **h.** $\dfrac{\$18}{4 \text{ lb}}$ **i.** $\dfrac{52.2 \text{ gal}}{9 \text{ min}}$

j. $\dfrac{30 \text{ servings}}{3 \text{ pans}}$ **k.** $\dfrac{\$7.77}{3 \text{ bunches}}$ **l.** $\dfrac{48 \text{ servings}}{4 \text{ pans}}$

m. $\dfrac{224 \text{ mi}}{8 \text{ gal}}$ **n.** $\dfrac{\$25.50}{2 \text{ h}}$ **o.** $\dfrac{188 \text{ km}}{8 \text{ L}}$

2. A single grizzly bear may eat 55 pounds of berries per day. Copy and complete the proportion below to show how many pounds of berries a grizzly bear may eat in one week.

$$\frac{55 \text{ lb}}{1 \text{ day}} = \frac{? \text{ lb}}{7 \text{ days}}$$

3. The total area of the district of Columbia is about 68 mi^2. The total population of the District of Columbia is about 600,000 people. Find the population density, or unit rate of people per square mile, for the District of Columbia.

4. To train for a cross country ski race, Frank wants to ski a total of 120 mi at an average rate no slower than 8 min/mi.

a. Copy and complete the table below to show the distance covered and cross country skiing times for a rate of 8 min/mi.

Time (min)	?	8	?	80	?
Distance (mi)	0.5	1	5	?	120

b. How many hours would it take Frank to cross country ski 120 mi at a rate of 8 min/mi?

5. Suppose Erin runs at the rates shown in the table below.

a. Copy and complete the table for 30 s and 60 s.

Time (s)	1	5	20	30	50
Distance (ft)	6	30	120	?	?

b. How far would you expect Erin to run in 50 s?

(continued)

MODULE 5 SECTION 1   **PRACTICE AND APPLICATIONS**

For use with Exploration 2

6. The table shows the number of minutes 20 students in Mr. Clement's class spent reading one night.

Student	Number of minutes	Student	Number of minutes
Jim	89	Doreen	94
Tim	76	Mary	88
Ralph	100	Bob	83
Keisha	85	Nick	79
Arnold	92	Matt	91
Barney	99	Liza	100
Alicia	89	Marty	89
Francine	88	Rosa	86
Buster	83	Janice	92
Arthur	90	Carter	96

a. Make a stem-and-leaf plot to show the number of minutes the students in Mr. Clement's class spent reading one night. Be sure to include a title and a key for your plot.

b. Use the stem-and-leaf plot to find the range, the mean, the median, and the mode of the number of minutes the students in Mr. Clement's class spent reading.

c. What would you consider an average time for the number of minutes the students in Mr. Clement's class spent reading?

For use with Exploration 3

7. The histogram shows the number of minutes students spent on their homework at Alta Junior High School.

a. How many minutes are included in each interval?

b. About how many students spend from 21–30 minutes on homework?

c. Is the number of students who spend more than one half hour on homework greater than, equal to, or less than the number of students who spend less than one half hour on homework?

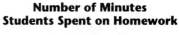

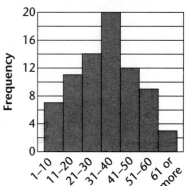

MODULE 5 SECTION 2 — PRACTICE AND APPLICATIONS

For use with Exploration 1

1. How many grams of protein are contained in 680 g of yogurt if 170 g of yogurt contain 7 g of protein?

2. How many grams of carbohydrate are contained in 448 g of pasta if 56 g of pasta contain 40 g of carbohydrate?

3. A horse eats about 75 lb of hay every 4 days. How many pounds of hay would you expect it to eat in 28 days?

4. Solve each proportion.

   a. $\dfrac{8}{15} = \dfrac{28}{x}$ **b.** $\dfrac{7}{n} = \dfrac{112}{384}$ **c.** $\dfrac{12}{76} = \dfrac{b}{171}$

   d. $\dfrac{36}{45} = \dfrac{y}{15}$ **e.** $\dfrac{m}{24} = \dfrac{51}{72}$ **f.** $\dfrac{3}{x} = \dfrac{24}{40}$

   g. $\dfrac{5}{12} = \dfrac{w}{30}$ **h.** $\dfrac{16}{c} = \dfrac{56}{105}$ **i.** $\dfrac{5}{9} = \dfrac{4.5}{t}$

   j. $\dfrac{4.5}{x} = \dfrac{18}{48}$ **k.** $\dfrac{5}{9} = \dfrac{z}{72}$ **l.** $\dfrac{14}{k} = \dfrac{56}{34}$

   m. $\dfrac{4}{18} = \dfrac{10}{x}$ **n.** $\dfrac{8}{14} = \dfrac{12}{n}$ **o.** $\dfrac{9}{15} = \dfrac{b}{75}$

5. A selection of the Morningside Café's breakfast menu is shown at the right with the average quantity of the items the restaurant usually uses in two days.

   a. How many pounds of pancake mix would you expect the Morningside Café to use in 7 days?

   b. How many gallons of orange juice would you expect the Café to use in 14 days?

   c. How many loaves of whole wheat bread would you expect the Café to use in 30 days?

   d. How many pounds of maple syrup would you expect the Café to use in 60 days?

Morningside Café Breakfast Menu

Item	Amount
bacon	35 lb
eggs	40 dozen
whole wheat bread	50 loaves
white bread	85 loaves
pancake mix	75 lb
maple syrup	12 lb
orange juice	15 gal

(continued)

Name _____   Date _____

For use with Exploration 2

6. Two real estate agents made the scatter plots below to show the relationship between the living area and selling prices of houses in a selected area. Choose the letter of the scatter plot that you think shows the better fitted line. Explain your choice.

A.

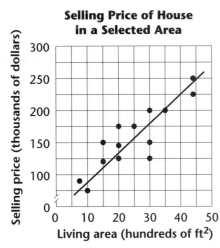

B.

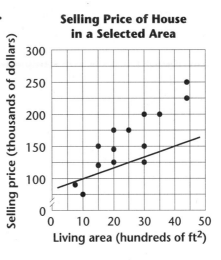

7. Use the scatter plot you chose in Exercise 6.

a. About what do you think the selling price of a 3500 ft^2 house in the selected area would be?

b. There are two houses with a living area of 3000 ft^2. One sells for $125,000 and the other sells for $150,000. Why do you think the selling prices are different?

For use with Exploration 3

8. Use the box-and-whisker plot shown.

a. Estimate the greatest amount of money a shopper spent at the grocery store.

b. Estimate the least amount of money a shopper spent at the grocery store.

c. Estimate the median amount of money a shopper spent at the grocery store.

d. Estimate the range in the amounts of money the shoppers spent at the grocery store.

Amount of Money Spent by 75 Shoppers in a Grocery Store

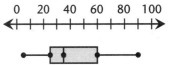

MODULE 5 SECTION 3 — PRACTICE AND APPLICATIONS

For use with Exploration 1

1. It is estimated that 9 out of 14 teenagers enrolled in Riviera Middle School play soccer. Estimate the percent of teenagers in Riviera Middle School who play soccer.

2. In a marketing survey of a new cereal, 8 out of every 17 people who responded gave the new cereal a rating of 9 or 10 on a scale of 1 to 10.

  a. What "nice" fraction can you use to estimate the percent of people who gave the cereal a rating of 9 or 10?

  b. Estimate the percent of people who gave the cereal a rating of 9 or 10.

3. Estimate the percent equivalent of each ratio.

  a. $\dfrac{9}{11}$ **b.** $\dfrac{11}{32}$ **c.** $\dfrac{7}{18}$

  d. $\dfrac{24}{35}$ **e.** $\dfrac{10}{24}$ **f.** $\dfrac{42}{85}$

  g. $\dfrac{17}{21}$ **h.** $\dfrac{42}{98}$ **i.** $\dfrac{34}{99}$

  j. $\dfrac{4}{19}$ **k.** $\dfrac{6}{49}$ **l.** $\dfrac{11}{45}$

For use with Exploration 2

4. Set up and solve a proportion to find the actual percent for Exercises 1 and 2. Round each answer to the nearest percent.

5. Write each ratio as a percent. Round each answer to the nearest tenth of a percent.

  a. $\dfrac{10}{12}$ **b.** $\dfrac{54}{135}$ **c.** $\dfrac{72}{96}$

  d. $\dfrac{75}{120}$ **e.** $\dfrac{21}{30}$ **f.** $\dfrac{45}{96}$

  g. $\dfrac{40}{150}$ **h.** $\dfrac{52}{160}$ **i.** $\dfrac{12}{72}$

  j. $\dfrac{28}{36}$ **k.** $\dfrac{25}{80}$ **l.** $\dfrac{14}{70}$

6. Of the 2628 new books purchased by the library, 525 were for teenagers. What percent of the new books were for teenagers?

(continued)

MODULE 5 SECTION 3   PRACTICE AND APPLICATIONS

For use with Exploration 3

7. Suppose 44% of students at a school do not like classical music. If 198 students do not like classical music, how many students are there in the school? Explain your reasoning.

8. Find each unknown number.

    a. 35% of a number is 17.5.   **b.** 42 is 70% of a number.

    c. 68% of a number is 578.   **d.** A number is 34% of 75.

    e. 18% of a number is 32.4.   **f.** A number is 23% of 16.

    g. 45% of a number is 117.   **h.** A number is 70% of 560.

    i. A number is 30% of 120.   **j.** 25% of a number is 21.

    k. 61% of a number is 91.5.   **l.** 60 is 48% of a number.

    m. A number is 40% of 40.   **n.** 5% of a number is 25.

    o. 75% of a number is 84.   **p.** 63% of a number is 56.7.

    q. 56 is 25% of a number.   **r.** A number is 4% of 75.

    s. 48% of a number is 172.8.   **t.** A number is 71% of 120.

    u. 60% of a number is 18.   **v.** 30% of a number is 45.

    w. A number is 55% of 300.   **x.** A number is 82% of 70.

9. A book costs $5.95. The tax on the book is 8% of the cost. What is the total cost of the book?

10. Jerry and Nadine had dinner at a Chinese restaurant. They left a 15% tip that was $2.70. How much did the meal cost before the tip?

11. An aerobics instructor maintains a strict diet of 2000 Calories per day. An 8 oz container of yogurt provides the instructor with 12% of her daily Calories. How many Calories does the yogurt provide?

12. In a school election, 285 students voted for Bill for the Student Council President. If 47.5% of the students voted for Bill, how many students voted in the election?

MODULE 5 SECTION 4   **PRACTICE AND APPLICATIONS**

For use with Exploration 1

1. Write each ratio as a fraction in lowest terms, a decimal, and a percent.

     a. $2:3$ **b.** $18:36$ **c.** $12:20$

     d. $9:25$ **e.** $3:9$ **f.** $28:40$

     g. $27:36$ **h.** $37:100$ **i.** $9.5:10$

For use with Exploration 2

2. Write each ratio, fraction, or decimal in percent form.

     a. $7:50$ **b.** $\dfrac{3}{4}$ **c.** 0.6

     d. $38:50$ **e.** $\dfrac{7}{8}$ **f.** 0.485

     g. $\dfrac{30}{80}$ **h.** $\dfrac{4}{25}$ **i.** $\dfrac{45}{125}$

3. Use mental math to write each fraction as a percent.

     a. $\dfrac{3}{20}$ **b.** $\dfrac{17}{25}$ **c.** $\dfrac{5}{20}$

     d. $\dfrac{1}{9}$ **e.** $\dfrac{32}{100}$ **f.** $\dfrac{222}{333}$

     g. $\dfrac{42}{84}$ **h.** $\dfrac{3.5}{50}$ **i.** $\dfrac{16}{32}$

4. To help the school dietician plan lunch menus, some students at a middle school took a survey of a random sample of their classmates to determine the top favorite lunch foods at their school. About 30% of the students surveyed chose pizza as their favorite lunch food. About 25% of the students surveyed chose sandwiches as their favorite lunch food. About 15% of the students surveyed chose pasta as their favorite lunch food. Suppose 600 students attend the school. How many of them would you expect to choose each food listed below?

     A. pizza   **B.** sandwiches   **C.** pasta

5. About 79% of American households have a microwave oven. Estimate the number of households that have a microwave oven in a population of 600,000 people.

(continued)

MODULE 5 SECTION 4   **PRACTICE AND APPLICATIONS**

For use with Exploration 3

6. Consider the experiment of flipping a coin and rolling a 6-sided die. Shade a grid to find the probability of each event.

    a. heads and the number 3
        b. tails and a number less than 4

    c. tails and an even number
        d. heads and a number greater than 1

    e. heads and a 5 or 6
        f. tails and a number less than 5

7. A bag contains one green marble and three yellow marbles. Three marbles are removed from the bag one after another. After each marble is removed, its color is recorded and the marble is put back into the bag before the next marble is removed.

Copy and complete the tree diagram at the right to show the outcomes of this experiment. Label each branch of the tree with the probability.

First marble
G
Y

8. Use the tree diagram from Exercise 7 to find the probability of each event. Round answers to the nearest tenth of a percent.

    a. drawing three green marbles
        b. drawing three yellow marbles

    c. drawing a green, a yellow, and a green marble
        d. drawing a yellow, a yellow, and a green marble

    e. drawing exactly two yellow marbles
        f. drawing exactly two green marbles

    g. drawing at least one yellow marble
        h. drawing at least one green marble

9. Suppose the probability that it will snow in Yellowstone this week is $\frac{3}{8}$ each day.

    a. What is the probability that it will not snow on a given day?

    b. Make a tree diagram to find all the possible outcomes for two consecutive days.

    c. Use a grid to find the probability of snow on two consecutive days.

    d. What is the probability that it will not snow on two consecutive days?

    e. What is the probability it will snow the first day and *not* snow the second day?

Name _____   Date _____

For use with Section 1

1. Write each rate as a unit rate.

a. $\dfrac{46 \text{ min}}{5 \text{ mi}}$ **b.** $\dfrac{243 \text{ mi}}{9 \text{ gal}}$ **c.** $\dfrac{\$.64}{8 \text{ min}}$

d. $\dfrac{176.4 \text{ km}}{6 \text{ L}}$ **e.** $\dfrac{38 \text{ min}}{4 \text{ mi}}$ **f.** $\dfrac{\$15}{4 \text{ lb}}$

g. $\dfrac{\$58.40}{4 \text{ h}}$ **h.** $\dfrac{\$4.08}{6 \text{ bunches}}$ **i.** $\dfrac{45 \text{ min}}{6 \text{ mi}}$

2. To celebrate her fiftieth birthday, Beatrice ran a 50 mile race. Her time for the race was about 14 h. Represent Beatrice's running pace as a unit rate. Round your answer to the nearest tenth.

3. Use the stem-and-leaf plot showing the spelling test scores for one class.

a. Do you notice any gaps or clusters in the data? Explain?

b. What is the range of the spelling test scores in the stem-and-leaf plot?

c. Find the median and mode of the data.

Spelling Test Scores

```
 6 | 9
 7 |
 8 | 0 0 2 5 6 7 8 8 9
 9 | 0 1 1 1 2 2 3 4 5 8
10 | 0
```

8 | 7 means 87

For use with Section 2

4. Solve each proportion.

a. $\dfrac{m}{8} = \dfrac{4.2}{2.4}$ **b.** $\dfrac{24}{18} = \dfrac{38.4}{s}$ **c.** $\dfrac{6}{y} = \dfrac{21}{52.5}$

d. $\dfrac{14}{5} = \dfrac{70}{c}$ **e.** $\dfrac{a}{20} = \dfrac{24}{96}$ **f.** $\dfrac{9}{p} = \dfrac{45}{18}$

g. $\dfrac{5}{16} = \dfrac{17.5}{t}$ **h.** $\dfrac{16}{20} = \dfrac{4}{x}$ **i.** $\dfrac{36}{54} = \dfrac{v}{40.5}$

j. $\dfrac{c}{3} = \dfrac{24}{48}$ **k.** $\dfrac{33}{15} = \dfrac{w}{45}$ **l.** $\dfrac{7}{25} = \dfrac{1.4}{r}$

5. A dog eats about 12 lb of dog food every 15 days. How many pounds of dog food would you expect it to eat in 60 days?

(continued)

MODULE 5 SECTIONS 1–4   PRACTICE AND APPLICATIONS

For use with Section 3

6. Estimate the percent equivalent of each ratio.

    a. $\dfrac{38}{79}$ **b.** $\dfrac{1}{9}$ **c.** $\dfrac{41}{52}$

    d. $\dfrac{21}{80}$ **e.** $\dfrac{63}{81}$ **f.** $\dfrac{22}{50}$

7. Write each ratio as a percent. Round each answer to the nearest tenth of a percent.

    a. $\dfrac{28}{60}$ **b.** $\dfrac{17}{85}$ **c.** $\dfrac{32}{128}$

    d. $\dfrac{11}{20}$ **e.** $\dfrac{23}{25}$ **f.** $\dfrac{42}{78}$

8. Find each unknown number.

    a. 25% of a number is 30.   **b.** 105 is 75% of a number.

    c. 60% of a number is 54.   **d.** A number is 42% of 65.

    e. A number is 36% of 150.   **f.** A number is 15% of 60.

9. Members of a running club had lunch at the Whole Grain Burger Palace. They left a 15% tip that totaled $9.30. How much did the meal cost?

For use with Section 4

10. Use mental math to write each fraction as a percent.

    a. $\dfrac{13}{20}$ **b.** $\dfrac{22}{25}$ **c.** $\dfrac{6}{24}$

11. About 76% of American households have a washing machine. Estimate the number of households that have a washing machine in a population of 200,000 people.

12. A box contains 1 red marker and 4 blue markers. Without looking, Danny reaches into the box and pulls out the first marker he touches. He puts the marker back into the box and then his sister Megan reaches into the box, without looking, and pulls out the first marker that she touches. What is the probability that both Danny and Megan pull out blue markers?

MODULE 5 SECTION 1   STUDY GUIDE

Run for Your Life   Ratios and Data Displays

GOAL **LEARN HOW TO:** • find unit rates
                      • set up proportions
                      • make and interpret stem-and-leaf plots
                      • interpret histograms

AS YOU: • explore running times
          • examine the results of a race

Exploration 1: Ratio and Proportions

Rates, Ratios, and Proportions

A **ratio** is a comparison of two quantities by
division. A ratio can be written in any of the   12 ft to 3 s $\frac{12 \text{ ft}}{3 \text{ s}}$ 12 ft : 3 s
three forms shown at the right.

A **rate** is a ratio that compares quantities measured in different units.

> **Examples**
>
> **a.** The ratio $\frac{35 \text{ mi}}{2 \text{ gal}}$ compares miles to gallons by division, so it is a rate.
>
> **b.** The ratio $\frac{3 \text{ min}}{60 \text{ min}}$ compares minutes to minutes, so it is *not* a rate.

A **proportion** is an equation stating that two ratios are equivalent. A **unit
rate** is the rate for one unit of a given quantity.

> **Example**
>
> Write $\frac{\$4.50}{6 \text{ cans}}$ as a unit rate.
>
> **Sample Response**
>
> Use a proportion to find the unit rate; that is, find the price for just 1 can.
>
> $$\frac{\$4.50}{6 \text{ cans}} = \frac{x}{1 \text{ can}}$$
>
> *Think*: What number must you divide the numerator and denominator by to change
> 6 cans to 1 can?
>
> $$\frac{\$4.50 \div 6}{6 \text{ cans} \div 6} = \frac{\$.75}{1 \text{ can}}$$
>
> The unit rate is $.75/can.

5-66 Math Thematics, Book 2

MODULE 5 SECTION 1   STUDY GUIDE

Exploration 2: Stem-and-Leaf Plots

Displays of Data

The **median** is the middle item when you order a data set from least to greatest. The **mode** is the item that appears most often in a set of data. The **range** of a data set is the difference between the greatest data value and the least data value.

Stem-and-leaf plots can be used to organize and display data. Stem-and-leaf plots show each data value. The *ones digit* of a data value is a *leaf*. The remaining digit or digits of the number form the *stem* for that leaf. The stems are written vertically in order from least to greatest. The leaves are then written horizontally next to the appropriate stem in order from least to greatest.

Medals Won by the Top 20 Countries in 1996 Olympics

```
 1 | 5 5 5 5 7 7 9
 2 | 0 1 2 3 5 7
 3 | 5 7
 4 | 1
 5 | 0
 6 | 3 5
 7 |
 8 |
 9 |
10 | 1
```

6 | 3 represents 63 medals.

Example

Find the mode, the median, and the range of the data shown in the stem-and-leaf plot above.

Sample Response

The mode is 15, because 15 occurs most often (4 times).

There are 20 data values in order in the plot. The median is the average of the 10th and 11th values found by counting from the first row of the plot. So, the median is $(22 + 23) \div 2$, or 22.5.

The greatest value is 101 and the least value is 15, so the range is $101 - 15$, or 86.

Exploration 3: Histograms

Frequency tables and **histograms** display frequencies in given intervals. A histogram is a bar graph with no spaces between the bars.

Weight of Puppies Sold at a Pet Store

Weight (lb)	Frequency
0.1–2.0	23
2.1–4.0	25
4.1–6.0	15
6.1–8.0	9
8.1–10.0	5

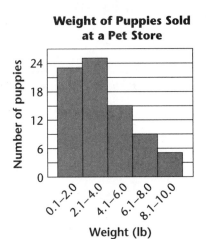

Weight of Puppies Sold at a Pet Store

Name _____   Date _____

Exploration 1

For Exercises 1–4, write each rate as a unit rate.

1. $\dfrac{\$13.80}{3 \text{ boxes}}$ **2.** $\dfrac{135 \text{ mi}}{5 \text{ gal}}$ **3.** $\dfrac{25¢}{4 \text{ min}}$ **4.** $\dfrac{3 \text{ mi}}{25 \text{ min}}$

5. A typical shower uses 4 gal of water per minute. How many gallons of water are used during a 15 min shower?

6. Long distance company X charges $2.70 for a 15 min call. Company Y charges $4.50 for a 27 min call. Which phone company has the best rates for its customers?

Exploration 2

7. a. This list gives the ages of the people enrolled in art classes at the museum: 15, 23, 18, 45, 63, 70, 34, 15, 28, 65, 65, 67, 19. Make a stem-and-leaf plot to show these ages. Be sure to include a title and a key for your plot.

    b. State the range, the median, and the mode of the data.

Exploration 3

Use the histogram at the right.

8. Is the number of students who read more than 3 hours per week *greater than*, *equal to*, or *less than* the number of students who read 3 hours or less per week?

9. How many students read at least 2 hours each week?

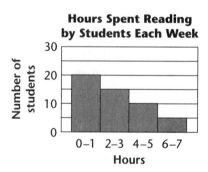

Spiral Review

Solve each equation. Check each solution. (Module 4, p. 300)

10. $3x + 5 = 26$ **11.** $6 + \dfrac{t}{3} = -3$ **12.** $\dfrac{y}{9} - 7 = 8$

Use mental math to find a reasonable estimate for the cost of each purchase. (Toolbox, pp. 582–583)

13. 2.5 lb of candy at $5.95 for 3 lb   **14.** 12 apples at $.39 per apple

Write each fraction in lowest terms. (Module 3, p. 170)

15. $\dfrac{24}{88}$ **16.** $\dfrac{9}{39}$ **17.** $\dfrac{20}{90}$ **18.** $\dfrac{6}{45}$

MODULE 5 SECTION 2 | STUDY GUIDE

Just for Fun   Proportions and Plots

GOAL **LEARN HOW TO:** • solve proportions using cross products
• make a scatter plot
• fit a line to a scatter plot
• interpret box-and-whisker plots

AS YOU: • explore the riders' experience on a roller coaster
• examine how much a rubber band stretches
• examine stone-skipping data

Exploration 1: Cross Products

You can use **cross products** to solve a proportion. Cross products are found by multiplying the numerator of one ratio in the proportion times the denominator of the other ratio.

The cross products of the proportion $\frac{1}{3} = \frac{4}{12}$ are $1 \cdot 12$ and $3 \cdot 4$.

Example

Solve the proportion $\frac{4}{5} = \frac{x}{15}$.

▨ Sample Response ▨

$$\frac{4}{5} = \frac{x}{15}$$

$4 \cdot 15 = 5 \cdot x$ ← Use cross products to write an equation.

$60 = 5x$

$\dfrac{60}{5} = \dfrac{5x}{5}$ ← Divide both sides by 5.

$12 = x$

Exploration 2: Scatter Plots

Scatter Plots and Fitted Lines

A **scatter plot** is a good way to explore how two sets of data are related. If the data values lie along a line, you can use a **fitted line** to make predictions.

For example, the fitted line on the scatter plot at the right can be used to predict that about 25 trees will be sold at $125 each.

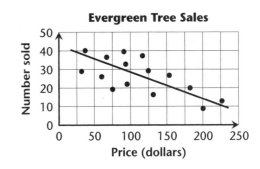

Evergreen Tree Sales

Name _____   Date _____

Exploration 3: Box-and-Whisker Plots

Box-and-whisker plots are useful for displaying a set of data. There are five important points represented in a box-and-whisker plot.

• The whisker on the left is called the *lower whisker*. The dot at the left end of the lower whisker represents the least value (the *lower extreme*).

• The whisker on the right is the *upper whisker* and the dot at its right end represents the greatest value (the *upper extreme*).

• The box between the two whiskers is divided into two parts by a vertical line. This vertical line represents the *median of the entire data set* (50% of the data are less than this value and 50% is greater).

• The point represented by the left end of the box is the median of the lower half of the data values. This point is called the *lower quartile* value.

• The point represented by the right end of the box is the median of the upper half of the data values. This point is called the *upper quartile* value.

Also, both of the whiskers and both parts of the box contain approximately 25% of the values in the data set.

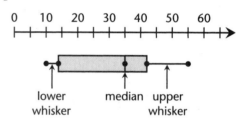

| **Example** |

Refer to the box-and-whisker plot above.

a. What is the greatest data value of the data set? the least data value?

b. What is the range of the data?

c. What is the median of the data?

d. About what percent of the data are greater than 14?

Sample Response

a. 55 (The value represented by the right end of the upper whisker.); 10 (The value represented by the left end of the lower whisker.)

b. 55 – 10, or 45

c. 35

d. Since 14 is the value represented by the lower end of the box, approximately 75% of the data values are greater than 14.

MODULE 5 SECTION 2 | PRACTICE & APPLICATION EXERCISES | STUDY GUIDE

Exploration 1

Solve each proportion.

1. $\dfrac{8}{22} = \dfrac{g}{33}$

2. $\dfrac{4}{k} = \dfrac{6}{21}$

3. $\dfrac{18}{24} = \dfrac{c}{40}$

4. $\dfrac{5}{12} = \dfrac{3.5}{x}$

Exploration 2

The scatter plots below shows the relationship between the monthly normal temperatures and the average precipitation for Boston, Massachusetts.

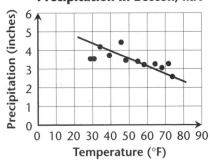

A. Monthly Normal Temperatures/ Precipitation in Boston, MA

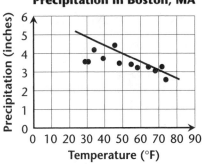

B. Monthly Normal Temperatures/ Precipitation in Boston, MA

5. Choose the letter of the scatter plot that you think shows the better fitted line. Explain your choice.

6. About how many inches of precipitation would you expect in Boston when the temperature averages 50°?

Exploration 3

Use the box-and-whisker plot at the right.

7. What is the age of the youngest swimmer?

8. About half of the swimmers are under what age?

Age of Swim Team Members (years)

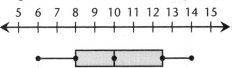

Spiral Review

Write each rate as a unit rate. (Module 5, p. 319)

9. $\dfrac{\$210}{3\ \text{books}}$

10. $\dfrac{75\ \text{min}}{5\ \text{pages}}$

11. $\dfrac{\$29}{2\ \text{dinners}}$

Write each product in exponential form. (Module 1, p. 20)

12. $6 \cdot 6$

13. $2 \cdot 2 \cdot 2 \cdot 2 \cdot 2$

14. $7 \cdot 7 \cdot 7 \cdot 7 \cdot 7 \cdot 7 \cdot 7$

Write each fraction in lowest terms. (Module 3, p. 170)

15. $\dfrac{16}{44}$

16. $\dfrac{5}{90}$

17. $\dfrac{34}{85}$

18. $\dfrac{39}{60}$

Name _____   Date _____

You Be the Critic   Percent

GOAL **LEARN HOW TO:** • estimate percents
                        • find percents
                        • find a missing part or a whole

AS YOU: • analyze movie ratings
           • find audience approval ratings
           • find how many people rated a movie

Exploration 1: Estimating Percents

Percent Bar Model

When solving problems involving percent, "nice" fractions can be used to
help estimate solutions. "Nice" fractions are fractions that can be
converted to percents easily. $\frac{1}{5}$, $\frac{1}{2}$, $\frac{3}{4}$, and $\frac{7}{10}$ are examples of "nice" fractions.

> **Example**
>
> Estimate the percent equivalent of 21 out of 40.
>
> **■ Sample Response ■**
>
> $\frac{21}{40}$ is slightly greater than the "nice" fraction $\frac{1}{2}$.
>
> Since $\frac{1}{2} = 50\%$, $\frac{21}{40}$ is a little more than 50%.

Exploration 2: Finding Percent

Proportions and Percents

You can find the percent equivalent for a ratio by using a proportion.

> **Example**
>
> Write the ratio $\frac{21}{40}$ as a percent.
>
> **■ Sample Response ■**
>
> $$\frac{21}{40} = \frac{x}{100}$$
>
> $$40 \cdot x = 21 \cdot 100$$
>
> $$40x = 2100$$
>
> $$x = 52.5 \qquad \text{So, } \frac{21}{40} = 52.5\%.$$

MODULE 5 SECTION 3   STUDY GUIDE

Exploration 3: Finding Parts or Wholes

You can use proportions to find a missing part or whole.

Example

Set up and solve a proportion to find the number that is 35% of 70.

Sample Response

$$
\begin{array}{cc}
\textbf{Percent} & \textbf{Number} \\
\end{array}
$$

Part → $\dfrac{35}{100} = \dfrac{x}{70}$ ← Part
Whole → $\phantom{\dfrac{35}{100}}$ ← Whole

Now solve the proportion.

$$\frac{35}{100} = \frac{x}{70}$$

$35 \cdot 70 = 100 \cdot x$ ← Use the cross products.

$2450 = 100x$

$\dfrac{2450}{100} = \dfrac{100x}{100}$ ← Divide both sides by 100.

$24.5 = x$

So, 35% of 70 is 24.5.

Example

36 is 45% of some number. Use a proportion to find the number.

Sample Response

$$
\begin{array}{cc}
\textbf{Percent} & \textbf{Number} \\
\end{array}
$$

Part → $\dfrac{45}{100} = \dfrac{36}{y}$ ← Part
Whole → $\phantom{\dfrac{45}{100}}$ ← Whole

Now solve the proportion.

$$\frac{45}{100} = \frac{36}{y}$$

$45 \cdot y = 100 \cdot 36$ ← Use the cross products.

$45y = 3600$

$\dfrac{45y}{45} = \dfrac{3600}{45}$ ← Divide both sides by 45.

$y = 80$

So, 36% of 45 is 80.

MODULE 5 SECTION 3 | PRACTICE & APPLICATION EXERCISES | STUDY GUIDE

Exploration 1

For Exercises 1–4, estimate the percent equivalent of each ratio.

1. $\frac{11}{23}$ **2.** $\frac{6}{21}$ **3.** $\frac{14}{17}$ **4.** $\frac{25}{26}$

5. A librarian estimated that 5 out every 13 library patrons ask the resource librarian a question. Estimate the percent of patrons who ask the resource librarian a question.

Exploration 2

For Exercises 6–9, write each ratio as a percent. Round each answer to the nearest tenth.

6. $\frac{40}{60}$ **7.** $\frac{15}{25}$ **8.** $\frac{11}{50}$ **9.** $\frac{7}{9}$

10. In Marta's class, 8 out of 28 students got 100% on a science exam. What percent of the class did *not* get 100%?

Exploration 3

Find each unknown number.

11. 13% of a number is 7.28.

12. A number is 27% of 44.

13. A number is 40% of 120.

14. 98% of a number is 98.

15. 80% of a number is 20.

16. A number is 75% of 150.

Spiral Review

Solve each proportion. (Module 5, p. 336)

17. $\frac{4}{5} = \frac{x}{25}$ **18.** $\frac{t}{7} = \frac{30}{280}$ **19.** $\frac{3}{m} = \frac{20}{100}$

Find the absolute value of each integer. (Module 2, p. 91)

20. −99   **21.** 58   **22.** −8   **23.** −1145

Write each fraction in lowest terms. (Module 3, p. 170)

24. $\frac{36}{180}$ **25.** $\frac{21}{35}$ **26.** $\frac{12}{15}$ **27.** $\frac{38}{44}$

MODULE 5 SECTION 4   **STUDY GUIDE**

Make Every Shot Count   Percent and Probability

GOAL   **LEARN HOW TO:** • write a fraction as a decimal or percent
  • estimate percents using "nice" fractions and mental math
  • use percents to make predictions
  • find theoretical probabilities for a multiple-stage experiment

  AS YOU: • test your free-throw ability
  • examine basketball statistics
  • analyze repeated free throws

Exploration 1: Fractions, Decimals, and Percents

Fraction-Decimal-Percent Equivalents

A ratio can be represented as a fraction, as a decimal, and as a percent.

Example

Write 24 out of 50 in ratio, fraction, decimal, and percent form.

Ratio form	Fraction form	Decimal form	Percent form
24 to 50 or 24 : 50	$\frac{24}{50}$	0.48	48%

Exploration 2: Predicting Using Percents

Percents can be used to predict future outcomes.

Example

John has hit the bull's-eye of a target with a dart on 15 of 65 throws. How many bull's-eyes can he expect to get in his next 10 throws?

Sample Response

original fraction: $\frac{15}{65} = \frac{3}{13}$ →   " nice" fraction: $\frac{3}{12} = \frac{1}{4}$

So, $\frac{15}{65} \approx \frac{1}{4} = 25\%$.

Since 25% of 10 = 0.25 • 10, or 2.5, John can expect to hit the bull's-eye 2 or 3 times in his next 10 throws.

Name _____ Date _____

Exploration 3: Multi-stage Experiments

Probability and Multi-stage Experiments

A **multi-stage experiment** consists of doing two or more events one after the other. You can find the probability of the outcomes of a multi-stage experiment by shading a grid or constructing a tree diagram.

Example

A spinner has three equal sectors numbered 1–3. If the spinner is spun twice, what is the probability that a 3 is spun both times?

■ Sample Response ■

There is a 1 in 3 chance of spinning a 3 on any spin.

Method 1: Use a 3×3 grid.

Start on the left and shade $\frac{1}{3}$ of the columns (1 column) to show the probability that a 3 is spun on the first spin.

Start at the top and shade $\frac{1}{3}$ of the rows (1 row) to show the probability that the second spin is a 3.

The probability that the first and the second spins will both be a 3 is represented by the region of the grid that was shaded twice. So, the probability is $\frac{1}{9}$.

Method 2: Use a tree diagram.

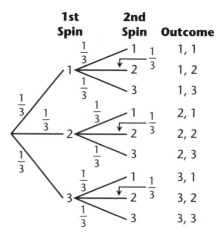

From the diagram, $P(3, 3) = \frac{1}{3} \cdot \frac{1}{3} = \frac{1}{9}$.

MODULE 5 SECTION 4 | **PRACTICE & APPLICATION EXERCISES** | **STUDY GUIDE**

Exploration 1

For Exercises 1–8, write each ratio as a fraction, as a decimal, and as a percent.

1. $2:5$ **2.** $12:36$ **3.** $8:40$ **4.** $18:100$

5. $25:500$ **6.** $5.4:21$ **7.** $18:24$ **8.** $25.8:200$

9. About 30% of 66 students during the first lunch period chose pizza over hamburgers. If a school enrolls 580 students, how many can they expect to eat pizza?

Use mental math to write each fraction as a percent.

10. $\dfrac{11}{33}$ **11.** $\dfrac{8}{32}$ **12.** $\dfrac{24}{400}$ **13.** $\dfrac{16}{24}$

Exploration 2

14. Thelma has earned an A on 24% of all her math tests so far this year. There will be 20 more math tests this year. Estimate the number of A's she can expect to earn on these remaining tests.

15. Petra ran 23 out of 35 cross country races in less than 18 min. Based on these results, how many times in the next 15 races would you expect him to finish in less than 18 min?

Exploration 3

16. A bag contains 4 green chips and 5 red chips. Two chips are removed from the bag one after another. After each chip is removed, its color is recorded and the chip is put back into the bag before the next chip is removed.

   a. Draw a 9×9 grid. Shade it to find the probability of drawing a green chip on the first pick and a red chip on the second pick.

   b. Draw a tree diagram to show the possible outcomes of this experiment. Label each branch of the diagram with the probability of the outcome represented by it.

   c. Use the tree diagram from part (b) to find the probability of drawing 2 red chips.

Spiral Review

Solve each proportion. (Module 5, p. 352)

17. $\dfrac{14}{36} = \dfrac{35}{m}$ **18.** $\dfrac{y}{100} = \dfrac{7}{25}$ **19.** $\dfrac{3}{t} = \dfrac{8}{48}$ **20.** $\dfrac{3}{11} = \dfrac{x}{231}$

MODULE 5 TECHNOLOGY

For Use with Section 2

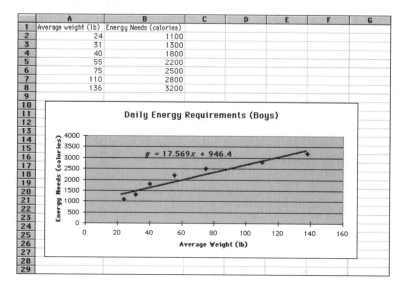

The scatter plot above shows the relationship between the average weight of a boy in pounds and his daily energy requirements in Calories. Spreadsheet software was used to enter the data and graph the data points.

The line in the graph is a fitted line for the the scatter plot. In order to have the software draw the fitted line for you, highlight the graph of the data points. In the **Chart** menu, click on **Add Trendline**. For the type of trend line, click on **Linear.**

1. Do the points of the graph seem to be close to the line?

_____

2. What is the energy requirement in Calories for a boy who weighs 70 pounds? _____

3. Estimate the weight of a boy who needs 3000 Calories a day.

_____

4. Estimate the daily Calorie requirements of a boy who weighs 160 pounds.

_____

Name _____   Date _____

Write each rate as a unit rate.

1. $18/4.5 lb   **2.** 442 mi/8.5 h   **3.** 0.2 in./50 min

4. The numbers of home runs hit by Triple Crown winners the year
they won the Triple Crown are 9, 14, 42, 39, 28, 48, 49, 31, 36, 32,
52, 49, and 44.

  a. Make a stem-and-leaf plot using the home run data.

  b. Find the range, median, and mode of the data.

5. The histogram shows average speeds of the winning
drivers in the Indianapolis 500.

  a. How many of the winning drivers drove 160 mi/h
  or faster?

  b. How many drivers drove between 140 mi/h and
  159 mi/h?

  c. Can you tell what was the fastest winning speed?
  Explain.

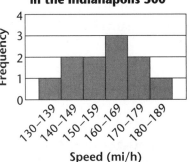

**Average Speed of Winning Drivers
in the Indianapolis 500**

Solve each proportion.

6. $\dfrac{14}{17} = \dfrac{42}{x}$ **7.** $\dfrac{11}{12} = \dfrac{x}{192}$ **8.** $\dfrac{2}{x} = \dfrac{9}{26}$ **9.** $\dfrac{x}{80} = \dfrac{42}{140}$

10. Refer to the table at the right.

  a. Make a scatter plot for the data.

  b. Draw a fitted line for your scatter plot.

  c. Predict the winning distance in the triple
  jump for the 2040 Olympics.

Winning Distances for Olympic Triple Jump

Year	Distance (rounded to nearest ft)
1900	47
1920	48
1936	52
1960	55
1980	57

11. The box-and-whiskers plot shows information about
the number of moves made in a series of games of
Tic-Tac-Toe played by two kindergarten students.
What is the median number of moves? What is the
range of the number of moves?

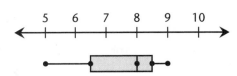

Name _____   Date _____

Write each rate as a unit rate.

1. 420 km/5 h   **2.** $13.50/3 lb   **3.** 26°F/3 h   **4.** 175 words/7 min

Use the table for Exercises 5–7. The table shows the number of hospitals in ten different states.

5. Make a stem-and-leaf plot of the data. Be sure to include a key and a title.

6. Find the range, the mean, the median, and the mode for the data.

7. Vermont has 15 hospitals. Suppose you include Vermont in the list. How would your stem-and-leaf plot change?

Number of Hospitals in Selected States

State	Number of hospitals
Arizona	60
Colorado	69
Idaho	41
Maryland	49
Montana	53
New Mexico	37
North Dakota	46
South Carolina	67
Utah	42
West Virginia	58

Use the histogram for Exercises 8 and 9.

8. How many triathletes finished the Ironman triathalon in less than 10 hours?

9. Can you tell the slowest time in which anyone finished the triathalon? Explain.

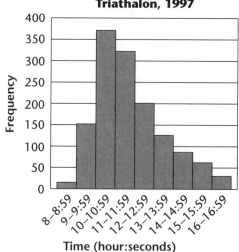

Solve each proportion.

10. $\dfrac{4}{13} = \dfrac{20}{x}$ **11.** $\dfrac{15}{y} = \dfrac{60}{75}$ **12.** $\dfrac{z}{92} = \dfrac{24}{138}$

MODULE 5 TEST FORM **A**

13. The fastest moving major glacier in the world is the Columbia Glacier in Alaska, which moves an average of 82 ft/day.

   a. How many days will it take for the glacier to move about 780 ft?

   b. How far will the glacier have moved in 2 weeks?

14. Use the data to make a scatter plot. Draw a fitted line for your scatter plot. Estimate the value of *y* when *x* is 8.

x	2	5	5	9	12	14	15	15	17	17	18	19
y	4	5	8	7	10	13	10	8	14	19	12	16

15. Use the box-and-whisker plot to estimate the median number of medals per country for top medal-winning countries in the 1996 Summer Olympics.

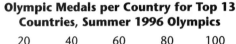

Olympic Medals per Country for Top 13 Countries, Summer 1996 Olympics

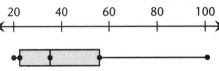

Estimate the percent equivalent of each ratio.

16. $\dfrac{65}{99}$ **17.** $\dfrac{6}{29}$ **18.** $\dfrac{59}{122}$ **19.** $\dfrac{151}{203}$

Write each ratio as a percent. Write each answer to the nearest tenth.

20. $\dfrac{5}{13}$ and $\dfrac{6}{14}$ **21.** $\dfrac{6}{7}$ and $\dfrac{36}{41}$

Solve for each unknown number.

22. 38% of a number is 171.   **23.** A number is 92% of 150.

24. A bag contains 5 tiles: 2 triangles and 3 squares. One tile is taken out of the bag without looking. The number of sides of the tile is recorded, and the tile is returned to the bag. Then the process is repeated once more. The outcome is the sum of the number of sides of the two shapes drawn.

   a. Draw a tree diagram that shows all the possible outcomes of the experiment. What is the theoretical probability that the outcome is 7?

   b. Suppose the experiment is done 200 times. About how many times would you expect to get a sum of 7?

MODULE 5 TEST   FORM (B)

Write each rate as a unit rate.

1. 540 km/8 h   **2.** $18.20/4 lb   **3.** 34°F/5 h   **4.** 360 mi/18 gal

Use the table for Exercises 5–7. The table shows the number of state legislators in ten selected states.

5. Make a stem-and-leaf plot of the data. Be sure to include a key and a title.

6. Find the range, the mean, the median, and the mode for the data.

7. New Hampshire has 424 legislators. Suppose you include New Hampshire on the list. How would your stem-and-leaf plot change?

Number of State Legislators for Selected States

State	Number of state legislators
Arkansas	135
Connecticut	187
Hawaii	76
Kentucky	138
Michigan	148
Montana	150
New Mexico	112
Oklahoma	149
Tennessee	132
Wisconsin	132

The Iditarod sled dog race is a 1049 mile race from Anchorage to Nome, Alaska. Use the histogram of winning times for the Iditarod for Exercises 8 and 9. (Note: The time 9:23 means 9 days 23 hours.)

8. In how many years was the winning time for the Iditarod faster than 12 days?

9. Can you tell the course record for the Iditarod? Explain.

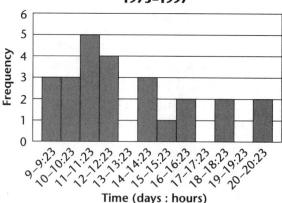

Winning Times for Iditarod Dog Sled Race, 1973–1997

Solve each proportion.

10. $\dfrac{6}{11} = \dfrac{30}{x}$ **11.** $\dfrac{y}{12} = \dfrac{12}{54}$ **12.** $\dfrac{z}{87} = \dfrac{15}{145}$

MODULE 5 TEST   FORM **B**

13. The fastest growing tree in the world grows at a rate of about 32.5 ft/yr.

   a. How many years would it take to grow 130 ft?

   b. About how many inches does it grow in 1 week?

14. Use the data below to make a scatter plot. Draw a fitted line for your scatter plot. Estimate the value of x when y is 10.

x	2	3	4	8	8	11	11	13	14	15	16	18
y	16	12	14	11	15	11	13	10	8	12	11	8

15. Use the box-and-whisker plot to estimate the median number of points per game for the NBA's Most Valuable Players for the years 1985–1996.

Points per Game for NBA Most Valuable Players, 1985–1996

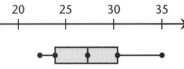

Estimate the percent equivalent of each ratio.

16. $\dfrac{3}{29}$ **17.** $\dfrac{19}{61}$ **18.** $\dfrac{161}{182}$ **19.** $\dfrac{118}{238}$

Write each ratio as a percent. Round each answer to the nearest tenth.

20. $\dfrac{11}{12}$ and $\dfrac{15}{17}$ **21.** $\dfrac{5}{9}$ and $\dfrac{35}{62}$

Solve for each unknown number.

22. A number is 36% of 650.   **23.** 68% of a number is 238.

24. A bag contains 5 tiles: 4 triangles and 1 pentagon. One tile is taken out of the bag without looking. The number of sides of the tile is recorded, and the tile is returned to the bag. Then the process is repeated once more. The outcome is the sum of the number of sides of the two shapes drawn.

   a. Draw a tree diagram that shows all the possible outcomes of the experiment. What is the theoretical probability that the outcome is 8?

   b. Suppose the experiment is done 150 times. About how many times would you expect to get a sum of 8?

Name _____   Date _____

1. Find the unit rate for 195.5 mi/8.5 gal.
  a. 25 mi/1 gal   **b.** 24 mi/1 gal
  c. 23 mi/1 gal   **d.** 22 mi/1 gal

2. Find the range of the data.

Spelling Test Scores

```
 5 | 9
 6 | 4 8
 7 | 2 5 5
 8 | 0 3 4 4 7 9
 9 | 0 0 2 8
10 | 0
```

5 | 9 represents a score of 59

  a. 39   **b.** 41
  c. 43   **d.** 44

3. If Christopher can type 65 words/min, how long will it take him to type a 3000-word essay?
  a. about 42 min   **b.** about 46 min
  c. about 50 min   **d.** about 54 min

4. Solve $\frac{4}{x} = \frac{30}{48}$.
  a. 2.5   **b.** 6.4
  c. 8.6   **d.** 360

5. Which of these is the best reason to use a scatter plot?
  a. to determine the relationship between two quantities and to make predictions
  b. to obtain the median of a set of data
  c. to determine the best way to organize the data
  d. to calculate the mean of a set of data

6. Which type of plot can be used to find the mode for a set of data?
  a. scatter plot
  b. histogram
  c. stem-and-leaf plot
  d. box-and-whisker plot

7. Estimate the percent equivalent $\frac{142}{358}$.
  a. 20%   **b.** 33%
  c. 40%   **d.** 50%

8. What percent study more than 3 h?

Time Spent Studying

Frequency vs *Time (min)*: bars at 0–60, 61–120, 121–180, 181–240, 241–300, over 300.

  a. about 14%   **b.** about 28%
  c. about 58%   **d.** about 64%

9. Which of the following fractions will give the largest result when written as a percent?
  a. $\frac{11}{14}$ **b.** $\frac{7}{9}$
  c. $\frac{8}{11}$ **d.** $\frac{5}{6}$

10. 323 is 38% of what number?
  a. 850   **b.** 436
  c. 249   **d.** 122.7

11. What is the median of the data shown in this box-and-whisker plot?

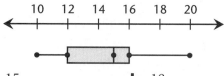

  a. 15   **b.** 18
  c. 20   **d.** 28

12. The probability that a certain basketball player will make a free throw is 82%. What is the approximate probability that she will miss 2 foul shots in a row?
  a. 3%   **b.** 8%
  c. 23%   **d.** 36%

MODULE 5   **MODULE PERFORMANCE ASSESSMENT**

A mobile is an intriguing way to display art or information. You can design a mobile if you understand proportions.

Each branch of a mobile is a carefully balanced *lever*, like a seesaw on the playground. Suppose Amy and Brian are sitting on opposite ends of a seesaw. It will not balance because Brian weighs more than Amy. What should they do? Many of us know from experience that the heavier person should move closer to the center.

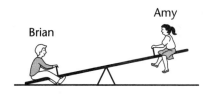

A seesaw is an example of a lever. The point on which it balances is called the *fulcrum*. The distance from the fulcrum to each object is inversely proportional to the weight of the objects. In other words, if two objects of different weights are on opposite ends of a lever balanced on a fulcrum, the heavier object will be closer to the fulcrum. So, for example, if Amy and Brian wish to balance on the seesaw, then the following must be true:

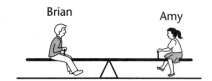

$$\frac{\text{Brian's weight}}{\text{Amy's weight}} = \frac{\text{Amy's distance from fulcrum}}{\text{Brian's distance from fulcrum}}$$

1. Ricky and Freddy are playing on a seesaw. Ricky weighs 75 pounds, and Freddy weighs 50 pounds. If Freddy sits 6 ft from the fulcrum, where should Ricky sit?

2. Look at the mobile shown below. Each set of weights must balance on its lever. Given the weights and distances shown, use proportions to find the unknown values.

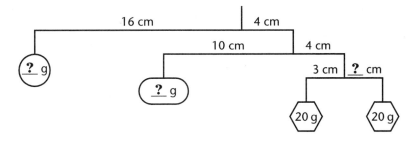

Answers

PRACTICE AND APPLICATIONS

Module 5, Section 1

1. a. 8.5 min/1 mi **b.** 23 mi/1 gal **c.** $2.80/1 lb
d. 8 servings/1 pan **e.** $.07/1 min
f. $.89/1 bunch **g.** 6.4 min/1 mi **h.** $4.50/1 lb
i. 5.8 gal/1 min **j.** 10 servings/1 pan
k. $2.59/1 bunch **l.** 12 servings/1 pan
m. 28 mi/1 gal **n.** $12.75/1 h **o.** 23.5 km/1 L
2. 55 lb/day = 385 lb/7 days
3. about 8824 people/1 mi^2
4. a.

Time (min)	4	8	40	80	960
Distance (mi)	0.5	1	5	10	120

b. 16 h
5. a.

Time (s)	1	5	20	30	50
Distance (ft)	6	30	120	180	300

b. 300 ft
**6. a. Number of Minutes
Students Spent Reading**

```
 7 | 6 9
 8 | 3 3 3 5 6 8 8 9 9
 9 | 0 1 2 2 2 4 6 9
10 | 0 0
```

8 | 5 = 85

b. 24; 89.45; 89; 88 and 89 **c.** 89 min
7. a. 10 min **b.** about 14 students **c.** greater than

Module 5, Section 2

1. 28 g
2. 320 g
3. 525 lb
4. a. 52.5 **b.** 24 **c.** 27 **d.** 12 **e.** 17 **f.** 5 **g.** 12.5
h. 30 **i.** 8.1 **j.** 12 **k.** 40 **l.** 8.5 **m.** 45 **n.** 21 **o.** 45
5. a. 262.5 **b.** 105 gal **c.** 750 loaves **d.** 360 lb
6. Sample Response: scatter plot A, because more of the points lie close to the line
7. a. Sample Response: about $200,000 **b.** Sample Response: One house is older than the other.
8. a. $90 **b.** $5 **c.** $35 **d.** $85

Module 5, Section 3

1. Sample Response: about 60%
2. a. $\frac{8}{16}$ or $\frac{1}{2}$ **b.** about 50%
3. Sample responses are given.
a. about 80% **b.** about 33% **c.** about 40%
d. about 70% **e.** about 40% **f.** about 50%
g. about 80% **h.** about 40% **i.** about 30%
j. about 20% **k.** about 10% **l.** about 25%

4. about 64.3%; about 47.1%
5. a. 83.3% **b.** 40% **c.** 75% **d.** 62.5% **e.** 70%
f. 46.9% **g.** 26.7% **h.** 32.5% **i.** 16.7% **j.** 77.8%
k. 31.3% **l.** 20%
6. about 20%
7. 450 students; The number of students can be found by solving $\frac{44}{100} = \frac{198}{x}$.
8. a. 50 **b.** 60 **c.** 850 **d.** 25.5 **e.** 180 **f.** 3.68
g. 260 **h.** 392 **i.** 36 **j.** 84 **k.** 150 **l.** 125 **m.** 16
n. 500 **o.** 112 **p.** 90 **q.** 224 **r.** 3 **s.** 360 **t.** 85.2
u. 30 **v.** 150 **w.** 165 **x.** 57.4
9. $6.43
10. $18
11. 240 Calories
12. 600 students

Module 5, Section 4

1. a. $\frac{2}{3}$, 0.6$\overline{6}$, 66$\frac{2}{3}$% **b.** $\frac{1}{2}$, 0.5, 50% **c.** $\frac{3}{5}$, 0.6, 60%
d. $\frac{9}{25}$, 0.36, 36% **e.** $\frac{1}{3}$, 0.3$\overline{3}$, 33$\frac{1}{3}$% **f.** $\frac{7}{10}$, 0.7, 70%
g. $\frac{3}{4}$, 0.75, 75% **h.** $\frac{37}{100}$, 0.37, 37% **i.** $\frac{9.5}{10}$, 0.95, 95%
2. a. 14% **b.** 75% **c.** 60% **d.** 76% **e.** 87.5%
f. 48.5% **g.** 37.5% **h.** 16% **i.** 36%
3. a. 15% **b.** 68% **c.** 25% **d.** 11$\frac{1}{9}$% **e.** 32%
f. 66$\frac{2}{3}$% **g.** 50% **h.** 7% **i.** 50%
4. a. 180 students **b.** 150 students **c.** 90 students
5. Sample Response: about 480,000
6. a. 8.3% **b.** 25% **c.** 25% **d.** 41.7% **e.** 16.7%
f. 33.3%
7.

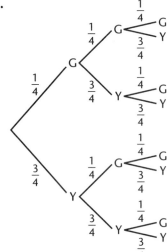

8. a. 1.6% **b.** 42.2% **c.** 4.7% **d.** 14.1% **e.** 42.2%
f. 1.4% **g.** 98.4% **h.** 57.8%

9. a. 62.5% **b.**

S < S / NS

NS < S / NS

c. about 14%

d. about 39% **e.** about 23.4%

Module 5, Sections 1–4

1. a. 9.2 min/1 mi **b.** 27 mi/1 gal **c.** \$.08/1 min
d. 29.4 km/1 L **e.** 9.5 min/1 mi **f.** \$3.75/1 lb
g. \$14.60/1 h **h.** \$.68/1 bunch **i.** 7.5 min/1 mi
2. 3.6 mi/1 h
3. a. Sample Response: a gap between 69 and 80; a cluster around 90 **b.** 31 **c.** 90, 91
4. a. 14 **b.** 28.8 **c.** 15 **d.** 25 **e.** 5 **f.** 3.6 **g.** 56
h. 5 **i.** 27 **j.** 1.5 **k.** 99 **l.** 5
5. 48 lb
6. a. about 50% **b.** about 10% **c.** about 80%
d. about 25% **e.** about 75% **f.** about 40%
7. a. 46.7% **b.** 20% **c.** 25% **d.** 55% **e.** 92%
f. 53.8%
8. a. 120 **b.** 140 **c.** 90 **d.** 27.3 **e.** 54 **f.** 9
9. \$62
10. a. 65% **b.** 88% **c.** 25%
11. about 152,000
12. 64%

STUDY GUIDE

Module 5, Section 1

1. $\dfrac{\$4.60}{1 \text{ box}}$

2. $\dfrac{27 \text{ mi}}{1 \text{ gal}}$

3. $\dfrac{6.25¢}{1 \text{ min}}$

4. $\dfrac{0.12 \text{ mi}}{1 \text{ min}}$

5. 60 gal
6. Company Y
7. a. **Ages of People Enrolled in Art Classes at the Museum**

1	5 5 8 9
2	3 8
3	4
4	5
5	
6	3 5 5 7
7	0

1 | 5 represents 15 years

b. range: 55; median: 34; modes: 15 and 65
8. less than
9. 30 students
10. $x = 7$
11. $t = -27$
12. $y = 135$
13. about \$5.00

14. about \$4.80
15. $\dfrac{3}{11}$
16. $\dfrac{3}{13}$
17. $\dfrac{2}{9}$
18. $\dfrac{2}{15}$

Module 5, Section 2

1. $g = 12$
2. $k = 14$
3. $c = 30$
4. $x = 8.4$
5. Sample Response: scatter plot A; approximately half of the points are plotted above the line and the other half are below it.
6. about 3.5 in.
7. 6 years
8. 10 years
9. $\dfrac{\$70}{1 \text{ book}}$
10. $\dfrac{15 \text{ min}}{1 \text{ page}}$
11. $\dfrac{\$14.50}{1 \text{ dinner}}$
12. 6^2
13. 2^5
14. 7^7
15. $\dfrac{4}{11}$
16. $\dfrac{1}{18}$
17. $\dfrac{2}{5}$
18. $\dfrac{13}{20}$

Module 5, Section 3

1–5. Sample Responses are given.
1. about 50%
2. about 30%
3. about 80%
4. about 100%
5. about 45%
6. 66.7%
7. 60%
8. 22%
9. 77.8%
10. about 71%
11. 56
12. 11.88
13. 48
14. 100
15. 25
16. 112.5
17. $x = 20$
18. $t = 0.75$
19. $m = 15$

20. 99

21. 58

22. 8

23. 1145

24. $\frac{1}{5}$

25. $\frac{3}{5}$

26. $\frac{4}{5}$

27. $\frac{19}{22}$

Module 5, Section 4

1. $\frac{2}{5}$, 0.4, 40%

2. $\frac{12}{36}$ or $\frac{1}{3}$, $0.\overline{3}$, 33%

3. $\frac{8}{40}$ or $\frac{1}{5}$, 0.2, 20%

4. $\frac{18}{100}$ or $\frac{9}{50}$, 0.18, 18%

5. $\frac{1}{20}$, 0.05, 5%

6. $\frac{54}{210}$ or $\frac{9}{35}$, about 0.257, about 25.7%

7. $\frac{3}{4}$, 0.75, 75%

8. $\frac{258}{2000}$ or $\frac{129}{1000}$, 0.129, 12.9%

9. Sample Response: about 170 students

10. $33\frac{1}{3}$%

11. 25%

12. 6%

13. $66\frac{2}{3}$%

14. 4 or 5 A's

15. 9 or 10 times

16. a.

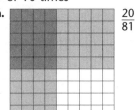

$\frac{20}{81}$

b.

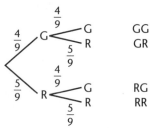

1st Draw	2nd Draw	Outcome

c. $\frac{25}{81}$

17. $m = 90$

18. $y = 28$

19. $t = 18$

20. $x = 63$

TECHNOLOGY

Module 5

1. Yes.

2. Sample Response: about 2200 Calories

3. Sample Response: about 117 lb

4. Sample Response: about 3750 Calories

ASSESSMENT

Mid-Module 5 Quiz

1. $4/1 lb

2. 52 mi/1 h

3. 0.004 in./1 min

4. a. Home Runs for Triple Crown Winners

```
0 | 9
1 | 4
2 | 8
3 | 1  2  6  9
4 | 2  4  8  9  9
5 | 2
```

3 | 6 means 36 home runs

b. 43, 39, 49

5. a. 6 drivers **b.** 4 drivers **c.** No; you can tell only that the fastest winning speed is in the interval from 180 mi/h to 189 mi/h.

6. 51

7. 176

8. $5\frac{7}{9}$

9. 24

10. a, b.

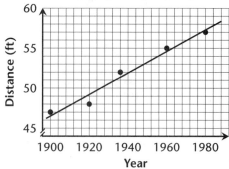

Winning Distance for Olympic Triple Jump

c. Sample Response: about 66 ft

11. median = 8; range = 4

Module 5 Test (Form A)

1. $\frac{84 \text{ km}}{1 \text{ h}}$

2. $\frac{\$4.50}{1 \text{ lb}}$

3. $\frac{8\frac{2}{3}°}{1 \text{ h}}$

4. $\dfrac{25 \text{ words}}{1 \text{ min}}$

5. Number of Hospitals per State in 10 Selected States

```
3 | 7
4 | 1 2 6 9
5 | 3 8
6 | 0 7 9
```

4 | 1 represents 41 hospitals

6. range = 32, mean = 52.2, median = 51, no mode

7. Vermont would be added to the top of the plot, changing the range to 54, the mean to about 48.8, and the median to 49.

8. Sample Response: about 170

9. No; you can tell only that the slowest time was between 16 and 17 hours.

10. 65

11. $18\dfrac{3}{4}$

12. 16

13. a. about $9\dfrac{1}{2}$ days **b.** about 1148 ft

14. Sample Response: When x is 8, y is about 8.

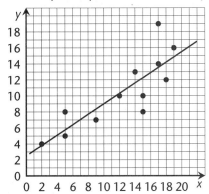

15. Sample Response: 35

16–19. Sample Responses are given.

16. about 67%

17. about 20%

18. about 50%

19. about 75%

20. 38.5%, 42.9%

21. 85.7%, 87.8%

22. 450

23. 138

24. a. $P(\text{sum is } 7) = \dfrac{12}{25}$

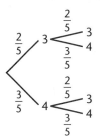

b. about 96 times

Module 5 Test (Form B)

1. $\dfrac{67.5 \text{ km}}{1 \text{ h}}$

2. $\dfrac{\$4.55}{1 \text{ lb}}$

3. $\dfrac{6.8°}{1 \text{ h}}$

4. $\dfrac{20 \text{ mi}}{1 \text{ gal}}$

5. Number of State Legislators in Selected States

```
 7 | 6
 8 |
 9 |
10 |
11 | 2
12 |
13 | 2 2 5 8
14 | 8 9
15 | 0
16 |
17 |
18 | 7
```

14 | 8 represents 148 legislators

6. range = 111, mean = 135.9, median = 136.5, mode = 132

7. New Hampshire would be added to the bottom of the plot, changing the range to 348, the mean to about 162, and the median to 138.

8. 11 years

9. No; you can only tell that the course record is between 9 and 10 days.

10. 55

11. $2\dfrac{2}{3}$

12. 9

13. a. about 4 years **b.** 7.5 in./wk

14.

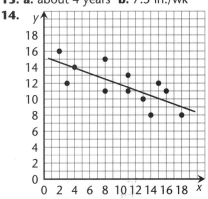

about 15

15. Sample Response: about 27

16–19. Sample Responses are given.

16. 10%

17. 33%

18. 90%

19. 50%

20. 91.7%, 88.2%

21. 55.6%, 56.5%

22. 234

23. 350

24. a. $P(\text{sum is }8) = \dfrac{8}{25}$

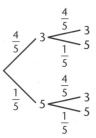

b. about 48 times

STANDARDIZED TEST

Module 5

1. c

2. b

3. b

4. b

5. a

6. c

7. c

8. c

9. d

10. a

11. a

12. a

MODULE PERFORMANCE ASSESSMENT

Module 5

1. Ricky should sit 4 ft from the fulcrum.

2.

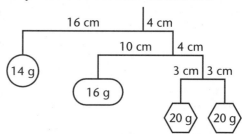

MIDDLE GRADES

MATH *Thematics*

MODULE 6 **Flights of Fancy**

MODULE 6

FLIGHTS of FANCY

Module Overview

Students will use mathematics to explore different aspects of flight and the problems involved in transporting a whale. Students use models to understand inequalities, similar figures, metric units, volume, geometric probability, networks, area, and relationships between angle measures.

Module Objectives

Section	Objectives	NCTM Standards
1	◆ Write simple and combined inequalities and graph them on a number line. ◆ Recognize concave and convex polygons and parallelograms. ◆ Find the area of a parallelogram, a triangle, and of shapes composed of them. ◆ Find probabilities of complementary events. ◆ Find geometric probabilities.	1, 2, 3, 4, 9, 11, 12
2	◆ Find principal and negative square roots of perfect squares. ◆ Estimate square roots to the nearest tenth. ◆ Sketch a net for a right prism. ◆ Find the surface area of a rectangular or triangular prism. ◆ Find the area of a circle.	1, 2, 3, 4, 5, 7, 12
3	◆ Recognize similar and congruent figures and identify corresponding parts. ◆ Use the scale of a drawing to find unknown measures. ◆ Classify triangles as acute, obtuse, or right. ◆ Find unknown measures in similar figures.	1, 2, 3, 4, 12
4	◆ Identify and find measures of angles formed by parallel lines and a transversal. ◆ Use the sum of the measures of the angles to find unknown angle measures in triangles and quadrilaterals.	1, 2, 3, 4, 12
5	◆ Find the volume of a prism. ◆ Use the relationship among metric units for volume, capacity, and mass of water. ◆ Convert among metric units of mass and among metric units of capacity. ◆ Interpret a weighted network.	1, 2, 3, 4, 12, 13

Topic Spiraling

Section	Connections to Prior and Future Concepts
1	Section 1 introduces writing and graphing of inequalities. Inequalities are solved in Module 7. Areas of parallelograms, areas of triangles, and geometric probability are reviewed from Modules 7 and 8 of Book 1. Geometric probability is revisited in Module 4 of Book 3.
2	Section 2 introduces square roots, which are revisited in Module 3 of Book 3. Nets and the area of a circle are covered, expanding on work with circumference in Module 4. Nets and circles are introduced in Module 7 of Book 1, and are revisited in Modules 1, 5, and 6 of Book 3.
3	Section 3 expands on the concepts of similarity and congruence introduced in Module 4. Relationships between corresponding parts are used to find unknown measures in similar figures, a topic introduced in Module 6 of Book 1 and revisited in Modules 3 and 6 of Book 3.
4	Section 4 introduces the relationships between angles formed by parallel lines and a transversal. The topic is revisited in Module 6 of Book 3. The sum of the measures of the angles of a triangle is introduced and applied to quadrilaterals. Module 4 of Book 3 covers the general case.
5	Section 5 expands on volume concepts reviewed in Module 1 to include volumes of prisms, a topic in Module 7 of Book 1. Volumes of other figures are explored in Modules 7 and 8. Volume, mass, and capacity relationships seen in Modules 3 and 8 of Book 1 are reviewed. Metric conversions seen in Module 3 are applied to mass and capacity. Networks are explored.

Integration

Mathematical Connections	1	2	3	4	5
algebra (including patterns and functions)	380–381, 388–390	394, 396, 402–409		432	437
geometry	382–389, 391–393	**394–409***	**410–421**	**422–435**	436–441, 445–447, 449–451
data analysis, probability, discrete math	381, 386–393				442–444, 446, 448–451
Interdisciplinary Connections and Applications					
social studies and geography	385, 390	394, 397, 405		422	448
reading and language arts	378		411		
science	379–384, 388, 390		418		436–437, 441, 447
flight	378–388, 390–391	394–401, 406, 407	410–412, 418	422, 433, 435	448
archery, painting, shipping and delivery, travel, world languages		407	420		436, 439, 442–444, 448

Bold page numbers indicate that a topic is used throughout the section.

MODULE 6

Guide for Assigning Homework

Regular Scheduling (45 min class period)

Section/ P&A Pages	Core Assignment	Extended Assignment	exercises to note		
			Additional Practice/Review	Open-ended Problems	Special Problems
1 pp. 389–393	**Day 1:** 1–12, SR 27–30	1–12, SR 27–34	EP, p. 393		
	Day 2: 13, 14, 16–18, SR 31–38	13, 14, Chal 15, 16–18, SR 35–38	TB, p. 593	PA 14	
	Day 3: 19–25, ROS 26	19–25, ROS 26		St Sk, p. 393	
2 pp. 405–409	**Day 1:** 1–10, SR 24–33	1–10, SR 24–33	EP, p. 409		
	Day 2: 11–14	11–14, *Chal 15			
	Day 3: 16–22, ROS 23	16–22, ROS 23		ROS 23	Mod Proj 1–3
3 pp. 418–421	**Day 1:** 1, 2, 5–10, SR 22–23	1, 2, 5–10, SR 22–23	EP, p. 421; PA 3, 4		
	Day 2: 11–19, *ROS 21, SR 24–30	11–19, *ROS 21, SR 24–30	PA 20, Career 31	PA 20	
4 pp. 430–435	**Day 1:** 1–7, 9, SR 24–26	1–7, Chal 8, SR 24–26	EP, p. 434; PA 10–15		
	Day 2: 16–22, ROS 23, SR 27–33	16, 18, 20, ROS 23, SR 27–33, *Ext 34–36		E^2, p. 435	Mod Proj 4–5; E^2, p. 435
5 pp. 446–451	**Day 1:** 1–6, SR 26–30	1–6, SR 26–30	EP, p. 450		
	Day 2: 7–19, SR 31–34	7–19, SR 31–34			
	Day 3: 20, 21, 23, 24, ROS 25	20, 21, Chal 22, 23, 24, ROS 25, *Ext 35–39		ROS 25; Std Test, p. 450	Mod Proj 6–9
Review/ Assess	Review and Assess (PE), Quick Quizzes (TRB), Mid-Module Quiz (TRB), Module Tests— Forms A and B (TRB), Standardized Assessment (TRB), Cumulative Test (TRB)				Allow 5 days
Enrich/ Assess	E^2 (PE) and Alternate E^2 (TRB), Module Project (PE), Module Performance Assessment (TRB)				
Yearly Pacing	**Mod 6:** 18 days	**Mods 1–6:** 109 days	**Remaining:** 31 days		**Total:** 140 days

Key: PA = Practice & Application; ROS = Reflecting on the Section; SR = Spiral Review; TB = Toolbox; EP = Extra Skill Practice; Ext = Extension; *more time

Block Scheduling (90 min class period)

	Day 1	Day 2	Day 3	Day 4	Day 5	Day 6	Day 7	
Teach	Sec 1 Expl 1–2	Sec 1 Expl 3; Sec 2 Expl 1	Sec 2 Expl 2–3	Sec 3	Sec 4	Sec 5 Expl 1–2	Sec 5 Expl 3	**Allow 2 days** review/assess/projects
Apply/ Assess (P&A)	Sec 1: 1–4, 6–9, 13, 14, 16–18, SR 27–38	Sec 1: 19–25, ROS 26 Sec 2: 1–10, SR 24–33	Sec 2: 12–14, 16–22, ROS 23	Sec 3: 1, 2, 5–8, 13–19, *ROS 21, SR 22–30	Sec 4: 1–7, 9, 16, 18, 20, ROS 23, SR 24–33	Sec 5: 1–19, SR 26–34	Sec 5: 20, 21, 23, 24, ROS 25	
Yearly Pacing	**Mod 6:** 9 days	**Mods 1–6:** 55 days		**Remaining:** 15 days			**Total:** 70 days	

Materials List

Section	Materials
1	3 in. by 11 in. strip of paper, ruler, 6–10 ice-cream sticks, tape, 3 in. by 5 in. index card, scissors, construction paper
2	Protractor, calculator, scissors, tape, centimeter grid paper, 2 centimeter cubes, Labsheet 2A, ruler, Project Labsheet A, balance scale (optional)
3	Labsheet 3A, ruler, protractor, Jenny cutouts from Exploration 1
4	Labsheets 4A and 4B, scissors, ruler, tape, index cards (3 in. by 5 in.), protractor, wing from Exploration 1, Project Labsheet A; for E^2: Extended Exploration Labsheet, ruler
5	48 centimeter cubes, Labsheet 5A

Support Materials in this Resource Book

Section	Practice	Study Guide	Assessment	Enrichment
1	Section 1	Section 1	Quick Quiz	Technology Activity
2	Section 2	Section 2	Quick Quiz	Technology Activity
3	Section 3	Section 3	Quick Quiz Mid-Module Quiz	
4	Section 4	Section 4	Quick Quiz	Alternate Extended Exploration
5	Section 5	Section 5	Quick Quiz	
Review/ Assess	Sections 1–5		Module Tests Forms A and B Standardized Assessment Module Performance Assessment Cumulative Test Modules 5–6	

Classroom Ideas

Bulletin Boards:
- pictorial history of airplanes and flight
- technical pictures of airplanes, wing span, and construction for flight
- diagrams of different "networks" (telephone, computer, migration patterns, and so on)

Student Work Displays:
- autogyros and Curtiss Jennys
- reports from the E^2
- gliders and test results from the Module Project

Interest Center:
- books on making kites and paper airplanes with materials to make them

Visitors/Field Trips:
- aeronautics engineer, skydiver
- airport

Technology:
- computer drawing software
- *Geometry Blaster* by Davidson & Associates, CD-ROM, Mac/Win

The Math Gazette
Flights of Fancy

Sneak Preview!

Over the next four weeks in our mathematics class, we will be writing and graphing inequalities, finding areas of polygons and circles, finding square roots, exploring prisms, and exploring similarity while completing a thematic unit on flight. Some of the topics we will be discussing are:

✗ wing design

✗ parawings and other types of kites

✗ barnstorming pilots

✗ the first successful powered airplane flight

✗ transporting a whale over 2000 miles

Ask Your Student

What are complementary events? (Sec. 1)

How can you find the surface area of a box? (Sec. 2)

What is a scale drawing? (Sec. 3)

Why did the Wright Flyer's wings have both vertical and diagonal struts? (Sec. 4)

What is the mass of one milliliter of water? (Sec. 5)

Connections

Social Studies:
Students will learn about different aspects of flight. They may be interested in finding out more about the history of human aviation, both powered and not powered. Possible sources include encyclopedias and biographies of inventors.

Literature:
Students will read excerpts from *Machines*, by Robert O'Brien and from *Barnstormers and Speed Kings*, by Paul O'Neil. They may be interested in reading these books or others about the history of flight and pioneering pilots.

Science:
Students will learn how Bernoulli's Principle relates to the theme of the module. They will also learn about the relationships among metric units of measure, which are universally used in scientific investigations. And they will learn how Keiko the whale was transferred from one aquarium to another.

E² Project

Following Section 4, students will have approximately one week to complete the E² project, *Locating the Hub*. Students will decide how to locate the hub city for a small airline.

Students may use the following materials for the project:

✗ large sheets of blank paper for drawing diagrams

✗ rulers for measuring distances

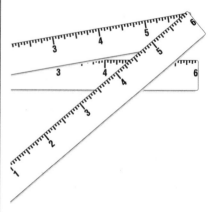

Flights of Fancy

Section Title	Mathematics Your Student Will Be Learning	Activities
1: Will It Fly?	◆ writing and graphing inequalities ◆ finding the area of a parallelogram and a triangle ◆ using areas of geometric figures to find probabilities of complementary events	◆ explore the effects of speed on air pressure ◆ model polygons with ice-cream sticks ◆ make an autogyro and use it to conduct a probability experiment
2: Go Fly a Kite!	◆ finding square roots ◆ identifying prisms and their parts ◆ finding the surface area of a prism ◆ finding the area of a circle	◆ investigate kite designs ◆ make nets for prisms ◆ use the area of a parallelogram to approximate the area of a circle ◆ construct a glider for the Module Project
3: Barnstorming	◆ identifying similar and congruent polygons ◆ finding the scale of a scale drawing ◆ classifying triangles by angle measures ◆ finding unknown lengths in similar figures	◆ create paper models of airplanes
4: Winging It!	◆ finding relationships among angles formed by parallel lines and a transversal ◆ finding sums of angle measures in triangles and quadrilaterals	◆ make a model wing ◆ measure angles formed by parallel lines and a transversal ◆ use the angles of a triangle to form a straight angle ◆ construct a larger glider for the Module Project ◆ measure distances to locate the hub city for an airline
5: A Whale of a Problem	◆ finding the volume of a prism ◆ learning relationships among metric units ◆ using weighted networks	◆ use centimeter cubes to compare sizes of pools for a whale ◆ use networks to analyze delivery routes ◆ complete the Module Project

MODULE 6

Activities to do at Home

◆ Find the area of a circular household object, such as a compact disc, the top of a can, or a wheel. (After Sec. 2)

◆ Make a scale drawing of your home or neighborhood. Include a scale and explain how you chose it. (After Sec. 3)

◆ Choose one room of your home and find its floor area in square centimeters. If the room were filled with water to a depth 1 cm, what would be the weight of the water? (After Sec. 5)

Related Topics

You may want to discuss these related topics with your student:

 Industrial design

 Mechanical drafting

 Maps and globes

Zoos and aquariums

Section ① Inequalities, Polygons, and Probability

Section Planner

DAYS FOR MODULE 6

1 2 3 4 5 6 7 8 9 10 11 12 13

SECTION 1

First Day
Setting the Stage, *p. 378*
Exploration 1, *pp. 379–381*

Second Day
Exploration 2, *pp. 382–384*

Third Day
Exploration 3, *pp. 385–387*
Key Concepts, *pp. 388–389*

Block Schedule

Day 1
Setting the Stage, Exploration 1, Exploration 2

Day 2
Exploration 3, Key Concepts
(Day 2 continues in Sec. 2.)

RESOURCE ORGANIZER

Teaching Resources
• Practice and Applications, Sec. 1
• Study Guide, Sec. 1
• Technology Activity, Sec. 1
• Warm-Up, Sec. 1
• Quick Quiz, Sec. 1

Section Overview

Section 1 begins with a discussion of the principles of flying. As they study the speeds at which birds fly, students will be introduced to inequalities. After listing and graphing discreet points that satisfy an inequality, students will learn the notation for an inequality and will graph inequalities on a number line. Students will also write and graph combined inequalities.

In Exploration 2, students will use polygons to model a bird's wing so they can estimate the area of the bird's wings for the purpose of determining how much weight the wings can carry. Convex and concave polygons, regular polygons, parallelograms, and quadrilaterals will be defined. Students will construct a parallelogram from a rectangle of equal area, helping them write a formula for the area of a parallelogram. Students will use the formulas for areas of parallelograms and triangles to find the areas of polygons that are composites of these shapes.

In Exploration 3, students will simulate a skydiving competition. Through this activity, students will learn how to find the geometric probability of an event, and will discover the relationship between the probabilities of complementary events.

SECTION OBJECTIVES

Exploration 1
• write simple and combined inequalities, and graph them on a number line

Exploration 2
• recognize parallelograms and concave and convex polygons
• find the area of a parallelogram, a triangle, and of shapes composed of them

Exploration 3
• find probabilities of complementary events
• find geometric probabilities

ASSESSMENT OPTIONS

Checkpoint Questions
• Question 9 on p. 381
• Question 15 on p. 384
• Question 28 on p. 387

Embedded Assessment
• For a list of embedded assessment exercises see p. 6-14.

Performance Task/Portfolio
• Exercises 6–9 on p. 390 (hummingbirds)
• Exercise 25 on p. 392
★Exercise 26 on p. 392 (visual thinking)
• Study Skills on p. 393 (making connections)

★ = a problem solving task that can be assessed using the Assessment Scales

SECTION 1 MATERIALS

Exploration 1
◆ 3 in. by 11 in. strip of paper

Exploration 2
◆ ruler
◆ 6–10 ice-cream sticks

Exploration 3
◆ tape
◆ 3 in. by 5 in. index card
◆ scissors
◆ construction paper

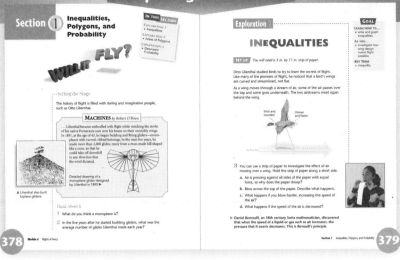

Setting the Stage

MOTIVATE

Read the Setting the Stage on page 378 about one of the early "fabulous flying machines" and address the questions as a class. The topic of flight will provide the context for the mathematics throughout this module. As this is a high interest topic, encourage students to locate additional information from the library, the Internet, or other resources. For this section, relevant areas of investigation include early flying machines, the flight of birds, the basics of wings, and Daniel Bernoulli (Bernoulli's principle).

Exploration I

PLAN

Classroom Management
Exploration 1 can best be performed in small groups, as the topic of Bernoulli's principle may be counterintuitive for some individual students. Still, make sure that all students have a strip of paper so they can try the experiment for themselves. Prepare 3 in. by 11 in. strips of paper ahead of time or have students cut, or crease and tear, strips from their notebook paper. You may want to guide or introduce the discussion in *Questions 4* and *8*. Address *Question 5* and the Example following it as a whole class to ensure that all students understand the basics of graphing an inequality on a number line.

GUIDE

Developing Math Concepts In *Question 3*, you will need to make sure that students are blowing *across* the paper strip instead of *against* it. If students begin thinking in terms of wind pushing an object, they may have trouble associating an *increase* in speed with a *decrease* in pressure.

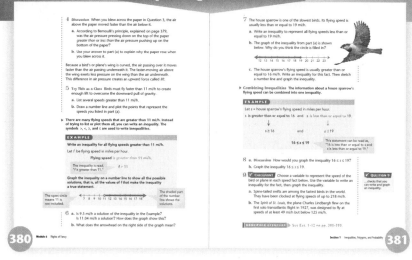

Exploration 1 continued

Logical Reasoning In *Question 4*, it may help students to think in terms of blowing the air *away from* above the strip. This may help them see that the air pressure will now be higher underneath the strip, which pushes up from below, causing the strip to rise.

Developing Math Concepts In the Examples on pages 380 and 381, emphasize the importance of making a clear statement describing the variable in an inequality. As in the Examples, encourage students to write brief sentences involving the variable to restate the situation before translating the sentences into mathematical language. This will strengthen their connections between words and symbols, and help them appreciate the efficiency of symbols. In the Example on page 381, some students may have difficulty going from "$s \geq 16$ and $s \leq 19$" to "$16 \leq s \leq 19$." Remind them that $s \geq 16$ and $16 \leq s$ are just two ways of saying the same thing.

Classroom Examples

Write an inequality for all flying speeds less than or equal to 28 mi/h.

Answer: Let f be flying speed in miles per hour.

Flying speed is less than or equal to 28 mi/h.

$$f \leq 28$$

Graph the inequality on a number line to show all the possible solutions.

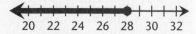

| | | | | | |
|20|22|24|26|28|30|32|

| The heavy line shows the solutions. | The closed circle means 28 is included. |

Classroom Examples

A peregrine falcon can fly at maximum speeds greater than 168 mi/h but less than 217 mi/h. Write an inequality to show the maximum flying speed of this falcon.

Answer: Let s = peregrine falcon's flying speed in miles per hour.

s is greater than 168	and	s is less than 217
↓		↓
$s > 168$	and	$s < 217$

$$168 < s < 217$$

Common Error In the Example on page 381 and later in setting up inequalities, students may get confused by the directions of the inequality symbols. Remind them that whether an arrow faces left or right, the arrow always points toward the smaller quantity and opens in the direction of the larger quantity. Visual learners may remember this in terms of having to "shrink" a number to move it through an arrow from the open end to the pointed end, or having to "expand" a number to move it through an arrow from the pointed end to the open end.

Checkpoint For *Question 9*, make sure that students state the variable in a sentence as in the Examples, and then are able to write a word statement of the problem and translate this correctly into symbols. You will also need to make sure that students distinguish correctly between open endpoints and closed endpoints, and that they interpret the inequality signs correctly when graphing.

▶ **HOMEWORK EXERCISES** ▶

See the Suggested Assignment for Day 1 on page 6-14. For Exercise Notes, see page 6-15.

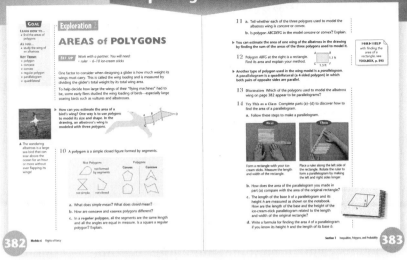

Exploration 2

PLAN	GUIDE

Classroom Management

Exploration 2 is best performed with students working in pairs. For *Question 14*, highlighted for a whole class activity, each pair of students will need 6–10 ice cream sticks to explore the area of a parallelogram. If ice cream sticks are not available, you can use anything similar in shape. *Question 16* is also highlighted for class work to ensure that students understand the formula for the area of a triangle. You may want to allow class time for students to participate in finding the areas of additional examples of parallelograms, triangles, and complex polygons that can be divided into simpler parts.

Developing Math Concepts

After *Question 10*, you may want to have students identify convex, concave, and regular polygons around the classroom. For *Question 12*, students will find the area of a rectangle. Have students find the area in terms of a base and a height, instead of in terms of a length and a width, so that they do not become confused when finding the area of a parallelogram.

Logical Reasoning

After *Question 12*, quadrilaterals and parallelograms are defined. You may want to use a flow chart or Venn diagram for classifying quadrilaterals to help students see the relationships among quadrilaterals (a square is a rectangle, but a rectangle may not be a square, and so on).

Developing Math Concepts

For *Question 14*, students should realize that because there is the same amount of wood or other material after rotating the ruler, the area does not change. You may want to ask students what happens to the perimeter of the figure as the ruler rotates (it increases, because the sides of the parallelogram have to "reach" to the same height, so they form diagonals of right triangles whose heights are the height of the parallelogram).

Common Error

For *Question 14* and those following, some students may confuse the height of a parallelogram with the length of its sides. Remind them that a height is always perpendicular to a base. Have students identify the base and height in several more parallelograms, including rectangles.

Classroom Examples
Find the area of the parallelogram.

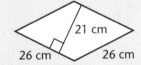

21 cm

26 cm   26 cm

Answer: $A = bh$
$= 26 \cdot 21$
$= 546$

The area of the parallelogram is 546 cm².

6-11

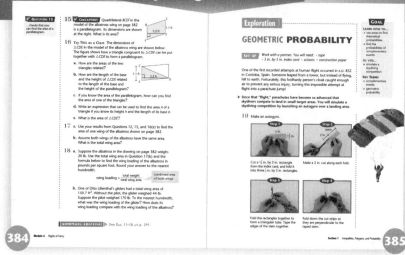

Exploration 2 continued

Checkpoint For *Question 15*, make sure that students can identify a base and a height, regardless of the orientation of a parallelogram. You may tell them that you can use one of either pair of opposite sides for a base (which means that there are two possible heights), but the area will be the same. Also, make sure that students always give area in terms of square units.

Classroom Examples
Find the area of the triangle.

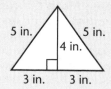

Answer: $A = \frac{1}{2}bh$

$= \frac{1}{2}(3 + 3)(4)$

$= \frac{1}{2}(6)(4)$

$= 12$

The area of the triangle is 12 in.^{2}.

HOMEWORK EXERCISES

See the Suggested Assignment for Day 2 on page 6-14. For Exercise Notes, see page 6-15.

Exploration 3

PLAN

Classroom Management
Exploration 3 is best performed in pairs. Each pair will construct an "autogyro" out of a 3 in. by 5 in. index card, and a landing area out of notebook paper and construction paper. Students will require enough time to construct these items, launch the autogyro ten times for each student, and record and analyze their results. If you are worried about time, you may want to consider having students construct the autogyros and landing areas outside of class. For this Exploration, pairs of students will also need enough unobstructed floor space to keep from interfering with each other.

Customizing Instruction

Alternative Approach 1 To demonstrate how area remains constant for rectangles and parallelograms with the same base and height, have students cut a rectangle from paper. Beginning at a bottom corner, have them cut on a straight line at any angle to the top of the rectangle. Sliding the resulting triangle to the opposite side forms a parallelogram from the same amount of paper (same area) as the original rectangle. Students can verify this using different rectangles and angles.

Alternative Approach 2 Using a geoboard, have students form different parallelograms with the same base and height, so that a portion of the top base of each is directly over a portion of its bottom base. On each parallelogram, have them place a separate band to cover the largest rectangular area between the base and the top. This should divide each parallelogram into a rectangle and two congruent triangles. Ask students what would happen to the overall shape if they moved the triangle from the right side to the left side. Then ask students what they notice about these rectangles.

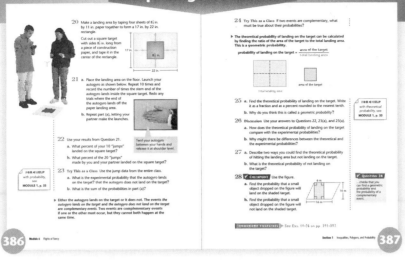

Exploration 3 continued

GUIDE

Developing Math Concepts
After *Question 23*, emphasize that for two complementary events, one or the other *must* occur. In the autogyro experiment we are not permitting the possibility that the target is missed completely or that there is a "tie," so the only possible events are landing on the target and *not* landing on the target. For *Question 24*, remind students that a probability of one means "a sure thing." For this experiment, it is a sure thing that the autogyro does or does not land on the target, so the probability is one. For *Question 25*, point out to students that this theoretical geometric probability depends upon the autogyro landing *randomly*; that is, it assumes that the autogyro will land on the target, but that you have no control over where on the target it lands. This may prompt a discussion with students about the meaning of *random* in this case.

Classroom Examples
Find the theoretical probability of landing on the shaded region.

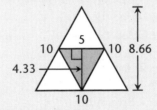

Answer:
probability of landing
on shaded region

$$= \frac{\text{area of shaded region}}{\text{area of large triangle}}$$

$$= \frac{\frac{1}{2}(5)(4.33)}{\frac{1}{2}(10)(8.66)}$$

$$= \frac{10.825}{43.3}$$

$$= \frac{1}{4}$$

The probability of landing on the shaded region is $\frac{1}{4}$, or 25%.

Writing For *Question 27(a)*, you may want students to write out a general rule for how to find the probability of one event whenever you know the probability of its complementary event. (If you know the probability of one of two complementary events, you can find the probability of the other one by subtracting the known probability from one.)

Checkpoint *Question 28* gives students the chance to apply the area formulas from Exploration 2. Make sure that the students recognize that the events in parts *(a)* and *(b)* are complementary.

HOMEWORK EXERCISES

See the Suggested Assignment for Day 3 on page 6-14. For Exercise Notes, see page 6-15.

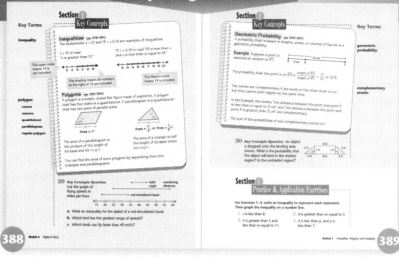

CLOSE

Closure Question State the formula for the area of a parallelogram and the formula for the area of a triangle. Then write an inequality describing the possible range of values for geometric probability.

Answer: area of a parallelogram: $A = bh$; area of a triangle: $A = \frac{1}{2}bh$; $0 \le p \le 1$, where p represents geometric probability.

SUGGESTED ASSIGNMENT

Core Course

Day 1: Exs. 1–12, 27–30
Day 2: Exs. 13, 14, 16–18, 31–38
Day 3: Exs. 19–26

Extended Course

Day 1: Exs. 1–12, 27–34
Day 2: Exs. 13–18, 35–38
Day 3: Exs. 19–26

Block Schedule

Day 1: Exs. 1–4, 6–9, 13, 14, 16–18, 27–38
Day 2: Exs. 19–26; Sec. 2, 1–10, 24–33

EMBEDDED ASSESSMENT

These section objectives are tested by the exercises listed.

Write simple and combined inequalities, and graph them on a number line.

Exercises 2, 4, 8

Recognize parallelograms and concave and convex polygons.

Exercises 13, 14

Find the area of a parallelogram, a triangle, and of shapes composed of them.

Exercises 16–18

Find probabilities of complementary events.

Exercises 22, 24

Find geometric probabilities.

Exercises 20, 24, 25

Customizing Instruction

Home Involvement Those helping students at home will find the Key Concepts on pages 388 and 389 a handy reference to the key ideas, terms, and skills of Section 1.

Absent Students For students who were absent for all or part of this section, the blackline Study Guide for Section 1 may be used to present the ideas, concepts, and skills of Section 1. If possible, have a student who already has an autogyro and landing area help the absent student conduct the experiment.

Extra Help For students who need additional practice, the blackline Practice and Applications for Section 1 provides additional exercises that may be used to confirm the skills of Section 1. The Extra Skill Practice on page 393 also provides additional exercises.

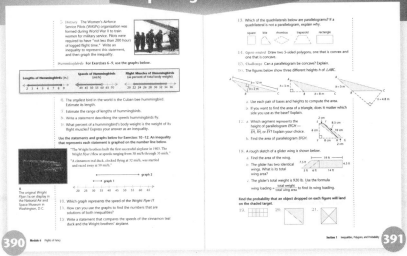

Practice & Application

EXERCISE NOTES

Reading *Ex. 5* requires that students read and correctly interpret the statement "not less than 200 hours." Have students rewrite this phrase in a positive manner, without the word *not* (for example, "at least 200 hours" or "200 hours or more") before writing an inequality.

Developing Math Concepts

Exs. 6–9 require students to be able to interpret the data displayed on an inequality graph and to write an inequality statement in the proper context given its graph. *Ex. 11* hints at systems of inequalities by illustrating that points can be solutions to more than one inequality statement at a time. For *Ex. 13*, you may want to encourage students to use flow charts or Venn diagrams to differentiate quadrilaterals. For *Ex. 15*, encourage students to try to draw a concave parallelogram to help them formulate their explanations. *Exs. 16–17* expose students to the fact that it isn't always possible to draw a height segment for a triangle or a parallelogram from a particular base to the opposite vertex or base. Remind them that the height is just a measure of how far a polygon extends in the direction perpendicular to the direction of a base.

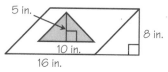

Practice & Application

Developing Math Concepts

Ex. 23 works well using the 4-step problem solving approach. First students must understand what information is given or immediately available (the square has a side length of 10, so its area is 10 • 10; the probability of landing in the circle is $\frac{3}{5}$, so the area of the circle is $\frac{3}{5}$ that of the square), and what is asked for (the area of the circle). Then students can plan to find the area of the circle in terms of that of the square by multiplying or writing a proportion. After carrying out their plan, students should reread the original problem situation to make sure that it still makes sense with their solution. For *Ex. 26*, encourage students to use manipulatives and sketches to see that the parallelograms formed from the square have a smaller height than that of the square. Because the base remains constant, the area must then decrease.

Closing the Section

Through the topic of flight, students have studied inequalities, including in the context of Bernoulli's principle. They have expanded their knowledge of polygons, including finding the areas of triangles, parallelograms, and polygons made from simpler polygons. The *Reflecting on the Section* exercise on page 392 explores the important distinction between parallelograms that have a fixed area and fixed base (as with the ice cream stick model) and those that have a fixed perimeter and a fixed base (as in this exercise). In this section, students have also addressed geometric probability from both an experimental and theoretical viewpoint.

QUICK QUIZ ON THIS SECTION

1. Write and graph an inequality to represent this statement: x is less than or equal to 18 and greater than 15.

2. Alyssa always spends at least 25 min a day practicing the tuba. Write an inequality to show how many minutes she practices in a week.

3. Use what you know about the areas of triangles and rectangles to find the area of this quadrilateral.

   15 cm

   4 cm

   18 cm

4. Find the theoretical probability that an object dropped on the figure below will land on the shaded target.

   5 in.

   8 in.

   10 in.

   16 in.

   What is the probability that it will fall outside the target?

For answers, see Quick Quiz blackline on p. 6-64.

Section ② Square Roots, Surface Area, and Area of a Circle

Section Planner

DAYS FOR MODULE 6

1 2 3 **4 5 6** 7 8 9 10 11 12 13

SECTION 2

First Day
Setting the Stage, p. 394
Exploration 1, pp. 395–397

Second Day
Exploration 2, pp. 397–400

Third Day
Exploration 3, pp. 401–403
Key Concepts, pp. 404–405

Block Schedule

Day 2 continued
Setting the Stage, Exploration 1

Day 3
Exploration 2, Exploration 3,
Key Concepts

RESOURCE ORGANIZER

Teaching Resources
• Practice and Applications, Sec. 2
• Study Guide, Sec. 2
• Technology Activity
• Warm-Up, Sec. 2
• Quick Quiz, Sec. 2

Section Overview

A discussion of the invention of the parawing will introduce students to the topics of Section 2, which include square roots, surface areas of prisms, and areas of circles. As students investigate the sail area of a parawing, they will find the area of a square. They will learn how to find the length of a side of a square given its area. In doing so, they will learn the definitions for square root, principal square root, and perfect square. Students will use mental math and calculators to estimate the square root of a number.

The Hargrave box kite will introduce students to prisms in Exploration 2. Students will learn the vocabulary for the parts of a prism. By constructing a net of a cube, students will discover how to find the surface area of prisms.

In Exploration 3, a centipede kite will model a set of circles. As they cut a circle into sectors and arrange the sectors to form a figure that approximates a parallelogram, students will learn the formula for the area of a circle. For help with the parts of a circle and circumference, refer students to Module 4, page 241.

SECTION OBJECTIVES

Exploration 1
• find principal and negative square roots of perfect squares
• estimate square roots to the nearest tenth

Exploration 2
• sketch a net for a right prism
• find the surface area of a rectangular or triangular prism

Exploration 3
• find the area of a circle

ASSESSMENT OPTIONS

Checkpoint Questions
Question 9 on p. 396
Question 11 on p. 397
Question 16 on p. 398
Question 21 on p. 400
Question 31 on p. 403

Embedded Assessment
• For a list of embedded assessment exercises see p. 6-23.

Performance Task/Portfolio
★Exercise 11 on p. 406 (visual thinking)
★Exercise 12 on p. 406 (visual thinking)
• Exercise 22 on p. 407
• Exercise 23 on p. 407 (oral report)
• Module Project on p. 408

★= a problem solving task that can be assessed using the Assessment Scales

SECTION 2 MATERIALS

Setting the Stage
◆ protractor

Exploration 1
◆ calculator

Exploration 2
◆ scissors
◆ tape

◆ centimeter grid paper
◆ two centimeter cubes

Exploration 3
◆ Labsheet 2A
◆ scissors
◆ tape
◆ ruler

Module Project on page 408
◆ Project Labsheet A
◆ ruler
◆ tape
◆ balance scale (optional)

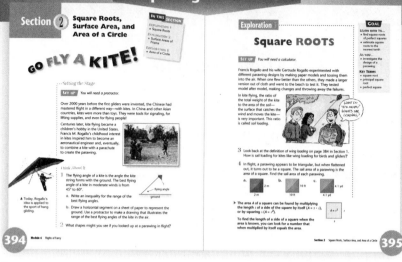

Setting the Stage

MOTIVATE

Kites have always held a fascination for both young and old. Their construction and flight also dovetail with mathematics in numerous ways. In this section, kite design leads into discussion of square roots, area, and surface area. Read the Setting the Stage as a class. Ask students to find out and bring in more information about the long history of kites, including how kites have been used to carry people both historically and in modern times. Students will need protractors to answer **Question 1**, which revisits the topic of inequalities addressed in the previous section.

Exploration 1

PLAN

Classroom Management
Exploration 1 can be performed in small groups or as a whole class. Monitor students to make certain they use mental math for **Question 7**. For **Question 10**, which is highlighted for whole-class participation, students will need calculators. You may want to work through additional examples with students before **Question 11**, so students can get more practice at recognizing perfect squares and at estimating.

GUIDE

Developing Math Concepts
For **Questions 4, 5**, and the *Example* between them, make sure that students are labeling units constantly and properly. Area involves multiplying a measure times a measure, so the answer is always square units. Finding the square root of an area, however, "undoes" this, so the units in the answer are no longer square units.

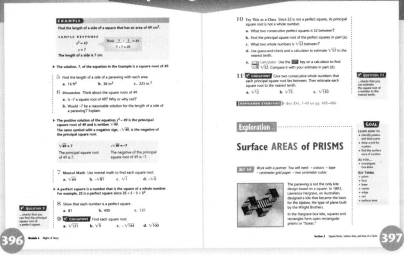

Exploration I continued

Classroom Examples
Find the length of the side of a square that has an area of 144 in.^{2}.

Answer:

$s^2 = 144$ in.^{2}

Think: $\underline{\ ?\ } \cdot \underline{\ ?\ } = 144$
$12 \cdot 12 = 144$
$s = 12$ in.

The length of a side is 12 in.

Developing Math Concepts
For *Question 6* and the exposition following, make sure that students are not confused by "throwing away" a negative square root in a real-life situation, and that they understand that the radical sign by itself always indicates only the positive square root. For *Question 8*, remind students that they are looking for a number to *multiply* by itself to obtain the indicated number. The first impulse of some students new to square roots may be to look first at half of the given number; they may be surprised that the square root is so small in relation to the original number.

Checkpoint *Question 9* allows you to check that students are correctly identifying the principal square root of a number and the opposite of this root.

Developing Math Concepts
For *Question 10*, you may want to have students list the first fifteen consecutive perfect squares and their principal square roots for reference. By making a pictorial representation of these perfect squares on graph paper, they will build a better sense for recognizing perfect squares and estimating square roots. You may also want them to work on a whole-class display of these perfect squares and their square roots.

Checkpoint For *Question 11*, make certain students are estimating. They should be using calculators only to check and refine their estimates. They can check their estimates using the square root function after they have completed their estimates to the nearest tenth.

HOMEWORK EXERCISES

See the Suggested Assignment for Day 1 on page 6-23. For Exercise Notes, see page 6-24.

Exploration 2

PLAN

Classroom Management
Students should complete Exploration 2 working in pairs. *Questions 12–16* involve mostly guided discussion. It will help while discussing *Question 14* if you have models of rectangular and triangular prisms that students can hold and examine. For *Questions 17–20*, students will need time and materials for constructing nets for centimeter cubes out of centimeter paper. As the concept of a two-dimensional net for a three-dimensional object is quite abstract, students will need plenty of hands-on time with covering prisms with nets. Expect students to need frequent guidance during this activity.

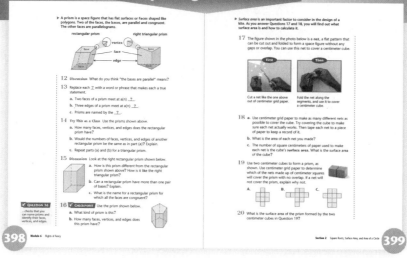

Exploration 2 continued

GUIDE

Developing Math Concepts

For **Question 12**, first review the definition of parallel lines (lines in a plane that never intersect). Have students point out parallel surfaces in the classroom, such as opposite walls or the floor and ceiling. For **Question 15(b)**, have students examine a book, box, or another model of a right rectangular prism.

Checkpoint *Question 16* will check that students can first identify the bases so that they can determine the name of the prism. They should notice that there is only one possible pair of bases here. Check students' ability to identify all the faces, vertices, and edges.

Developing Math Concepts

For *Question 17*, make sure that students understand that there can be no overlap in a net when constructing a space figure. For *Question 18(a)*, ask students how many squares any net of the cube will have and why (6; the cube has 6 sides, each a square one centimeter on an edge). Tell students that two nets are considered the same if you can form one from the other by rotating it or flipping it (some students may be familiar with this idea from experience with pentominoes). For *Question 19*, encourage students actually to copy, cut out, and try to cover the two-cube prism with the nets. For *Question 20*, remind students that because the surface area is a sum of other areas, the answer will still be in terms of square units.

Customizing Instruction

Visual Learners Provide several rectangular and tri-angular prisms for students to hold and examine for this section. If possible, have faces (including bases), edges, and vertices labeled on at least one of each type of prism. You may also want to have students construct several different sizes and types of labeled prisms out of sturdy materials. If removable tape is used, students can fold and unfold each prism to help them understand its net.

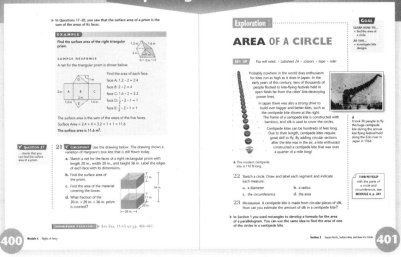

Exploration 2 continued

Classroom Examples
**Find the surface area of the
rectangular prism below.**

Answer: A net for the rectangular
prism is shown below.

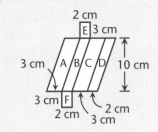

Find the area of each face.
face A: 3 • 10 = 30
face B: 2 • 10 = 20
face C: 3 • 10 = 30
face D: 2 • 10 = 20
face E: 2 • 3 = 6
face F: 2 • 3 = 6

The surface area is the sum of
the areas of the six faces.
Surface Area
= 30 + 20 + 30 + 20 + 6 + 6 = 112
The surface area is 112 cm^2.

Managing Time For the
Example, allow time for students
to make a net similar to the one
shown. On the net, they can
label all dimensions and areas of
each of the polygons before
folding the net into a prism. The
more nets and prisms they construct, the better students'
understanding of surface area
will become.

Estimation Encourage students
to use estimation when finding
the surface area of prisms. As an
illustration, in the Example, the
surface area must be more than
five times the area of the smallest polygon in the net and less
than five times the area of the
largest. Or, students might
decide polygon A is an "average" size polygon in the net, so
the surface area should be about
5 • 2.4 = 12 m^2, which agrees
with the answer.

Checkpoint *Question 21*
requires students to make a net of
a rectangular prism, and use this to
find the surface area. Make sure
students distinguish between the
surface area of the whole prism
itself and the area that is covered
by material. You may want to have
them indicate the material-covered
portion of the prism on the net.

HOMEWORK EXERCISES ▶

See the Suggested Assignment
for Day 2 on page 6-23. For
Exercise Notes, see page 6-24.

Exploration 3

PLAN

Classroom Management
Exploration 3 can be completed
as individuals, in pairs, or in
small groups. Each student will
need Labsheet 2A, scissors, tape,
and a ruler to estimate the area
of a circle. *Question 26* is highlighted for the whole class, but
the discussion-oriented *Question
27* (as well as *Questions 28* and
29) will also require close guidance to ensure that students
understand the process of using
parallelograms to approximate
the area of a circle. *Question 30*
is also marked for whole-class
participation to ensure that students gain comfort in dealing
with π both as an exact number
and as an approximation.

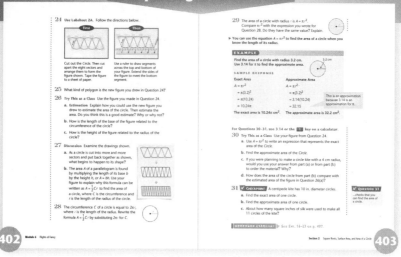

Exploration 3 continued

GUIDE

Developing Math Concepts

For **Question 26(b)**, you may want to have students highlight the portions of the sectors that were part of the original circle to help them make the connection between the circumference of the circle and the base of the parallelogram. For **Question 26(c)**, make sure students see that a segment from the vertex of each upward-pointing sector straight down to the base of the parallelogram is a radius. For **Question 28**, remind students that π is the ratio of the circumference of any circle to its diameter, $\pi = C/d$, or $C = \pi d = \pi(2r) = 2\pi r$. For the Example on page 403, if time permits, you may want to perform the activity using cylindrical containers, a ruler, and string to strengthen students' comprehension that π is a little more than 3. For **Question 30**, remind students that π is a *number*, not a variable. We just use the symbol because we could never write out the decimal form of π, $\pi = 3.1415926535898....$

Classroom Examples

Find the area of a circle with radius 10.5 m. Use 3.14 for π to find the approximate area.

Answer:

Exact Area   Approximate Area
$A = \pi r^2$ $A = \pi r^2$
$= \pi(10.5)^2$ $= \pi(10.5)^2$
$= \pi(110.25)$ $\approx (3.14)(110.25)$
$= 110.25\pi$ ≈ 346.185

The exact area is 110.25π m², or about 346.185 m².

Checkpoint *Question 31* checks that students can find both the exact and approximate area of a circle.

▌ HOMEWORK EXERCISES ▶

See the Suggested Assignment for Day 3 on page 6-23. For Exercise Notes, see page 6-24.

CLOSE

Closure Question State the formulas for the area of a square and the area of a circle. Explain a concept that these formulas have in common.

Sample Response: The formula for the area of a square with side s is $A = s^2$. The formula for the area of a circle with radius r is $A = \pi r^2$. Both formulas involve finding squares of numbers; in one case, the side of the square and, in the other, the radius of the circle.

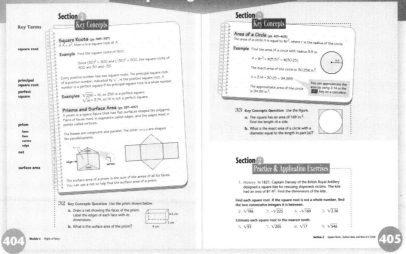

SUGGESTED ASSIGNMENT

Core Course
Day 1: Exs. 1–10, 24–33
Day 2: Exs. 11–14
Day 3: Exs. 16–23

Extended Course
Day 1: Exs. 1–10, 24–33
Day 2: Exs. 11–15
Day 3: Exs. 16–23

Block Schedule
Day 2: Sec. 1, Exs. 19–26;
      Exs. 1–10, 24–33
Day 3: Exs. 12–14, 16–23

EMBEDDED ASSESSMENT

These section objectives are tested by the exercises listed.

Find principal and negative square roots of perfect squares.
Exercises 2, 4

Estimate square roots to the nearest tenth.
Exercises 6, 8, 10

Sketch a net for a right prism.
Exercises 12a, 12b, 13a

Find the surface area of a rectangular or triangular prism.
Exercises 12c–f, 13b, 13c, 14

Find the area of a circle.
Exercises 16, 22

Customizing Instruction

Home Involvement Those helping students at home will find the Key Concepts on pages 404–405 a handy reference to the key ideas, terms, and skills of Section 2.

Absent Students For students who were absent for all or part of this section, the blackline Study Guide for Section 2 may be used to present the ideas, concepts, and skills of Section 2. It will help students who missed the portion on nets and prisms if they have physical models they can take home and manipulate.

Extra Help For students who need additional practice, the blackline Practice and Applications for Section 2 provides additional exercises that may be used to confirm the skills of Section 2. The Extra Skill Practice on page 409 also provides additional exercises.

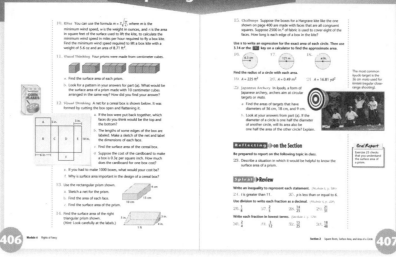

Practice & Application

| EXERCISE NOTES |

Developing Math Concepts
For *Ex. 10*, the formula may
seem confusing to students. To
clarify it, you may want to use
some simple examples. For
example, let $A = 1$ and let
$w = 1$, 9, and 25. Students
should see that the heavier the
kite, the faster the wind must be
for a given area. Similarly, let
$w = 100$ and let $A = 1$, 4, and 25
to show that the greater the area
for a given weight, the lower the
wind speed can be. For *Ex. 11*,
encourage students to use tables.
It will help some students to use
actual cubes to find the pattern,
while some may want to draw
nets. Make sure students explain
their solutions in detail. For *Ex.
12(a)*, some students may still
need to copy and cut out a net
like the one shown. In part *(c)*,
encourage students to write a
plan or rule for finding the surface area before they start their
calculations.

Writing For *Ex. 12(f)*, have
students give their explanations
in complete sentences, with reference to the results of parts
(c)–(e).

Challenge For *Ex. 15*, encourage students to use the 4-step
problem solving approach, pay-
ing special attention to what
information they know and
what they need to find.

Developing Math Concepts
For *Ex. 18*, students may be confused at π being used for a diameter. Point out that the area is
always π times the square of the
radius, no matter what the
radius is. For *Exs. 19–21*, it may
help students understand what
they are looking for if they
replace each A with πr^2. For *Ex.
22(b)*, ask students to describe
any relationships that they do
find (the area will be one fourth
the area of the original circle).

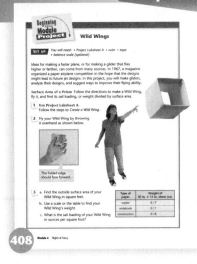

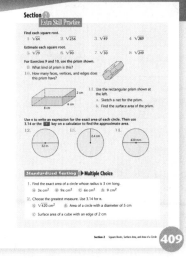

In this project, students will first make a glider called a "Wild Wing." Later they will construct a larger, similar glider. Finally, after analyzing the two gliders, they will recommend ways to make a faster-, farther-, or higher-flying glider. Students will each need a copy of Project Labsheet A for directions on how to construct their own Wild Wing. Make sure students label their gliders before flying them. To fly the gliders, students will need a large, unobstructed area. *Question 3* asks students to find the surface area and sail loading (discussed on page 395) of their gliders. As students will be continuing this project in Sections 4 and 5, you will want to collect or make sure students keep their labsheets, gliders, and solutions.

Closing the Section

Through examining the shapes and surfaces of kites, including the concept of sail loading, students have gained knowledge about procedures for finding square roots, finding areas of circles, and finding the surface area of various prisms. This has included using two-dimensional nets to represent three-dimensional figures. Through the *Reflecting on the Section* exercise on page 407, students will consider situations where it is important to use surface area. Let students know your expectations for any reports. Encourage students to use illustrations and models to present any examples they suggest.

QUICK QUIZ ON THIS SECTION

1. Find $\sqrt{400}$.

2. Estimate $\sqrt{22}$ to the nearest tenth.

3. What is the name of this prism? How many faces, edges, and vertices does it have?

4. What is the surface area of a rectangular prism with base 10 cm by 12 cm and height 20 cm?

5. Find the area of a circle with diameter 2.4 in. Round to the nearest tenth.

For answers, see Quick Quiz blackline on p. 6-65.

Section ③ Triangles and Similarity

Section Planner

DAYS FOR MODULE 6

| 1 | 2 | 3 | 4 | 5 | 6 | 7 | 8 | 9 | 10 | 11 | 12 | 13 |

SECTION 3

First Day
Setting the Stage, p. 410
Exploration 1, pp. 411–413

Second Day
Exploration 2, pp. 414–416
Key Concepts, p. 417

Block Schedule

Day 4
Setting the Stage, Exploration 1, Exploration 2, Key Concepts

RESOURCE ORGANIZER

Teaching Resources
• Practice and Applications, Sec. 3
• Study Guide, Sec. 3
• Mid-Module Quiz
• Warm-Up, Sec. 3
• Quick Quiz, Sec. 3

Section Overview

In Section 3, students will examine two scale models of the Curtiss JN-4, or *Jenny*, a favorite airplane of Bessie Coleman, the first female African-American pilot. Students will discover that because the models have the same shape, they can align the models in their line of sight so that the smaller model exactly obscures the larger model. In Module 4, students were introduced informally to similar figures when they investigated transformations on the coordinate plane. As they identify the ratios of the lengths of corresponding sides and the measures of corresponding angles of the two scale models, students will learn the formal definition of similar figures. They will discover that a scale drawing produces a figure similar to the original figure. Students will find the scale of a drawing and use the scale to find unknown measurements by solving proportions.

As they investigate similar triangles, students will classify triangles by their angle measures. Key terms include acute triangle, obtuse triangle, and right triangle. Students will also explore the relationship between similar and congruent polygons in this section.

SECTION OBJECTIVES

Exploration 1
• recognize similar and congruent figures, and identify corresponding parts
• use the scale of a drawing to find unknown measures

Exploration 2
• classify triangles as acute, obtuse, or right
• find unknown measures in similar figures

ASSESSMENT OPTIONS

Checkpoint Questions
• Question 10 on p. 413
• Question 12 on p. 413
• Question 19 on p. 416

Embedded Assessment
• For a list of embedded assessment exercises see p. 6-31.

Performance Task/Portfolio
• Exercise 20 on p. 419 (open-ended)
★ Exercise 21 on p. 419 (visual thinking)
• Standardized Testing on p. 421

★ = a problem solving task that can be assessed using the Assessment Scales

SECTION 3 MATERIALS

Exploration 1
♦ Labsheet 3A
♦ ruler
♦ protractor
♦ scissors
♦ tape

Exploration 2
♦ Jenny cutouts from Exploration 1
♦ ruler
♦ protractor
♦ tape

Practice and Application Exercises
♦ protractor
♦ ruler

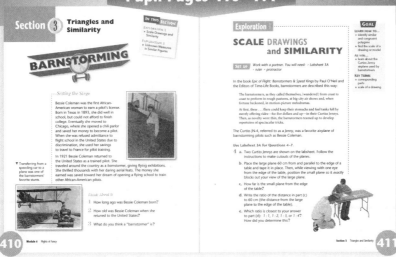

Setting the Stage

MOTIVATE

Read the Setting the Stage and address the questions as a class. Many students will have seen old black-and-white film footage of early barnstormers, perhaps even including scenes of pilots actually flying planes through open barns! You may want to encourage students to do library or Internet research on Bessie Coleman or other early barnstormers.

Exploration 1

PLAN

Classroom Management
Exploration 1 is best performed in student pairs. The partners will need Labsheet 3A, scissors, tape, a protractor, and a ruler. You can either read the introduction to the Exploration as a class or have student pairs read it. As students begin on the activity with the plane cutouts in *Question 4*, inform them that the cutouts will be collected after *Question 12* for use in Exploration 2. You may want a few extra copies of Labsheet 3A on hand for those who make errors in cutting and for Exploration 2. For *Question 4*, students will need tables they can use or desks that are at least 2 feet wide. *Questions 8* and *9* are highlighted for whole-class discussion to ensure that students understand what makes two figures similar, and that they can identify corresponding parts and angles of similar figures regardless of the orientation of the figures.

GUIDE

Developing Math Concepts
For *Question 4*, make sure students are viewing with their eyes at the table's edge, so that their results will be accurate. In part *(d)*, some students may need reminding that the ratio of quantity *A* to quantity *B* is *A* : *B*, or *A/B*. Make sure students are not writing the ratio in reverse order. For part *(e)*, encourage students to use rounding and estimation, as they are looking for an approximate ratio.

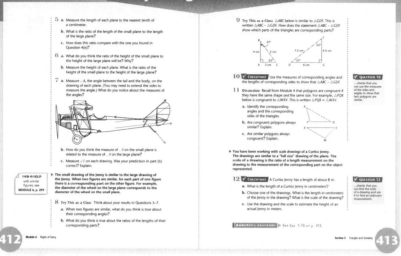

Exploration 1 continued

Cooperative Learning After discussing *Question 8*, ask students to use this information to offer a definition of similar polygons (two polygons are similar if their corresponding angles are congruent and the ratios of their corresponding sides are all equal). Have different students offer their own definitions, refining the definitions of others until they can agree on the best definition.

Developing Math Concepts In *Question 9*, it will help students see the similarity by redrawing one of the triangles rotated 90° to the same orientation as the other.

Checkpoint *Question 10* makes sure that students can identify congruent corresponding angles and proportional corresponding sides of two polygons to show that they are similar. They will also have to write and simplify ratios to show the proportionality.

Developing Math Concepts For *Question 11*, emphasize the difference between the symbols for similarity and congruence. Before parts *(b)* and *(c)*, have students modify the definition of congruent polygons as having the same shape and same size to define similar polygons (polygons that have the same shape, though not necessarily the same size.) You may want to represent this relationship with a Venn diagram.

Checkpoint For *Question 12*, students will find a scale factor by comparing the length of one of the drawings to the actual length of the plane. Check that students can set up the proper proportion in part *(c)* to find the height of the plane. Remind students to label all measures. You may want to suggest that one partner use the small plane and the other the large plane. Then partners can compare their answers and discuss why their results for the plane's height are about the same.

| HOMEWORK EXERCISES |

See the Suggested Assignment for Day 1 on page 6-31. For Exercise Notes, see page 6-31.

Customizing Instruction

Alternative Approach 1 Provide students multiple, labeled polygons drawn on a page such that there are sets of similar figures. Have students identify sets of similar polygons. Encourage students to cut out and reorient the polygons, laying them over one another to check for similarity. This will increase students' experience and ability in recognizing similar figures, especially for visual and tactile learners. Finally, have students measure to estimate the ratio of corresponding sides in pairs of similar figures, checking that each pair of corresponding sides has the same ratio.

Alternative Approach 2 Have students present other examples of scale drawings or models they have seen (models of planes or cars, a drawing of the Statue of Liberty or Eiffel Tower, a drawing or model of a cell or integrated circuit). Have students bring in the pictures or models. Then use the scale factor and the measurements of the drawing or model to find the actual size of the object.

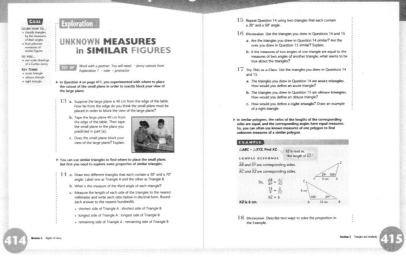

Exploration 2

PLAN

Classroom Management

Students continue working with their partner and cut-out planes from Exploration 1. They will again need a ruler, a protractor, and tape. Have students keep the cutouts set up throughout the Exploration, as they will be used in *Questions 13* and *21–23*. *Question 17* is highlighted for the whole class to ensure that all students understand how to classify triangles. As the whole class addresses *Question 21*, make sure that students understand how the diagram corresponds to their displays of the planes on the table.

GUIDE

Developing Math Concepts

For *Questions 14–15*, encourage students to be as accurate as possible when drawing their triangles and finding the ratios of corresponding sides to increase their confidence in their answers to *Question 16*.

Managing Time If time is short, you may have one student from each pair complete *Question 14* while the other completes *Question 15*. Then they can share their results with each other before discussing *Question 16*.

Classroom Examples

$\triangle KLM \sim \triangle NOP$. Find *KL*.

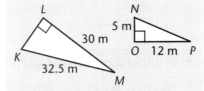

Answer:
$\overline{LM}$ and $\overline{OP}$ are corresponding sides.
$\overline{KL}$ and $\overline{NO}$ are corresponding sides.

So, $\dfrac{LM}{OP} = \dfrac{KL}{NO}$

$\dfrac{30}{12} = \dfrac{KL}{5}$

$KL = 12.5$

Developing Math Concepts

For *Question 16(b)*, some students may already be aware that the sum of the measures of the angles of a triangle is 180°, so that the third angle must be 180° minus the sum of the other two angles. This topic will be addressed in Section 4. For *Question 17*, have students identify and classify triangles around the classroom and common triangles outside the classroom. You may want to ask students if a triangle can have two right angles (no). For *Question 18*, make sure that students feel confident solving the proportion both with cross products and using equivalent fractions.

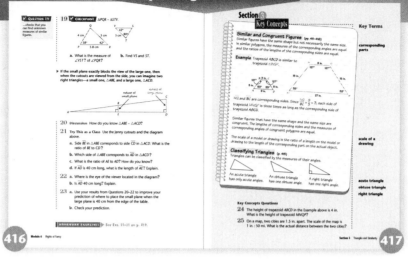

MODULE 6 ◆ SECTION 3

Exploration 2 continued

Checkpoint For *Question 19*, students must be able to identify corresponding angles and sides. While finding the missing angles requires no calculation, finding the missing side lengths requires setting up and solving proportions as shown in the previous Example.

Developing Math Concepts
For *Question 21(a)*, remind students to measure and compare the heights of the plane cutouts instead of measuring and comparing the vertical segments on the diagram, since we are basing the diagram on the cutouts.

Visual Learners For *Question 22(a)*, you can use a yardstick or meter stick as in the Plan section to illustrate the position of the eye in the diagram. If you move the small plane forward and backward while holding the rule in place, students can see how the small plane exactly blocks the view of the large plane when the top of the small plane just touches the diagonal connecting the eye and the top of the large plane.

HOMEWORK EXERCISES

See the Suggested Assignment for Day 2 on page 6-31. For Exercise Notes, see page 6-31.

CLOSE

Closure Question What is needed to show that two triangles are similar? How is this different from showing that two triangles are congruent?

Sample Response: For similarity, show that the measures of corresponding angles are equal and that the ratios of the lengths of corresponding sides are equal. For congruence, the measures of the corresponding angles must be equal and the lengths of the corresponding sides must also be equal.

Customizing Instruction

Home Involvement Those helping students at home will find the Key Concepts on page 417 a handy reference to the key ideas, terms, and skills of Section 3.

Absent Students For students who were absent for all or part of this section, the blackline Study Guide for Section 3 may be used to present the ideas, concepts, and skills of Section 3. You may want to save some of the cutouts and drawings of the triangles in *Questions 14–15* for students who have been absent to view and manipulate.

Extra Help For students who need additional practice, the blackline Practice and Applications for Section 3 provides additional exercises that may be used to confirm the skills of Section 3. The Extra Skill Practice on page 421 also provides additional exercises.

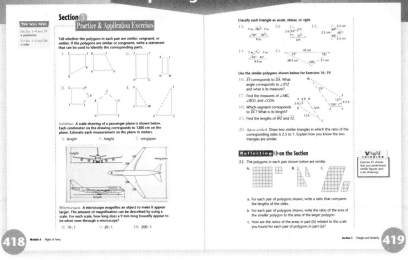

Core Course

Day 1: Exs. 1, 2, 5–10, 22, 23

Day 2: Exs. 11–19, 21, 24–30

Extended Course

Day 1: Exs. 1, 2, 5–10, 22, 23

Day 2: Exs. 11–19, 21, 24–30

Block Schedule

Day 4: Exs. 1, 2, 5–8, 13–19, 21–30

These section objectives are tested by the exercises listed.

Recognize similar and congruent figures, and identify corresponding parts.

Exercises 1, 2

Use the scale of a drawing to find unknown measures.

Exercises 6, 8

Classify triangles as acute, obtuse, or right.

Exercises 13–15

Find unknown measures in similar figures.

Exercises 16, 18

Practice & Application

EXERCISE NOTES

Common Error For *Exs. 5–7,* students who do not read closely may answer improperly even if they set up and solve the correct proportion because they don't convert their answers from centimeters to meters.

Developing Math Concepts

For *Exs. 8–10,* remind students that, as described before in *Question 12* on page 413, the first number of the ratio represents the measurement on the drawing, model, or image, while the second number represents the measurement on the actual object. So, a scale of 10 : 1 means that the representation is 10 times larger than the actual object, while a scale of 1 : 10 means that the representation is one tenth as large as the actual object. For *Exs. 16–19,* encourage students first to write a statement that can be used to identify the corresponding parts of the similar polygons. This will help them keep the corresponding parts organized as they answer the questions. They may also want to sketch the labeled polygons oriented in the same way for clarity.

Writing For *Ex. 20,* encourage students to write out the steps they used to draw the two triangles. This will help them realize that it is not possible for them to draw non-similar triangles satisfying the given ratio.

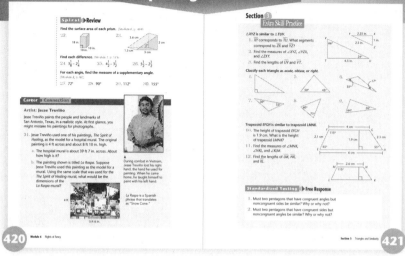

Closing the Section

Through scale drawings of a Curtiss *Jenny* airplane, students have explored the relationships of corresponding parts of similar figures, while learning to distinguish congruence from similarity. They have used the ratio of corresponding sides of similar polygons to find the scale of a drawing and to write and solve proportions for missing side lengths. Along the way, they have identified the distinctions among acute, obtuse, and right triangles. The *Reflecting on the Section* exercise on page 419 gives students more practice in finding the ratio of corresponding sides of similar polygons. Students then test their understanding of similarity by examining the relationship of side-length ratios to area ratios between similar figures.

QUICK QUIZ ON THIS SECTION

1. Draw two obtuse triangles that are similar but not congruent.

2. The two pentagons below are similar. Write a statement that can be used to identify the corresponding parts.

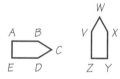

3. If ∠*BCD* in Question 2 is 60°, what can you say about another angle measure or side length in pentagon *VWXYZ*?

4. The Statue of Liberty is 152 ft tall. Luis drew a scale drawing of the statue with a scale of 1 in. = 8 ft. How many inches tall was his drawing?

5. △ *ABC* ~ △ *XYZ*. Find the missing lengths.

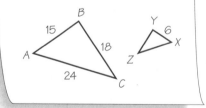

For answers, see Quick Quiz blackline on p. 6-66.

Section ④ Parallel Lines and Angles of Polygons

Section Planner

DAYS FOR MODULE 6

`1 2 3 4 5 6 7 8 9 10 11 12 13`

SECTION 4

First Day
Setting the Stage, p. 422
Exploration 1, pp. 423–425

Second Day
Exploration 2, pp. 426–428
Key Concepts, p. 429

Block Schedule

Day 5
Setting the Stage, Exploration 1, Exploration 2, Key Concepts

RESOURCE ORGANIZER

Teaching Resources
• Practice and Applications, Sec. 4
• Study Guide, Sec. 4
• Warm-Up, Sec. 4
• Quick Quiz, Sec. 4

Section Overview

In Section 4, students will make wing models to explore why vertical struts and diagonal wires were important to the structure of wings in early airplanes. Students will use their models to investigate the relationships between the pairs of alternate interior angles, alternate exterior angles, vertical angles, and corresponding angles that are formed by a transversal intersecting two parallel lines.

When they create a second wing model, this time using diagonal supports, students will explore the effect of triangular supports on wing design. They will apply the information they learn about parallel lines and transversals to find the sum of the measures of the angles of a triangle. Then they will confirm their finding by examining physical models of the angles of a triangle. As they explore the relationship between a rectangle and a triangle, students will find the sum of the measures of the angles of a rectangle. Their investigation of rectangles will lead them to discover the sum of the measures of the angles of any quadrilateral.

SECTION OBJECTIVES

Exploration 1
• identify and find measures of angles formed by parallel lines and a transversal

Exploration 2
• use the sum of the measures of the angles to find unknown angle measures in triangles and quadrilaterals

ASSESSMENT OPTIONS

Checkpoint Questions
• Question 11 on p. 425
• Question 21 on p. 428

Portfolio Assessment
• Extended Exploration on p. 435

Embedded Assessment
• For a list of embedded assessment exercises see p. 6-38.

Performance Task/Portfolio
• Exercise 8 on p. 430 (challenge)
• Exercise 9 on p. 430
★ Exercise 23 on p 431 (visual thinking)
★ Exercises 34–36 on p. 432 (extension)
★ Module Project on p. 433
• Standardized Testing on p. 434
★ Extended Exploration on p. 435

★ = a problem solving task that can be assessed using the Assessment Scales

SECTION 4 MATERIALS

Exploration 1
♦ Labsheets 4A and 4B
♦ scissors
♦ ruler
♦ tape
♦ 2 index cards (3 in. by 5 in.)
♦ protractor

Exploration 2
♦ scissors
♦ ruler
♦ tape
♦ 4 index cards (3 in. by 5 in.)
♦ Labsheet 4A
♦ wing from Exploration 1

Module Project on page 433
♦ Project Labsheet A
♦ ruler and tape

Extended Exploration on page 435
♦ Extended Exploration Labsheet
♦ ruler

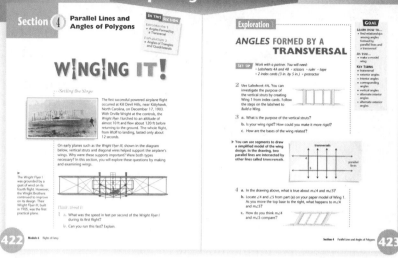

Setting the Stage

MOTIVATE

Have students watch the clock for 12 seconds. Now ask them to close their eyes and open them when they think 12 seconds have passed. Read the first paragraph of the Setting the Stage as a class. Many students will have heard of the flight, but they may be surprised that it lasted only 12 seconds and covered only 120 feet. Complete the reading and have students examine the photo carefully. Many students will be aware of the strengthening effects of triangular supports and braces. Ask students for other examples they have seen of triangular and diagonal supports (buildings, bridges, radio towers, and so on). After answering *Questions 1(a)* and *(b)*, students may be amazed that the first powered flight ever got off the ground at such a speed!

Exploration I

PLAN

Classroom Management
Exploration 1 is best performed in student pairs. Students will need copies of Labsheets 4A and 4B, the materials for constructing the wings, and a protractor. Collect Labsheet 4A and the wings if students break before *Question 13*, as both will be needed for Exploration 2. Many new terms are introduced in this Exploration, especially in *Questions 5–8*. Encourage students to describe their understanding of these terms to each other, and to try to find all examples of each type of angle in the diagrams. In *Question 9*, students will use Labsheet 4B to draw a transversal and measure angles. For *Question 10*, include the whole class to ensure that students can distinguish among the different pairs of angles and can identify the congruence relationships when a transversal intersects two parallel lines.

GUIDE

Developing Math Concepts
For *Question 3(a)*, point out to students that because the struts are all the same length, the top and bottom wings are everywhere the same distance apart, that is, they are parallel.

Developing Math Concepts
For *Question 4*, ask students what quantities remain the same for each of the parallelograms formed by the wings and the struts no matter what the angle (the base and the perimeter). Then ask them what quantities change as the angle changes (the height and the area).

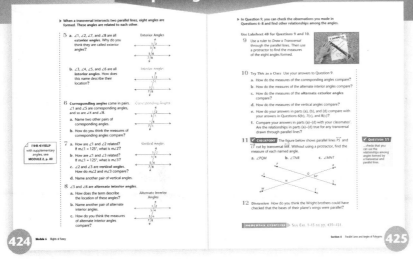

Exploration I continued

Classroom Examples
In the figure below, line *t* intersects parallel lines *m* and *n*. Name all angles that you know to be congruent.

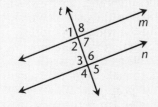

Answer:
∠1 ≅ ∠7 and ∠2 ≅ ∠8 because they are vertical angles;
∠1 ≅ ∠3 and ∠2 ≅ ∠4 because they are corresponding angles;
∠1 ≅ ∠5 because they are alternate exterior angles;
∠2 ≅ ∠6 because they are alternate interior angles

So ∠1 ≅ ∠7 ≅ ∠3 ≅ ∠5 and ∠2 ≅ ∠4 ≅ ∠6 ≅ ∠8.

Developing Math Concepts
For *Questions 9–10*, make sure that students recognize that when a transversal cuts a pair of parallel lines, all of the angles formed have one of only two possible measures. Students should realize that for each type of angle—corresponding, vertical, alternate interior, and alternate exterior—there will be pairs that take on each of these two angle measures. Also, a given angle can be a vertical angle, a corresponding angle, and an alternate interior or exterior angle to different angles simultaneously. For *Question 10(f)*, it is important that student pairs see the results of other student pairs from *Question 9* to reinforce that these same relationships hold for all other transversals of the pair of parallel lines given.

Checkpoint
For *Question 11*, students will use vertical angle and alternate interior or corresponding angle relationships for parts *(a)* and *(b)*. For part *(c)*, they will have to use the fact that the two angles that form a straight angle (supplementary angles) must have a total measure of 180°. You may want to encourage students to label all of the angles on the diagram for practice.

Developing Math Concepts
For *Question 12*, point out that not only do the struts act like transversals for the wings, but the wings act like transversals for the lines containing the struts.

HOMEWORK EXERCISES

See the Suggested Assignment for Day 1 on page 6-38. For Exercise Notes, see page 6-38.

MODULE 6 ◆ SECTION 4

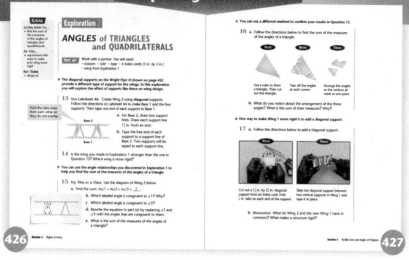

Exploration 2

PLAN

Classroom Management Have students perform Exploration 2 in the same pairs as in Exploration 1. Students will again need Labsheet 4A and the wings from Exploration 1, and will need the materials for making new wings and modifying the old ones. *Questions 15* and *19* are highlighted for whole class discussion to make certain that students understand the logic for why the sum of the measures of the angles is 180° in a triangle and 360° in a quadrilateral.

GUIDE

Reading For *Question 14*, make sure students are not reading *strong* and *rigid* just as synonymns. The strength refers more to the load that the wing can sustain without breaking, while the rigidity refers to the stiffness of the wing, or how easily the wing can be distorted from its intended shape. Students should see that the diagonal supports make the wing much less susceptible to sideways forces.

Developing Math Concepts

For *Question 15*, it will help students see the connection between the Wing 2 diagram and the angle relationships between parallel lines and transversals if they sketch the diagram and extend the wing support segments so that they are more recognizable as transversals. Also, check to make sure that students can use proper notation regarding angles. For example, if $m\angle 3 = 65°$ and $m\angle 1 = 65°$, then $m\angle 3 = m\angle 1$, and so $\angle 3 \cong \angle 1$. Encourage students to try *Question 16* with more than one triangle to confirm the results.

MODULE 6 ◆ SECTION 4

Customizing Instruction

Alternative Approach Geoboards allow students to make many different triangles and quadrilaterals. Students can measure the angles in geoboard triangles to confirm the 180° sum. By placing different colored bands in the shape of triangles over bands marking quadrilaterals, students can confirm the 360° sum of the angle measures of a quadrilateral.

Technology Geometry software programs exist that can make drawing polygons and measuring their angles very easy. Once the students know the basics of the software, this allows them to draw, manipulate, and examine a large number of figures in a short period of time.

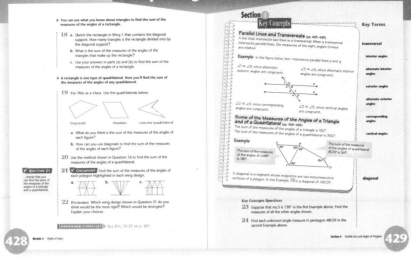

Exploration 2 continued

Developing Math Concepts

For *Question 19*, you may want to challenge students to try to draw a quadrilateral that can't be divided into two triangles. For the concave quadrilateral shown, make sure that students recognize that an angle in a polygon can be greater than 180°.

Classroom Examples
Find the measure of $\angle R$ below.

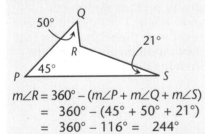

$m\angle R = 360° - (m\angle P + m\angle Q + m\angle S)$
$\quad = 360° - (45° + 50° + 21°)$
$\quad = 360° - 116° = 244°$

Checkpoint *Question 21*

checks not only that students recognize the 180° and 360° angle measure sums in triangles and quadrilaterals, but that they can use combinations of these shapes to find the sum of the angle measures in a more complicated polygon.

> **HOMEWORK EXERCISES**

See the Suggested Assignment for Day 2 on page 6-38. For Exercise Notes, see page 6-38.

> **CLOSE**

Closure Question Name four types of angle relationships formed when two parallel lines are cut by a transversal. Then state the sum of the measures of the angles of a triangle and the sum of the measures of the angles of a quadrilateral.

Possible answers: interior angles, exterior angles, alternate interior angles, alternate exterior angles, corresponding angles, and vertical angles; The sum of the measures of the angles of a triangle is 180°, and the sum of the measures of the angles of a quadrilateral is 360°.

Customizing Instruction

Home Involvement Those helping students at home will find the Key Concepts on page 429 a handy reference to the key ideas, terms, and skills of Section 4.

Absent Students For students who were absent for all or part of this section, the blackline Study Guide for Section 4 may be used to present the ideas, concepts, and skills of Section 4. You may also want to encourage students to lend the wings they have constructed from *Labsheet 4A* and the angles they have measured in *Labsheet 4B* to students who have missed these activities.

Extra Help For students who need additional practice, the blackline Practice and Applications for Section 4 provides additional exercises that may be used to confirm the skills of Section 4. The Extra Skill Practice on page 434 also provides additional exercises.

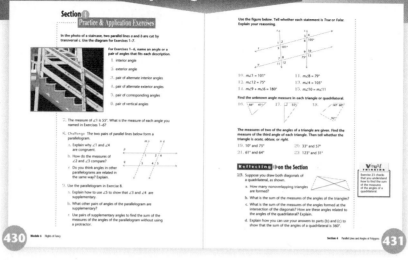

SUGGESTED ASSIGNMENT

Core Course
Day 1: Exs. 1–7, 9, 24–26
Day 2: Exs. 16–23, 27–33

Extended Course
Day 1: Exs. 1–8, 24–26
Day 2: Exs. 16, 18, 20, 23,
27–36

Block Schedule
Day 5: Exs. 1–7, 9, 16, 18, 20,
23–33

EMBEDDED ASSESSMENT

These section objectives are
tested by the exercises listed.

**Identify and find measures
of angles formed by parallel lines and a transversal.**

Exercises 3–7

**Use the sum of the mea-
sures of the angles to find
unknown angle measures
in triangles and quadrilaterals.**

Exercises 16, 18, 20

Practice & Application

EXERCISE NOTES

Developing Math Concepts
For *Exs. 1–6*, students are
required to give only one angle
or pair of angles as answers, but
make sure they realize that there
are four each of interior and
exterior angles, pairs of corresponding angles, and pairs of
vertical angles, and two pairs
each of alternate interior angles
and alternate exterior angles.

Challenge
For *Ex. 8*, it may
help students if they first write
down all the congruence relationships they can identify from
the diagram. Turning the diagram sideways may help them
see that lines *p* and *q* are transversals to the parallel lines *m*
and *n*.

Writing
For *Ex. 9(a)*, encour-
age students to write their explanations as short sentences in
paragraph form. They should
start with what they know from
the diagram, and then make sure
that each statement follows logi-
cally from previous statements.

Developing Math Concepts
For *Exs. 10–15*, remind students
that it may take more than one
step to find the measure of a
given angle. They should always
begin with the relationships that
they can immediately identify
from the diagram.

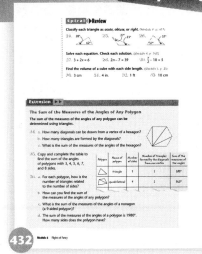

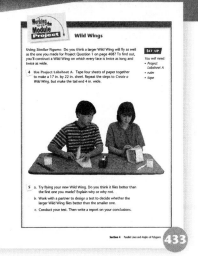

Working on the Module Project

Students will need Project Labsheet A and Wild Wing from the first part of this project (page 408). They will now construct another Wild Wing twice as long and wide as the first. With a partner, they will devise and carry out a test to compare the two Wild Wings. When writing up their conclusions for *Question 5(c)*, stress that students should clearly describe the intended purposes of their test, any materials they used, the steps they used to conduct the test, and any measurements they made. Then students should present their data in a clear way, using appropriate means of representation, followed by any conclusions they can draw from their test data. Remind students that they will need these results and both Wild Wings for the conclusion of the Module Project at the end of Section 5.

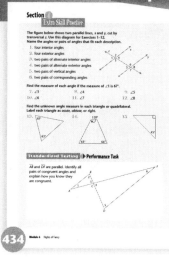

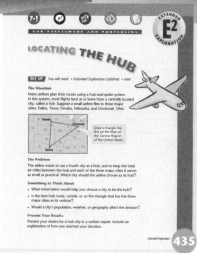

Closing the Section

Through examining the wing structure of early Wright Brothers' planes, students have been introduced to the relationships of the angles formed by a transversal and a pair of parallel lines. They have also discovered the patterns in the sums of the measures of angles in various polygons. The *Reflecting on the Section* exercise on page 431 ties together the measures of supplementary angles and the measures of the angles in a triangle to demonstrate again that the sum of the angle measures in a quadrilateral is 360°. Finally, the *Standardized Testing Performance Task* on page 434 provides an efficient way for students to demonstrate their knowledge of the angles formed by a transversal.

QUICK QUIZ ON THIS SECTION

For Questions 1–3, use the diagram. Lines r and s are parallel.

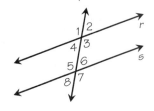

1. Name a pair of vertical angles.

2. Name a pair of alternate interior angles.

3. List four congruent angles in the figure.

4. Find the unknown angle measure in the quadrilateral.

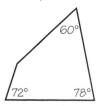

5. Two of the angles of a triangle are 45° and 56°. What is the measure of the third angle? Is the triangle acute, obtuse, or right?

For answers, see Quick Quiz blackline on p. 6-67.

Extended Exploration

The problem of traveling between cities as efficiently as possible has attracted mathematicians for centuries. For an airline, routing hundreds of flights through scores of cities, this problem alone is immense, without even considering factors like weather, economics, and people's travel needs and habits. This Extended Exploration addresses these problems by looking at an airline's use of hubs. As students explore this field, they will need to keep detailed records of any criteria they are using for their decisions. They will need to provide displays of any mathematical methods they have used to minimize travel distances. You may want to encourage students to approach this problem as if they were executives for an airline facing a presentation to the board about where to locate their new hub. This may help them realize the importance of being clear and well prepared!

MODULE 6 ◆ SECTION 4

Section ⑤ Volume of a Prism and Metric Relationships

Section Planner

DAYS FOR MODULE 6

1 2 3 4 5 6 7 8 9 10 **11 12 13**

SECTION 5

First Day
Setting the Stage, *p. 436*
Exploration 1, *pp. 437–439*

Second Day
Exploration 2, *pp. 439–441*

Third Day
Exploration 3, *pp. 442–444*
Key Concepts, *pp. 445–446*

Block Schedule

Day 6
Setting the Stage, Exploration 1,
Exploration 2

Day 7
Exploration 3, Key Concepts

RESOURCE ORGANIZER

Teaching Resources
• Practice and Applications, Sec. 5
• Study Guide, Sec. 5
• Warm-Up, Sec. 5
• Quick Quiz, Sec. 5
• Module Test Forms A and B
• Standardized Assessment
• Module Performance
  Assessment
• Cumulative Test Modules 5 and 6

Section Overview

Students will begin their work in Section 5 by comparing the the the volumes of two pools that have been the home for Keiko, the star of the movie Free Willy. To learn about the volume of a prism, students will build rectangular prisms from centimeter cubes. As they add layers to their prisms, students will investigate the relationship between the area of a prism's base and its height. Students will also apply this activity to triangular prisms.

In Exploration 2, students will study the relationship between mass, capacity, and volume as they explore Keiko's mass, the mass of water in the container in which he was shipped to the Oregon Coast Aquarium, and the volume of the container. The metric units milliliter, gram, liter, and kilogram will all be introduced, and students will convert metric units of mass, volume, and capacity.

In Exploration 3, students will identify arcs and vertices of a network as they examine the routes a package might travel to get to its destination. They will also interpret the meaning of the arcs and the vertices. Students will learn how routes on a network can be weighted so that drivers' routes can be planned efficiently.

SECTION OBJECTIVES

Exploration 1
• find the volume of a prism
Exploration 2
• use the relationship among metric units for volume capacity and mass of water
Exploration 3
• interpret a weighted network

ASSESSMENT OPTIONS

Checkpoint Questions
• Question 10 on p. 438
• Question 16 on p. 440
• Question 20 on p. 441
• Question 25 on p. 443
• Question 28 on p. 444

Embedded Assessment
• For a list of embedded assessment exercises see p. 6-47.

Performance Task/Portfolio
• Exercise 25 on p. 448
  (visual thinking)
★ Exercises 35–39 on p. 449
  (extension)
• Standardized Testing on p. 450
★ Module Project on p. 451

★ = a problem solving task that can be assessed using the Assessment Scales

SECTION 5 MATERIALS

Exploration 1
◆ 48 centimeter cubes

Exploration 3
◆ Labsheet 5A

Practice and Application Exercises
◆ Labsheet 5B

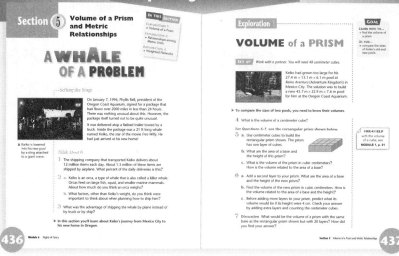

Setting the Stage

MOTIVATE

A container holding a 21 ft whale is not your typical express package! Read the introductory paragraphs as a class. Ask how many students have seen the movie *Free Willy*. You may want to have a student very briefly summarize the movie. As you discuss *Questions 1–3*, encourage students to try to imagine all the logistical problems that had to be overcome to transport Keiko. Considering some of these problems will lead students into exploring the volume of prisms and studying relationships among metric units, especially those of mass and capacity. The more general transportation problem will introduce an exploration of weighted networks. If students want to know more about Keiko, have them do research in a library or on the Internet and report their findings.

Exploration 1

PLAN

Classroom Management
Students perform Exploration 1 in pairs. Each pair of students will need 48 centimeter cubes, so you may want to have sets of cubes prepared beforehand. Students will be assembling prisms from the cubes throughout Exploration 1, so they will need plenty of time to perform the manipulations and record the results. You may want to monitor the discussion in *Question 7* to ensure that students are observing the pattern correctly. *Question 9* is highlighted for the whole class. You will probably want to take the time to combine students' results from *Question 8* in a class table to have more complete data for observing surface area patterns. *Question 12* is also marked for whole-class discussion to ensure that students can properly generalize how to find the volume of any prism using their tables from *Question 11*. Have several students present their observations and methods in parts *(a)–(c)* of *Question 12* before deciding as a class on a general method for part *(d)*.

GUIDE

Developing Math Concepts
Question 4 provides a review of the most basic unit of volume. Make sure that students understand the notation for cubic units: (units)(units)(units) = units^3.

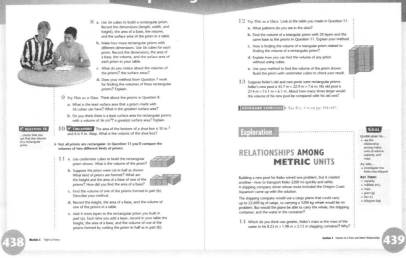

Exploration 1 continued

Developing Math Concepts

For *Question 8(b)*, encourage students to use different combinations of dimensions instead of just different alignments. For example, a 3 by 3 by 4 prism is the same form as a 3 by 4 by 3 prism. For *Question 9(b)*, ask students what shape they think the rectangular prism with a volume of 36 and the least surface area would take (a cube). It may be hard for students to understand that there is no greatest surface area. It may help to use a two-dimensional example. For example, a 6-by-6 rectangle has an area of 36 and a perimeter of 24, but a 360,000-by-0.0001 rectangle also has an area of 36, while its perimeter is 720,000.0002!

Developing Math Concepts

For *Question 12*, make sure students realize that the formula $V = B \cdot h$ is the most efficient statement of volume for a prism. This way, whatever the shape of the base, a triangle, rectangle, or whatever, you can just use the formula for the area of that shape and then multiply by the height of the prism. If the base is a more complicated polygon that can be divided into simpler ones, then you can still start by just piecing together the area of the base.

HOMEWORK EXERCISES

See the Suggested Assignment for Day 1 on page 6-47. For Exercise Notes, see page 6-47.

Exploration 2

PLAN

Classroom Management You may want to have students continue to work in the same pairs for Exploration 2 as for Exploration 1. *Question 15* is highlighted for the whole class to make sure students understand the important relationships among mass, capacity, and volume in the metric system. If possible, have a centimeter cube, a gram mass, and a small container that measures in milliliters on hand for students to examine. For *Question 17*, it will help to have a cube 10 cm on an edge, a kilogram mass, and a container that measures in liters.

Customizing Instruction

Alternative Approach If there are not enough centimeter cubes, students can use any other type of cubes and label the volume as cubic units instead of cubic centimeters.

Visual Learners To visualize half of a rectangular prism for *Question 11*, it may help some students to cover a diagonal half with a piece of paper, or to lay a piece of string diagonally across the top of the prism.

Career Information Have students conjecture about all the different types of careers the work with Keiko involved and how they might involve mathematics. For example, there are many different careers related to making movies, biology, working with shipping companies, or working with a commercial aquarium.

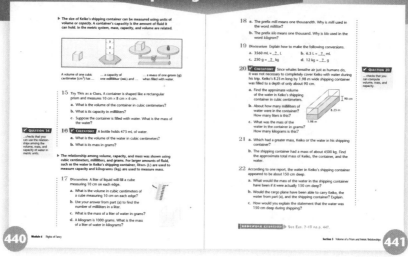

Exploration 2 continued

GUIDE

Developing Math Concepts
For *Question 15*, some students may feel uncomfortable with metric units. Remind them, however, that if these quantities were in cubic inches, fluid ounces, and ounces for weight, these problems would be much more difficult.

Checkpoint *Question 16* asks students only to recognize the direct connection among milliliters of water, cubic centimeters, and grams.

Common Error In *Question 17* and those following, students who don't have a sense for the measures are much more likely to make errors. Have students weigh and measure objects around the classroom to give them more experience with these measures. Help students develop benchmarks for metric units (a plastic liter container of spring water, which also weighs a bit over a kilogram because of the container; a meter is about the height of my waist; and so on).

Developing Math Concepts
For *Question 19*, remind students to use their number sense to guide them. When you convert from a small unit to a larger unit, you will need fewer of the larger units, so you divide; when you convert from a large unit to a smaller unit, you will need more of the smaller units, so you multiply. Encourage students always to label units and to use conversion fractions when they are trying to describe a quantity in different units from those given.

Checkpoint For *Question 20*, students will need to pay especially close attention to the different units of measure as they find different measures for the amount of water in Keiko's container.

HOMEWORK EXERCISES

See the Suggested Assignment for Day 2 on page 6-47. For Exercise Notes, see page 6-47.

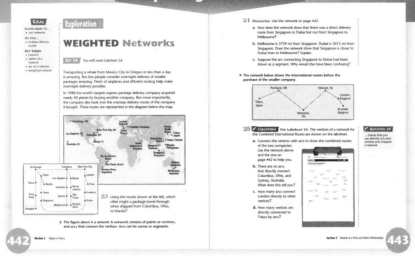

Exploration 3

PLAN

Classroom Management Each student will need a copy of Labsheet 5A. Exploration 3 can be completed as individuals or with a partner. Students should discuss *Question 24* with at least one other student to ensure understanding. For *Question 25*, all of the work is done on the labsheet, so you can collect students' work if you want to check their progress. *Question 27* is highlighted for the whole class to make sure students can follow a path on a network and can interpret the weightings on each path correctly.

GUIDE

Developing Math Concepts
For *Question 23*, make sure students understand that the question does not ask for the shortest or simplest route, but the package can only visit any given city once. For *Question 24*, the network referred to is not drawn to scale, so in this way it is not useful for directions and distances like a map is. By not having to draw to scale, it is easier to arrange vertices so that arcs meet only at vertices.

Checkpoint Students should complete *Question 25*, using Labsheet 5A, on their own. Remind them that the arcs should not cross so that there is no confusion about possible routes.

Customizing Instruction

Alternative Approach Have students think of portions of their lives they can represent by networks (going to their favorite shops in a mall or shopping center, visiting several friends, going on a weekend trip or vacation). Students can draw their own networks and create a problem that can be solved using weightings on their networks, such as finding the minimum travel time.

Visual Learners It will help some students to copy the networks and use colored pencils to trace their routes. As they trace a route, they should record the vertices they encounter and any weightings on the path to help them keep track.

MODULE 6 ◆ SECTION 5

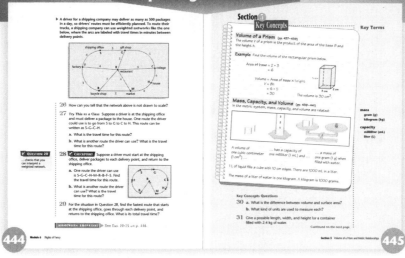

Exploration 3 continued

Developing Math Concepts

For *Question 26*, help students realize that the weights on a weighted network function like a scale on a map, in that they give you the context you need to interpret the diagram.

Checkpoint For *Question 28*, students will use the network at the top of the page to find the travel time on a route, and to find an alternate route and its travel time.

Developing Math Concepts

For *Question 29*, students will be looking for the fastest route. Encourage them to make an organized list of the routes and travel times so that they don't skip promising routes or retrace their steps. Encourage students to break the problem into smaller problems. For example, to avoid having to retrace a path, they need to enter and leave the shipping office on different paths. Likewise, they will have to travel both paths that connect to the House. If they go to the Factory first, they can find the quickest path from there to the Market that contains both the Restaurant and the Bicycle shop without having to worry yet about what path they will follow after leaving the Market.

HOMEWORK EXERCISES

See the Suggested Assignment for Day 3 on page 6-47. For Exercise Notes, see page 6-47.

CLOSE

Closure Question Name two other metric measures that are equivalent to one cubic centimeter (1 cm^3). Then explain what is meant by a network.

Answer: a capacity of one milliliter (1 mL) and a mass of one gram of water (1 g); *Sample Response:* A network is a set of points, called vertices, that are connected by lines or arcs, called paths.

Customizing Instruction

Home Involvement Those helping students at home will find the Key Concepts on pages 445–446 a handy reference to the key ideas, terms, and skills of Section 5.

Absent Students For students who were absent for all or part of this section, the blackline Study Guide for Section 5 may be used to present the ideas, concepts, and skills of Section 5.

Extra Help For students who need additional practice, the blackline Practice and Applications for Section 5 provides additional exercises that may be used to confirm the skills of Section 5. The Extra Skill Practice on page 450 also provides additional exercises.

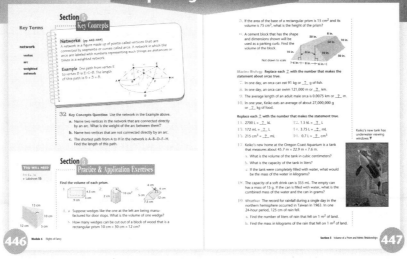

446 Module 6 *Flights of Fancy*

Section 5 *Volume of a Prism and Metric Relationships* 447

SUGGESTED ASSIGNMENT

Core Course
Day 1: Exs. 1–6, 26–30
Day 2: Exs. 7–19, 31–34
Day 3: Exs. 20, 21, 23–25

Extended Course
Day 1: Exs. 1–6, 26–30
Day 2: Exs. 7–19, 31–34
Day 3: Exs. 20–25, 35–39

Block Schedule
Day 6: Exs. 1–19, 26–34
Day 7: Exs. 20, 21, 23–25

EMBEDDED ASSESSMENT

These section objectives are tested by the exercises listed.

Find the volume of a prism.
Exercises 2, 4, 6

Use the relationship among metric units for volume, capacity, and mass of water.
Exercises 16–18

Convert among metric units of mass and among metric units of capacity.
Exercises 7, 10, 12, 14

Interpret a weighted network.
Exercises 20, 23

Practice & Application

EXERCISE NOTES

Developing Math Concepts
For *Exs. 1–4*, remind students to use what they know, first deciding on a base and finding its area. For *Ex. 6*, some students may have trouble recognizing the trapezoidal shape as a base, but they can still add the volumes of one rectangular prism and two triangular prisms. Other students may notice that "cutting off" one of the triangular wings and repositioning it on the opposite side will give them one rectangular prism with a base that measures 14 in. by 8 in. For *Exs. 7–16*, remind students to use their number sense to make sure their answers are reasonable. For *Ex. 17*, encourage students to write out the equivalencies they use in each step to avoid confusion.

MODULE 6 ♦ SECTION 5

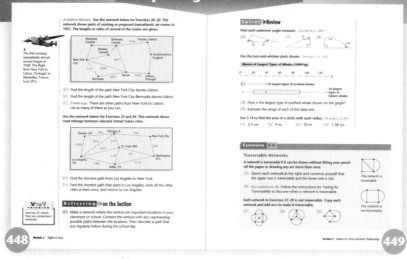

Practice & Application

Challenge For *Ex. 22*, encourage students to keep an organized list to keep track of the paths. It will also help if students make multiple copies of the network and then use a colored pencil or marker to highlight each path that they find.

Developing Math Concepts
For *Ex. 23*, again encourage students to solve simpler problems first. For example, if they fly through Chicago, what is the shortest path?; if they fly through Dallas, what is the shortest path?; and so on. For *Ex. 24*, you may want to point out to students that because the path must go through Denver and New York, they cannot avoid flying each of the legs between Los Angeles and Denver, Denver and Chicago, Chicago and New York, and New York and Washington, D.C. unless they retrace a portion of their trip. If they mark these legs at the beginning, it will help them approach the problem.

Extension For *Exs. 36–39*, students will need Labsheet 5B. After students have completed the labsheet, you may want to discuss with them why there must be two odd vertices. (If a vertex is odd, this means that you must leave it one time more than you enter it, or you must enter it one more time than you leave it. In the first case, that vertex must be a starting point. In the second case, that vertex must be a finishing point. Since you can't start and finish at the same odd vertex, there must be two odd vertices—one (and only one) to start at, and one (and only one) to finish at.)

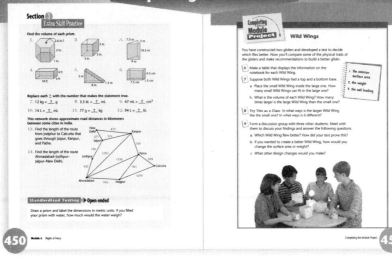

Closing the Section

The relocation of Keiko the whale from Mexico City to his new home in Oregon has introduced students to the concept of finding the volume of a prism. By treating the volume as just the base times the height, students can find the volumes even of some complex prisms. This also sets the stage for further mathematics, such as finding the volume of a cylinder. In dealing with considerations of volume, capacity, and mass, students have also gained experience with the elegance of the metric system. Students have also begun an exploration of networks and weighted networks, which they can apply to their everyday lives through carrying out the Reflecting on the Section exercise on page 448.

QUICK QUIZ ON THIS SECTION

1. Find the volume of the prism.

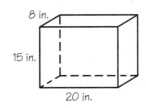

8 in.

15 in.

20 in.

2. If a triangular prism has volume 1860 cm^3 and height 12 cm, what is the area of each triangular base?

3. How many cm^3 are in 1.8 L?

4. If a swimming pool 18 m by 12 m by 2 m is filled completely with water, what is the mass of the water in kilograms?

5. Use the weighted network below to find the shortest path from A to D. How long is that path?

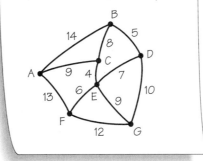

For answers, see Quick Quiz blackline on p. 6-68.

**Completing
the
Module
Project**

Students will need both of their Wild Wings from the earlier sections of the Module Project, as well as their comparison test results from *Question 5* on page 433. Students will make a physical comparison of their Wild Wings in which they have a chance to compare measures such as volume, surface area, and wing loading. Finally, they will have a chance to discuss their flight test results in groups and brainstorm ways to make a better Wild Wing. You may want to extend the project by having students create and test a better Wild Wing. Students should verify that it is better by repeating their earlier flight tests. You may even want to consider a Wild Wing design and flying contest among students.

Name _____ Date _____

(Use with Section 2, Exploration 2.)

MODULE 6

Circle   (Use with Question 24 on page 402.)

Directions

• Cut out the circle.

• Cut apart the eight sectors and arrange them to form the figure shown below.

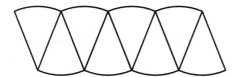

• Tape the figure to a sheet of paper.

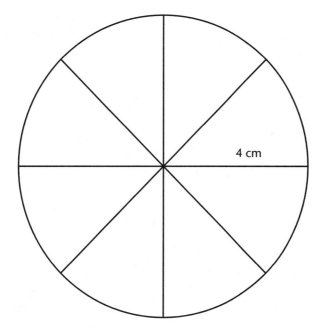

4 cm

MODULE 6   **PROJECT LABSHEET** **A**

Create a Wild Wing

(Use with Project Question 1 on page 408 and Project Question 4 on page 433.)

Step 1 Draw a line 2 in. from the top of an $8\frac{1}{2}$ in. by 11 in. sheet of paper. This will be the tail of your Wild Wing.

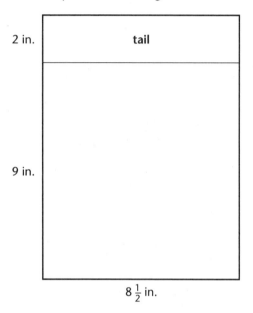

2 in.

tail

9 in.

$8\frac{1}{2}$ in.

Step 2 Bring the bottom edge of the paper up to meet the line you drew. Fold and crease the paper. Repeat this step three more times.

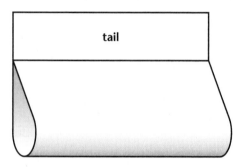

tail

Step 3 To create a rectangular Wild Wing, fold the paper in fourths. Here is one way to do this: first, fold the paper in half, next, open the paper, and then fold each side into the middle.

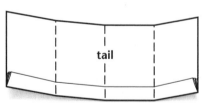

tail

To create a triangular Wild Wing, fold the paper in thirds.

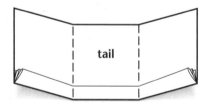

tail

Step 4 Bring the ends together and tape the seam. The folded edge should be in the interior of your Wild Wing.

rectangular Wild Wing

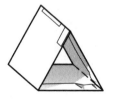

triangular Wild Wing

MODULE 6 **LABSHEET 3A**

Curtiss Jennys (Use with Questions 4–7 on pages 411–412.)

Directions

- Carefully cut out each airplane along the solid lines. Include the tabs on the sides and bottom of the plane. Be careful not to bend the drawings.

- Fold back the tabs along the dotted lines. Align the side tabs evenly with the bottom tab and tape them together. Do this carefully so both planes stand up straight.

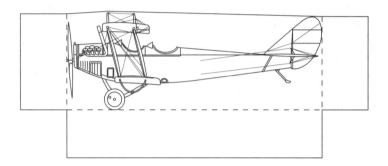

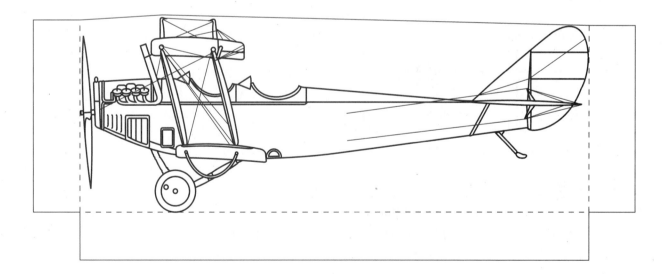

MODULE 6   **LABSHEET 4A**

Build a Wing

(Use with Question 2 on page 423 and Question 13 on page 426.)

Construct the bases.

First   Cut out two $1\frac{1}{2}$ in. $\times$ 5 in. bases.

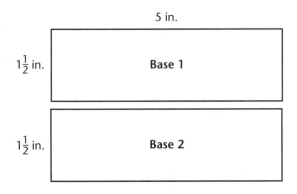

Then   Draw support lines at 1 in. intervals on both bases.

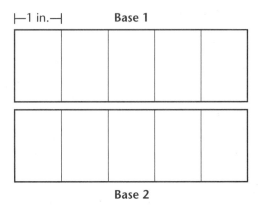

Construct the supports.

First   Cut out four $1\frac{1}{2}$ in. $\times$ 2 in. supports.

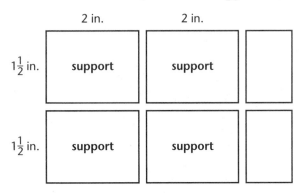

Then   Fold $\frac{1}{4}$ in. tabs on each support.

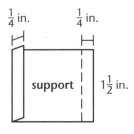

Construct Wing 1.

First   Tape one end of a support to a support line on Base 1. Wrap tape around the tab and the base to secure the support. Repeat for the other three supports

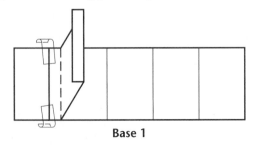

Then   Tape the free ends of the supports to Base 2.

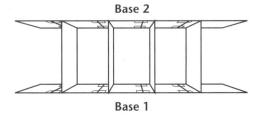

MODULE 6   **LABSHEET 4B**

Draw a Transversal   (Use with Questions 9 and 10 on page 425.)

Directions

- Draw a transversal. Then label the angles formed by the parallel lines and the transversal as ∠1, ∠2, ∠3, ∠4, ∠5, ∠6, ∠7, and ∠8.

- Measure each angle and record the measurements in the table.

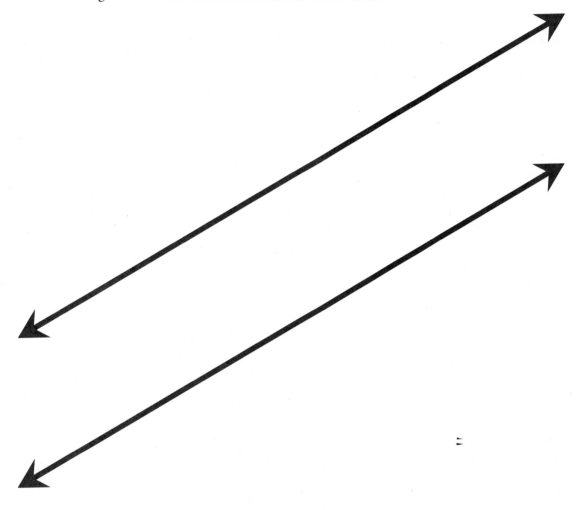

Angle	Measure	Angle	Measure
∠1		∠2	
∠3		∠4	
∠5		∠6	
∠7		∠8	

Name _____   Date _____

Map of the Central Region of the United States

(Use with the Extended Exploration on page 435.)

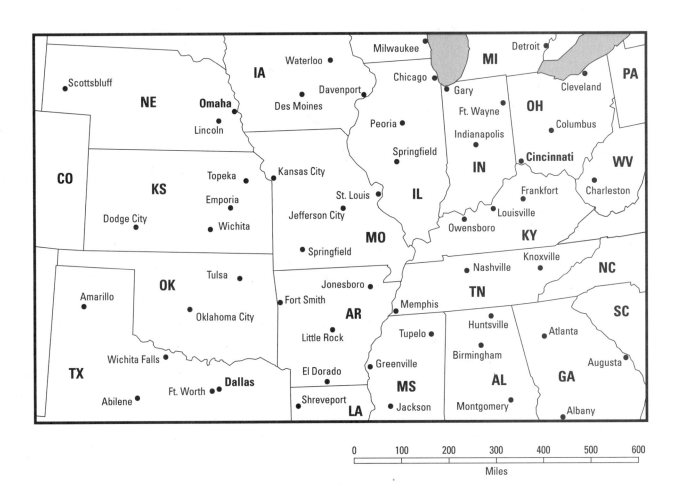

MODULE 6   LABSHEET **5A**

Combined International Routes
(Use with Question 25 on page 443.)

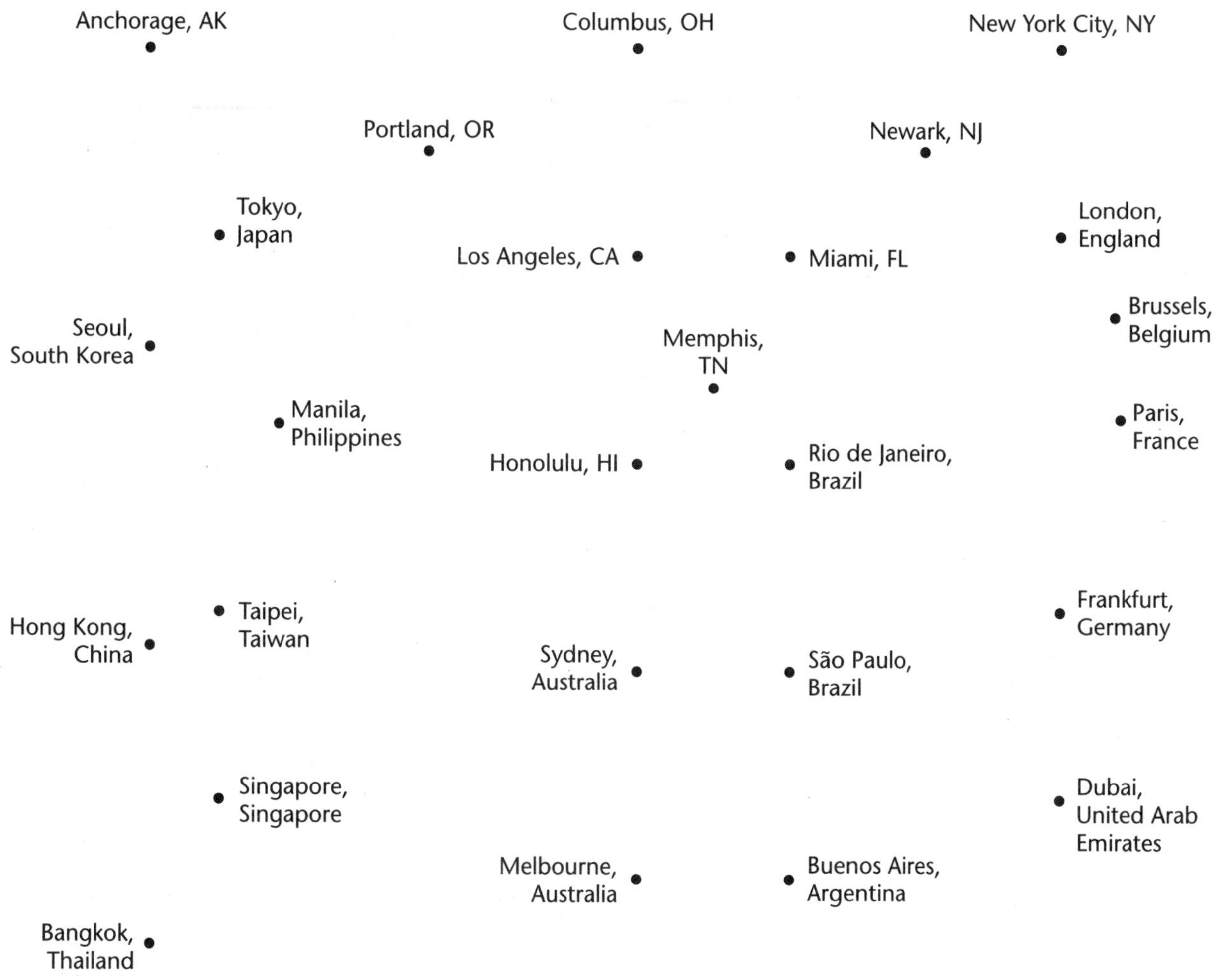

Anchorage, AK
•

Columbus, OH
•

New York City, NY
•

Portland, OR
•

Newark, NJ
•

Tokyo,
• Japan

Los Angeles, CA •

• Miami, FL

London,
• England

Seoul,
South Korea •

Memphis,
TN
•

• Brussels,
Belgium

Manila,
• Philippines

Honolulu, HI •

• Rio de Janeiro,
Brazil

• Paris,
France

Hong Kong,
China •

• Taipei,
Taiwan

Sydney,
Australia •

• São Paulo,
Brazil

• Frankfurt,
Germany

Singapore,
• Singapore

• Dubai,
United Arab
Emirates

Melbourne,
Australia •

• Buenos Aires,
Argentina

Bangkok, •
Thailand

MODULE 6   **LABSHEET** (**5B**)

Testing for Traversability (Use with Exercise 36 on page 449.)

Directions
Complete the table.

> An odd vertex is a vertex at which an odd number of arcs meet.

> An even vertex is a vertex at which an even number of arcs meet.

Network	Number of odd vertices	Number of even vertices	Traversable? (*yes* or *no*)

a. Make a conjecture about when a network is traversable and when a network is not traversable.

b. Test your conjecture by drawing and testing a network fitting each description.

   • 0 odd vertices   • 2 odd vertices   • 4 odd vertices   • 6 odd vertices

c. Did your conjecture work in every case you tested? Explain.

Name _____   Problem _____

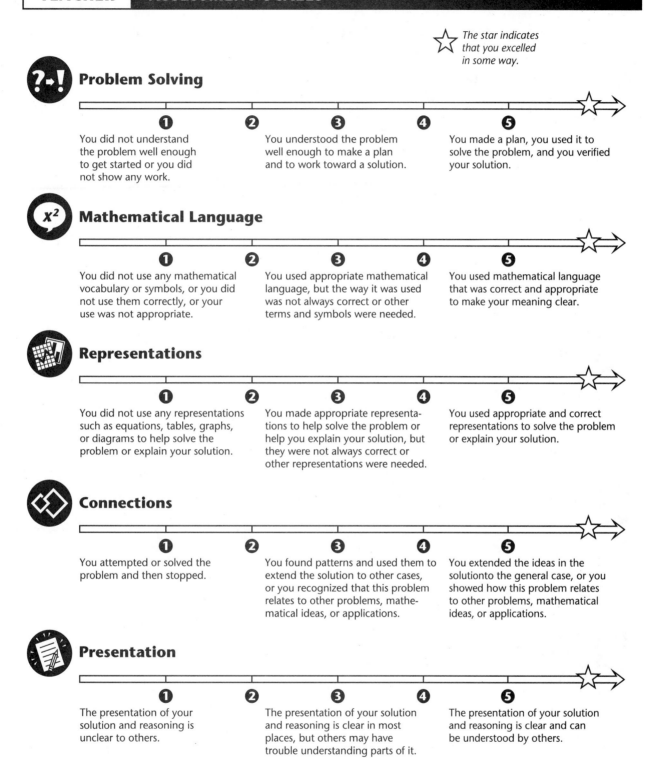

☆ The star indicates
that you excelled
in some way.

Problem Solving

① ② ③ ④ ⑤ ☆

① You did not understand
the problem well enough
to get started or you did
not show any work.

③ You understood the problem
well enough to make a plan
and to work toward a solution.

⑤ You made a plan, you used it to
solve the problem, and you verified
your solution.

x^2 Mathematical Language

① ② ③ ④ ⑤ ☆

① You did not use any mathematical
vocabulary or symbols, or you did
not use them correctly, or your
use was not appropriate.

③ You used appropriate mathematical
language, but the way it was used
was not always correct or other
terms and symbols were needed.

⑤ You used mathematical language
that was correct and appropriate
to make your meaning clear.

Representations

① ② ③ ④ ⑤ ☆

① You did not use any representations
such as equations, tables, graphs,
or diagrams to help solve the
problem or explain your solution.

③ You made appropriate representations to help solve the problem or
help you explain your solution, but
they were not always correct or
other representations were needed.

⑤ You used appropriate and correct
representations to solve the problem
or explain your solution.

Connections

① ② ③ ④ ⑤ ☆

① You attempted or solved the
problem and then stopped.

③ You found patterns and used them to
extend the solution to other cases,
or you recognized that this problem
relates to other problems, mathematical ideas, or applications.

⑤ You extended the ideas in the
solutionto the general case, or you
showed how this problem relates
to other problems, mathematical
ideas, or applications.

Presentation

① ② ③ ④ ⑤ ☆

① The presentation of your
solution and reasoning is
unclear to others.

③ The presentation of your solution
and reasoning is clear in most
places, but others may have
trouble understanding parts of it.

⑤ The presentation of your solution
and reasoning is clear and can
be understood by others.

Content Used: _____   Computational Errors: Yes ☐ No ☐

Notes on Errors: _____

_____

STUDENT   SELF-ASSESSMENT SCALES

If your score is in the shaded area, explain why on the back of this sheet and stop.

The star indicates that you excelled in some way.

Problem Solving

① I did not understand the problem well enough to get started or I did not show any work.

② ③ I understood the problem well enough to make a plan and to work toward a solution.

④ ⑤ I made a plan, I used it to solve the problem, and I verified my solution.

Mathematical Language

① I did not use any mathematical vocabulary or symbols, or I did not use them correctly, or my use was not appropriate.

② ③ I used appropriate mathematical language, but the way it was used was not always correct or other terms and symbols were needed.

④ ⑤ I used mathematical language that was correct and appropriate to make my meaning clear.

Representations

① I did not use any representations such as equations, tables, graphs, or diagrams to help solve the problem or explain my solution.

② ③ I made appropriate representations to help solve the problem or help me explain my solution, but they were not always correct or other representations were needed.

④ ⑤ I used appropriate and correct representations to solve the problem or explain my solution.

Connections

① I attempted or solved the problem and then stopped.

② ③ I found patterns and used them to extend the solution to other cases, or I recognized that this problem relates to other problems, mathematical ideas, or applications.

④ ⑤ I extended the ideas in the solution to the general case, or I showed how this problem relates to other problems, mathematical ideas, or applications.

Presentation

① The presentation of my solution and reasoning is unclear to others.

② ③ The presentation of my solution and reasoning is clear in most places, but others may have trouble understanding parts of it.

④ ⑤ The presentation of my solution and reasoning is clear and can be understood by others.

Locating the Hub (E² on textbook page 435)

This is an open-ended problem that can be approached in a number of ways. All of the *Math Thematics* Assessment Scales can be used to assess students' solutions, but the problem does not provide much opportunity to use mathematical language or different representations, so you may not want to score students on the Mathematical Language and Representations Scales.

The sample response below shows part of a student's solution.

Partial Solution

First, I went to the library and found an atlas that had a map with Omaha, Cincinnati, and Dallas on it. I made a copy of the map and drew the triangle with these cities at its vertices on it.

I decided that the best place to locate the hub is at one of the larger cities inside the triangle. I decided the hub should be inside the triangle because I wanted to keep the sum of the distances from the hub to each of the major cities as small as possible.

The next thing I did was to use the scale on the map to find the distance from each of the possible hubs to each of the three major cities. For example, the scale is 6.5 cm = 500 miles and the distance from Omaha to Springfield, IL, on the map is 4.5 cm, so

$$\frac{500}{6.5} = \frac{x}{4.5}$$
$$6.5x = 2250$$
$$x \approx 346 \text{ miles}$$

The possible cities I chose, their populations, and their distance from each of the three major cities are listed in the table. I looked up the populations in an almanac.

	Kansas City, Missouri 435,146	Saint Louis, Missouri 396,685	Springfield, Illinois 105,227	Tulsa, Oklahoma 367,302	Fort Smith, Arkansas 72,798	Springfield, Missouri 140,494	Jefferson City, Missouri 35,481
Cincinnati	534	305	279	660	603	492	412
Dallas	450	549	618	244	221	358	481
Omaha	160	351	346	344	416	313	267
Total miles	1144	1205	1243	1248	1240	1163	1160

I decided that it is also important to keep the lengths of the three flights as close to each other as possible. My recommendation is to use Springfield, Missouri, as the hub. It isn't as large as Kansas City, but it is close to Branson, Missouri, which is a major entertainment center and that might help attract passengers to the airline.

MODULE 6   ALTERNATE E²

It's Raining Cats and Dogs

The Situation

People often use the expression "it's raining cats and dogs" to describe a heavy rainfall.

The Problem

If the expression "it's raining cats and dogs" was true, how many cats and dogs would have a mass equal to the mass of 2 cm of rain falling on a 10 m × 12 m rectangular garden plot?

Something to Think About

- The mass of cats range from 2.2 kg to 6.4 kg.
- The mass of a dog depends on its breed. Several examples are given in the table.

Chihuahua	0.5–2.7 kg
Dachsund	2–9 kg
Poodle-toy	2.7 kg
Poodle-miniature	6.4–7.3 kg
Poodle-standard	18.1–24.9 kg
Scottish Terrier	8.2–10 kg
Cocker Spaniel	11.3 kg
Dalmation	15.9–22.7 kg
Irish Setter	22.7–31.8 kg
Collie	22.7–34 kg
Golden Retriever	27.2–34.1 kg
Doberman Pinscher	27–34 kg
German Shepherd	27.2– 38.5 kg
Saint Bernard	64–77 kg
Great Dane	up to 68.1 kg

Source: *The Concise Columbia Encyclopedia*

Present Your Results

Explain how you determined the mass of the water, and the reasoning you used to determine the number of cats and dogs.

It's Raining Cats and Dogs

Solutions to this problem will vary depending on how students interpret and use the data given. All of the *Math Thematics* Assessment Scales can be used to assess students' solutions.

The sample response below shows part of a student's solution.

Partial Solution

The first thing I did was to find the mass of the water falling on the garden plot.

$10 \text{ m} = 10 \text{ m} \cdot 100 \text{ cm/m} = 1000 \text{ cm}$

$12 \text{ m} = 12 \text{ m} \cdot 100 \text{ cm/m} = 1200 \text{ cm}.$

Volume of the rain $= 1000 \text{ cm} \cdot 1200 \text{ cm} \cdot 2 \text{ cm} = 2{,}400{,}000 \text{ cm}^3$

Since 1 cm^3 of water has a mass of 1 gram,

Mass of the rain $= 2{,}400{,}000 \text{ g} = 2{,}400{,}000 \text{ g} \div 1000 \text{ g/kg} = 2400 \text{ kg}$

Since the mass of a cat is between 2.2 and 6.4 kg, I decided to use the mean of these masses or 4.3 kg for the average mass of a cat. I did the same thing for the masses of the dogs in the table.

Dog breed	Masses	Average mass	
Chihuahua	0.5–2.7 kg	1.6 kg	1.6
Dachsund	2–9 kg	5.5 kg	2.7
Poodle-toy	2.7 kg	2.7 kg	5.5
Poodle-miniature	6.4–7.3 kg	6.85 kg	6.85
Poodle-standard	18.1–24.9 kg	21.5 kg	9.1
Scottish Terrier	8.2–10 kg	9.1 kg	11.3
Cocker Spaniel	11.3 kg	11.3 kg	19.3
Dalmation	15.9–22.7 kg	19.3 kg	**21.5** — median
Irish Setter	22.7–31.8 kg	27.25 kg	27.25
Collie	22.7–34 kg	28.35 kg	28.35
Golden Retriever	27.2–34.1 kg	30.65 kg	30.5
Doberman Pinscher	27–34 kg	30.5 kg	30.65
German Shepherd	27.2–38.5 kg	32.85 kg	32.85
Saint Bernard	64–77 kg	70.5 kg	68.1
Great Dane	up to 68.1 kg	up to 68.1 kg	70.5

I wasn't sure what to use for the average for Great Danes, but since 68.1 and 70.5 are very large in comparison to the other averages, I decided the median of the average masses, 21.5 kg, would be the best average to use for the mass of a dog.

I decided the number of dogs and the number of cats should be the same, so I let $x =$ number of dogs and $x =$ the number of cats.

$4.3x + 21.5x = 2400$

$25.8x = 2400$

$x \approx 93$

So, if "it's raining cats and dogs," about 90 cats and 6 of each kind of dog ($90 \div 15$) named in the table will fall on the garden plot.

Write each inequality in words.

1. $2s > 8$

2. $b \leq 14$

3. State the formula for the area of a square.

4. State the formula for the area of a rectangle.

Find each probability.

5. picking an even number from the numbers 0–9

6. selecting a red pen if there are 2 red pens, 2 blue pens, and 1 black pen in a container

MODULE 6 SECTION 1   **QUICK QUIZ**

1. Write and graph an inequality to represent this statement: x is less than or equal to 18 and greater than 15.

2. Alyssa always spends at least 25 min a day practicing the tuba. Write an inequality to show how many minutes she practices in a week.

3. Use what you know about the areas of triangles and rectangles to find the area of this quadrilateral.

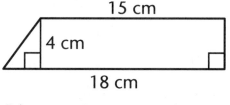

4. Find the theoretical probability that an object dropped on the figure at the right will land on the shaded target. What is the probability that it will fall outside the target?

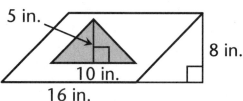

ANSWERS

Warm-Ups: 1. Two times s is greater than 8.   **2.** b is less than or equal to 14.   **3.** $A = s^2$, where s is the length of the side of the square.   **4.** $A = lw$, where l is the length and w is the width of the rectangle.   **5.** $\frac{1}{2}$ **6.** $\frac{2}{5}$

Quick Quiz: 1. $15 < x \leq 18$ **2.** $t \geq 175$, where t is the number of minutes Alyssa practices in a given week.   **3.** 66 cm² **4.** $\frac{25}{128}$, or about 19.5%; $\frac{103}{128}$, or about 80.5%

Find each value when *m* = 4.

1. m^2 **2.** $3m^3$

Find the area of each figure.

3. a triangle with base of 16 in. and a height of 7 in.

4. a rectangle with base of 13 m and a height of 4 m

5. a square with side lengths of 2.5 cm

1. Find $\sqrt{400}$.

2. Estimate $\sqrt{22}$ to the nearest tenth.

3. What is the name of this prism? How many faces, edges, and vertices does it have?

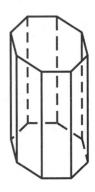

4. What is the surface area of a rectangular prism with base 10 cm by 12 cm and height 20 cm?

5. Find the area of a circle with diameter 2.4 in. Round to the nearest tenth.

ANSWERS

Warm-Ups: 1. 16   **2.** 192   **3.** 56 in.^{2} **4.** 52 m^2 **5.** 6.25 cm^2

Quick Quiz: 1. 20   **2.** 4.7   **3.** octagonal prism; 10, 24, 16   **4.** 1120 cm^2 **5.** 4.5 in.^{2}

Write each ratio in two other ways.

1. 3 : 4

2. $\dfrac{2}{7}$

3. 6 to 1

Solve each proportion.

4. $\dfrac{8}{12} = \dfrac{20}{y}$

5. $\dfrac{x}{4} = \dfrac{5}{6}$

6. $\dfrac{9}{5} = \dfrac{m}{12}$

1. Draw two obtuse triangles that are similar but not congruent.

2. The two pentagons at the right are similar. Write a statement that can be used to identify the corresponding parts.

3. If ∠BCD in Question 2 is 60°, what can you say about another angle measure or side length in pentagon *VWXYZ*?

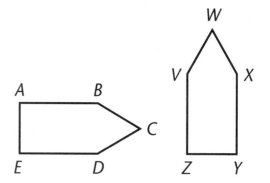

4. The Statue of Liberty is 152 ft tall. Luis drew a scale drawing of the statue with a scale of 1 in. = 8 ft. How many inches tall was his drawing?

5. △*ABC* ~ △*XYZ*. Find the missing lengths.

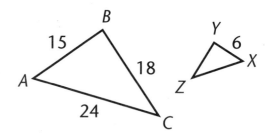

ANSWERS

Warm-Ups: 1. $\frac{3}{4}$; 3 to 4 **2.** 2 : 7; 2 to 7 **3.** $\frac{6}{1}$; 6 : 1 **4.** 30 **5.** $\frac{10}{3}$ **6.** 21.6

Quick Quiz: 1. Check students' work. **2.** *ABCDE* ~ *ZVWXY* **3.** ∠*VWX* is also 60°.
4. 19 in. **5.** *XZ* = 9.6, *YZ* = 7.2

Use a protractor to find the measure of the angles in each figure.

a. $m\angle 1$ **b.** $m\angle 2$ **c.** $m\angle 3$ **d.** $m\angle 4$

1.

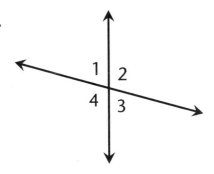

2.

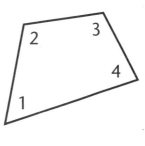

For Questions 1–3, use the diagram at the right. Lines *r* and *s* are parallel.

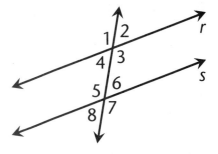

1. Name a pair of vertical angles.

2. Name a pair of alternate interior angles.

3. List four congruent angles in the figure.

4. Find the unknown angle measure in the quadrilateral at the right.

5. Two of the angles of a triangle are 45° and 56°. What is the measure of the third angle? Is the triangle acute, obtuse, or right?

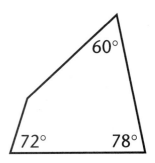

<u>**ANSWERS**</u>

Warm-Ups: 1. a. 75° **b.** 105° **c.** 75° **d.** 105° **2. a.** 61° **b.** 109° **c.** 110° **d.** 80°

Quick Quiz: 1. $\angle 1$ and $\angle 3$, $\angle 2$ and $\angle 4$, $\angle 5$ and $\angle 7$, or $\angle 6$ and $\angle 8$ **2.** $\angle 3$ and $\angle 5$ or $\angle 4$ and $\angle 6$ **3.** $\angle 1$, $\angle 3$, $\angle 5$, and $\angle 7$, or $\angle 2$, $\angle 4$, $\angle 6$, and $\angle 8$ **4.** 150° **5.** 79°; acute

Find the volume of each figure.

1. a cube with side lengths of 6.2 cm

2. a rectangular block with a length of 3 m, a width of 2.5 m, and a height of 8 m

Convert each measure.

3. 1 m = ___?___ cm

4. 1000 g = ___?___ kg

5. 1000 mL = ___?___ L

1. Find the volume of the prism.

2. If a triangular prism has volume 1860 cm^3 and height 12 cm, what is the area of each triangular base?

3. How many cm^3 are there in 1.8 L?

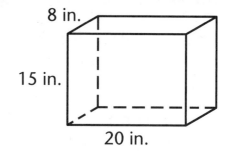

4. If a swimming pool 18 m by 12 m by 2 m is filled completely with water, what is the mass of the water in kilograms?

5. Use the weighted network at the right to find the shortest path from A to D. How long is that shortest path?

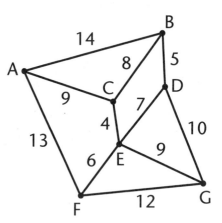

ANSWERS

Warm-Ups: **1.** 238.328 cm^3 **2.** 60 m^3 **3.** 100 **4.** 1 **5.** 1

Quick Quiz: **1.** 2400 in.^{3} **2.** 155 cm^2 **3.** 1800 **4.** 432,000 kg **5.** A–B–D; 19

MODULE 6 SECTION 1   **PRACTICE AND APPLICATIONS**

For use with Exploration 1

1. Write an inequality to represent each statement. Then graph the inequality on a number line.

a. *x* is less than 5.

b. *b* is greater than or equal to 7.

c. *h* is greater than 6 and less than or equal to 14.

d. 2 is less than *p*, and *p* is less than 9.

e. *a* is greater than 3.

f. *k* is less than or equal to 6.

g. *r* is greater than 2 and less than 5.

h. *s* is greater than 4 and less than 17.

i. 4 is less than *t*, and *t* is less than or equal to 16.

j. *b* is greater than 8 and less than or equal to 10.

2. Use the graph below.

Lengths of North American Owls (in inches)

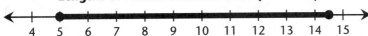

a. One of the smallest owls in North America is the elf owl. Estimate its length.

b. Estimate the range of sizes of the owls represented in the graph.

For use with Exploration 2

3. Tell whether each quadrilateral is a parallelogram. If a quadrilateral is not a parallelogram, explain why not.

a.

b.
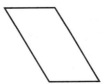

c.

4. Classify each polygon as concave or convex.

a.

b.

c.

5. Draw two 6-sided polygons, one that is convex and one that is concave.

(continued)

MODULE 6 SECTION 1   PRACTICE AND APPLICATIONS

For use with Exploration 3

6. Find the probability that a small object dropped on each figure will land on the shaded target.

a.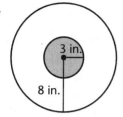

b.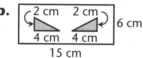

c.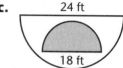

d.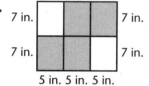

e.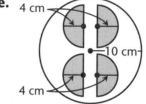

f.

7. Suppose the probability that an object dropped onto the square shown at the right will land inside the shaded star is $\frac{3}{4}$.

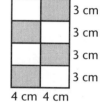

a. What is the probability that the object will land in the unshaded area?

b. What is the area of the star?

8. A small object is tossed onto a game board. If the object lands on the shaded area, Player I wins. If not, Player II wins.

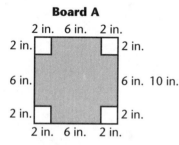
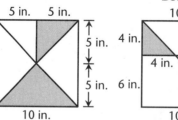

Board A   **Board B**   **Board C**

a. Which game board is fair to both players, that is, makes their chances of winning equal?

b. If you want Player I to have a greater chance of winning, which game board should you choose?

MODULE 6 SECTION 2 | **PRACTICE AND APPLICATIONS**

For use with Exploration 1

1. Show that each number is a perfect square.

   a. 49   **b.** 900   **c.** 225

2. Find each square root.

   a. $\sqrt{144}$ **b.** $\sqrt{36}$ **c.** $\sqrt{0}$

   d. $\sqrt{169}$ **e.** $-\sqrt{16}$ **f.** $-\sqrt{100}$

   g. $\sqrt{400}$ **h.** $-\sqrt{121}$ **i.** $-\sqrt{81}$

   j. $-\sqrt{196}$ **k.** $\sqrt{324}$ **l.** $-\sqrt{256}$

   m. $\sqrt{289}$ **n.** $-\sqrt{25}$ **o.** $-\sqrt{1}$

   p. $\sqrt{64}$ **q.** $-\sqrt{0}$ **r.** $\sqrt{361}$

3. Give two consecutive whole numbers that each principal square root lies between. Then estimate each square root to the nearest tenth.

   a. $\sqrt{18}$ **b.** $\sqrt{46}$ **c.** $\sqrt{115}$

   d. $\sqrt{30}$ **e.** $\sqrt{7}$ **f.** $\sqrt{140}$

4. Estimate each square root to the nearest tenth.

   a. $\sqrt{72}$ **b.** $\sqrt{160}$ **c.** $\sqrt{28}$

   d. $\sqrt{230}$ **e.** $\sqrt{56}$ **f.** $\sqrt{415}$

   g. $\sqrt{80}$ **h.** $\sqrt{39}$ **i.** $\sqrt{249}$

   j. $\sqrt{50}$ **k.** $\sqrt{130}$ **l.** $\sqrt{260}$

   m. $\sqrt{20}$ **n.** $\sqrt{110}$ **o.** $\sqrt{61}$

   p. $\sqrt{136}$ **q.** $\sqrt{209}$ **r.** $\sqrt{42}$

5. A square playground in the center of a park has an area of 784 ft². Karen wants to walk along one side of the playground. How far does she walk?

(continued)

MODULE 6 SECTION 2   **PRACTICE AND APPLICATIONS**

For use with Exploration 2

6. Use the prism shown.

   a. What kind of prism is this?

   b. How many faces, vertices, and edges does this prism have?

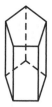

7. Use the prism shown.

   a. What kind of prism is this?

   b. How many faces, vertices, and edges does this prism have?

8. Use the rectangular prism shown.

   a. Sketch a net for the prism.

   b. Find the surface area of the prism.

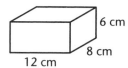

9. A box of macaroni and cheese is 7 in. tall, 4 in. long, and 2 in. wide. What is the surface area of the box?

For use with Exploration 3

10. Use π to write an expression for the exact area of each circle. Then use 3.14 or the ⬚π⬚ key on a calculator to find the approximate area to the nearest hundredth.

a.

23 in.

b.

4.2 cm

c.

12 m

d.

30 m

e.

16.4 cm

f.

25 ft

11. A circular window has a diameter of 18 in. What is the area of the window?

Name _____   Date _____

For use with Exploration 1

1. Tell whether the polygons in each pair are *similar, congruent,* or *neither.* If the polygons are similar or congruent, write a statement that can be used to identify the corresponding parts.

   a.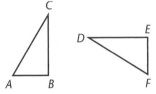

   b.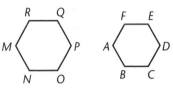

   c.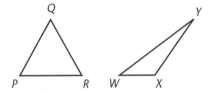

   d.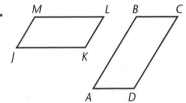

2. A scale drawing of a tree is shown at the right. Each centimeter on the drawing corresponds to 120 cm on the tree. Estimate each measurement of the tree in meters.

   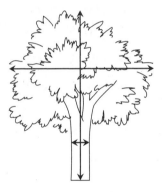

   a. height

   b. width of trunk

   c. center width of foliage

3. A magnifying glass makes an object appear larger. The amount of magnification can be described by using a scale. For each scale, how long does a 6 mm long ant appear to be when seen through the magnifying glass?

   a. 2 : 1   **b.** 5 : 1   **c.** 10 : 1

   d. 15 : 1   **e.** 18 : 1   **f.** 20 : 1

4. On a map, two cities are 3.5 in. apart. The scale of the map is 1 in. : 60 mi. What is the actual distance between the two cities?

   (continued)

Name _____ Date _____

For use with Exploration 2

5. Classify each triangle as *acute*, *obtuse*, or *right*.

a.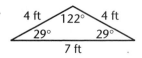

b.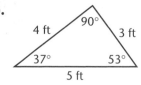

c.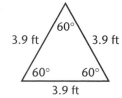

d.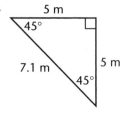

e.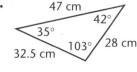

6. △*MNO* is similar to △*PQR*.

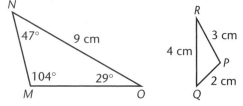

   a. $\overline{OM}$ corresponds to $\overline{RP}$. What segments correspond to $\overline{MN}$ and $\overline{NO}$?

   b. Find the measures of ∠*QPR*, ∠*PRQ*, and ∠*RQP*.

   c. Find the lengths of $\overline{NM}$ and $\overline{MO}$.

7. Use the similar polygons shown at the right.

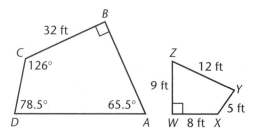

   a. $\overline{AB}$ corresponds to $\overline{ZW}$. What angle corresponds to ∠*ABC* and what is its measure?

   b. Find the measures of ∠*WXY*, ∠*YZW*, and ∠*XYZ*.

   c. Which segment corresponds to $\overline{XY}$? What is its length?

   d. Find the lengths of $\overline{AB}$ and $\overline{AD}$.

8. Rectangle *ABCD* is similar to rectangle *QRST*. The length of one side of rectangle *ABCD* is three times the width of the rectangle. The length of rectangle *QRST* is half the length of rectangle *ABCD*. What is the length of rectangle *QRST* if the width of rectangle *ABCD* is 6 cm?

Name _____   Date _____

For use with Exploration 1

1. The figure below shows two parallel lines, *c* and *d*, cut by transversal *t*. Name the angles or the pairs of angles that fit each description.

   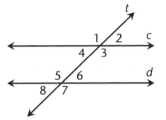

   a. four interior angles

   b. four exterior angles

   c. two pairs of alternate interior angles

   d. two pairs of alternate exterior angles

   e. two pairs of vertical angles

   f. two pairs of corresponding angles

2. Use the figure in Exercise 1. Find the measure of each angle if the measure of $\angle 8$ is 53°.

   a. $\angle 1$ **b.** $\angle 2$ **c.** $\angle 3$

   d. $\angle 4$ **e.** $\angle 5$ **f.** $\angle 6$

3. Use the figure below. The figure shows two parallel lines, *a* and *b*. Tell whether each statement is *True* or *False*.

   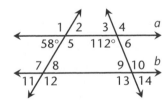

   a. $m\angle 2 = 58°$ **b.** $m\angle 5 = 122°$ **c.** $m\angle 6 = 58°$

   d. $m\angle 5 + m\angle 8 = 180°$ **e.** $m\angle 7 = m\angle 10$ **f.** $m\angle 9 = 68°$

   g. $m\angle 14 = 112°$ **h.** $m\angle 3 = m\angle 9$ **i.** $m\angle 4 = 112°$

   j. $m\angle 1 = m\angle 12$ **k.** $m\angle 8 = 58°$ **l.** $m\angle 11 = m\angle 13$

(continued)

MODULE 6 SECTION 4   **PRACTICE AND APPLICATIONS**

For use with Exploration 2

4. Find the unknown angle measure in each triangle or quadrilateral.

a.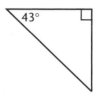
43°

b.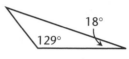
18°
129°

c.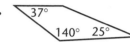
37°
140° 25°

d.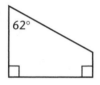
62°

e.
41°   56°

f.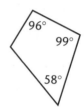
96°
99°
58°

g.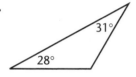
31°
28°

h.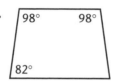
98°   98°
82°

i.
60°
60°

j.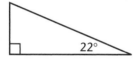
22°

k.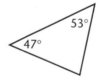
53°
47°

l.
63°
75°

5. The measures of two of the angles of a triangle are given. Find the measure of the third angle of each triangle, and tell whether the triangle is *acute, obtuse,* or *right.*

  a. 15° and 65°   **b.** 42° and 54°

  c. 46° and 69°   **d.** 118° and 41°

  e. 72° and 26°   **f.** 32° and 58°

  g. 38° and 14°   **h.** 59° and 27°

  i. 11° and 90°   **j.** 73° and 29°

  k. 21° and 36°   **l.** 47° and 62°

6. A window is in the shape of a triangle. One of the angles of the triangle measures 32°. The other two angles of the triangle have the same measure. Find each angle measure.

Name _____   Date _____

For use with Exploration 1

1. Find the volume of each prism.

a.

2.5 cm
6 cm   1.5 cm

b.

18 ft
7 ft   6 ft

c.

3.5 m
4.1 m
3.2 m

d.

15 m²
4.8 m

e.

22 in.²
6.5 in.

f.

36 cm²
9 cm

g.

3.2 cm
7 cm
1.8 cm

h.

8 m
16 m
6 m

i.

10 in.
12 in.
5 in.

2. a. Suppose blocks like the one at the right are being manufactured for pedestals. What is the volume of one pedestal?

b. How many pedestals can be cut out of a block of wood that is a rectangular prism 6 in. × 20 in. × 9 in.?

4 in.
3 in.
6 in.

3. a. If the area of the base of a rectangular prism is 24 cm² and its volume is 144 cm³, what is the height of the prism?

b. If the height of a rectangular prism is 8 cm and its volume is 128 cm³, what is the area of the base of the prism?

c. What is the length of each side of the base of the rectangular prism in part (b) if the base is a square?

(continued)

MODULE 6 SECTION 5   **PRACTICE AND APPLICATIONS**

For use with Exploration 2

4. Replace each ___?___ with the number that makes the statement true.

    a. 24 kg = ___?___ g

    b. 55,000 m = ___?___ km

    c. 0.0028 km = ___?___ m

    d. 3500 L = ___?___ kL

    e. 6.4 kL = ___?___ L

    f. 283 mL = ___?___ L

    g. 4.71 L = ___?___ mL

    h. 0.8 kg = ___?___ g

    i. 0.6 L = ___?___ cm^3

    j. 19 kg = ___?___ g

    k. 4.3 kL = ___?___ mL

    l. 31 mL = ___?___ cm^3

    m. 63 L = ___?___ mL

    n. 59 g = ___?___ kg

    o. 85 L = ___?___ kL

5. The dimensions of a salt water tank at a city aquarium are 2.5 m × 3.4 m × 1.2 m.

    a. What is the volume of the tank in cubic centimeters?

    b. What is the capacity of the tank in liters?

    c. If the tank were completely filled with water, what would be the mass of the water in kilograms?

6. The capacity of a can of juice is 185 mL. The empty can has a mass of 12 g. If the can is filled with water, what is the combined mass of the water and the can in grams?

For use with Exploration 3

7. This network shows approximate road distances in miles between some cities in Canada.

    a. Find the length of the path from Nipigon to Montreal that goes through Sault Ste. Marie, North Bay, and Ottawa.

    b. Find the length of the path Ottawa-North Bay-Cochrane-Hearst-Geraldton.

    c. How much longer is the path Hearst-Cochrane-Montreal than the path Hearst-Cochrane-North Bay-Ottawa-Montreal?

    d. Do you think the network is drawn to scale? Explain.

Geraldton 152 Hearst
99 133 Cochrane
Nipigon
235 593
368 North Bay Montreal
264 226
Sault Ste. Marie Ottawa 128

| **MODULE 6 SECTIONS 1–5** | **PRACTICE AND APPLICATIONS** |

For use with Section 1

1. Tell whether each quadrilateral is a parallelogram. If a quadrilateral is not a parallelogram, explain why not.

a.   **b.**   **c.**

2. Classify each polygon as concave or convex.

a.   **b.**   **c.**

For use with Section 2

3. Use π to write an expression for the exact area of each circle. Then use 3.14 or the 🔲 π key on a calculator to find the approximate area. Round approximate answers to the nearest hundredth.

a.   **b.**   **c.**

5.5 in.   8.3 cm   42 m

For use with Section 3

4. Tell whether the polygons in each pair are *similar, congruent,* or *neither.* If the polygons are similar or congruent, write a statement that can be used to identify the corresponding parts.

a. 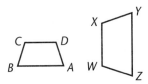   **b.**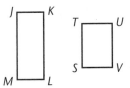

5. On a map, two cities are 4 in. apart. The scale of the map is 1 in. : 75 mi. What is the actual distance between the two cities?

(continued)

Name _____   Date _____

For use with Section 3

6. The scale 5000 : 1 describes the setting for the magnification on an electron microscope. How long does a 0.003 mm long speck of asbestos appear to be when seen through the electron microscope?

7. Trapezoid *ABCD* is similar to trapezoid *EHGF*.

    a. Find the measures of ∠*FGH*, ∠*GHE*, and ∠*HEF*.

    b. Find the lengths of $\overline{AD}$, $\overline{AB}$, and $\overline{DC}$.

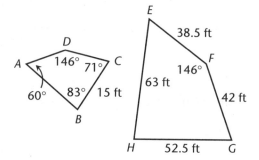

For use with Section 4

8. The figure below shows parallel lines $\overleftrightarrow{AB}$ and $\overleftrightarrow{CD}$ cut by transversal $\overleftrightarrow{SW}$. Find the measure of each named angle.

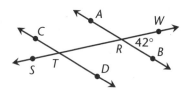

    a. ∠*ART*   **b.** ∠*DTR*   **c.** ∠*STD*

    d. ∠*CTR*   **e.** ∠*CTS*   **f.** ∠*ARW*

For use with Section 5

9. The network shown below gives road distances in miles between several U.S. cities.

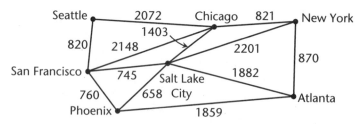

    a. Find the length of the path Seattle-San Francisco-Phoenix.

    b. Find the length of the path San Francisco-Salt Lake City-Atlanta.

    c. Find the shortest path from San Francisco to New York.

    d. Find the shortest path from Seattle to Atlanta.

Name _____   Date _____

Will It Fly?   Inequalities, Polygons, and Probability

GOAL **LEARN HOW TO:** • write and graph inequalities
• find the areas of polygons
• use areas to find theoretical probabilities
• find the probabilities of complementary events

AS YOU: • investigate how wing design makes flight possible
• study the wing of an albatross
• simulate skydiving competition

Exploration 1: Inequalities

A mathematical sentence that contains one or more of the symbols
$>, <, \geq,$ or $\leq$ is an **inequality**.

Example

Write an inequality to represent each statement. Then graph the inequality.

a. y is less than 5.

b. 3 is less than or equal to x, and x is less than or equal to 6.

▇ Sample Response ▇

a. $y < 5$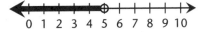

The open circle means 5 is not included.

b. $3 \leq x \leq 6$

The solid circles mean 3 and 6 are included.

Exploration 2: Areas of Polygons

Polygons

A **polygon** is a simple, closed, flat figure made of segments.
A polygon can be either **convex** or **concave**. If a polygon is
convex, every line that contains two of its vertices passes
through the interior of the polygon. For a concave polygon,
there is at least one line containing two vertices that does not
pass through the interior of the polygon. In a **regular** polygon,
all the segments are the same length and all the angles are
equal in measure.

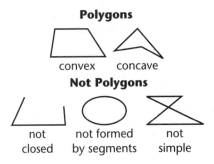

MODULE 6 SECTION 1 | **STUDY GUIDE**

A polygon that has *four sides* is a **quadrilateral**. A **parallelogram** is a quadrilateral that has *two pairs of parallel sides*.

Quadrilateral   **Parallelogram**

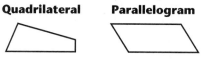

The area of a parallelogram is the product of the length of its base and its height. The area of a triangle is half the length of its base times its height.

Parallelogram

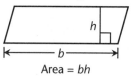

Area = bh

You can find the area of some polygons by separating them into triangles and parallelograms.

Triangle

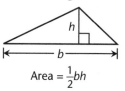

Area = $\frac{1}{2}bh$

Exploration 3: Geometric Probability

A probability that is based on lengths, areas, or volumes of figures is a **geometric probability**.

Example

Find the probability that a point selected at random on $\overline{PR}$ is on $\overline{QR}$.

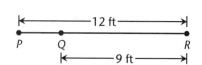

Sample Response

The probability that a point which is on $\overline{PR}$ is located on $\overline{QR}$ is:

$$\frac{\text{length of } \overline{QR}}{\text{length of } \overline{PR}} = \frac{9}{12} = \frac{3}{4}, \text{ or } 75\%.$$

Two events are **complementary events** if one or the other must occur, but they cannot both happen at the same time. The sum of the probabilities of two complementary events is 1.

Example

The events *rolling an even number* and *rolling an odd number* when a number cube is rolled are complementary events.

The events *landing heads* and *landing tails* when a coin is flipped are complementary events.

When selecting a card at random from a standard deck of cards, the events *drawing a red card* and *drawing a black card* are complementary events.

Name _____ Date _____

Exploration 1

Write an inequality to represent each statement. Then graph the inequality on a number line.

1. w is greater than 5.

2. j is less than or equal to 13.

3. 1 is less than y, and y is less than 4.

4. r is greater than 3 and less than or equal to 7.

Exploration 2

Tell whether each quadrilateral is a parallelogram. If a quadrilateral is not a parallelogram, explain why not.

5.

6.

Classify each polygon as *convex* or *concave*.

7.

8.

Exploration 3

9. Suppose a point on $\overline{XZ}$ is selected at random. Find the probability that the point is on $\overline{XY}$.

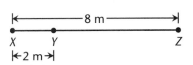

10. Find the probability that a small object dropped on the parallelogram will land on the shaded region.

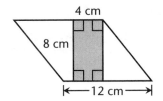

Spiral Review

Use mental math to write each fraction as a percent.
(Module 5, p. 366)

11. $\dfrac{11}{26}$

12. $\dfrac{39}{51}$

13. $\dfrac{41}{83}$

14. $\dfrac{27}{90}$

Find the prime factorization of each number. (Module 3, p. 156)

15. 20

16. 45

17. 50

18. 130

Write each power in standard form. (Module 1, p. 21)

19. 3^2

20. 4^2

21. 7^2

22. 8^2

Go Fly a Kite!   Square Roots, Surface Area, and Area of a Circle

GOAL   **LEARN HOW TO:** • find square roots of perfect squares
• estimate square roots to the nearest tenth
• identify prisms and their parts
• draw a net for a prism
• find the surface area of a prism
• find the area of a circle

AS YOU: • investigate the design of a parawing
• investigate box kites
• investigate kite designs

Exploration 1: Square Roots

One of two equal factors of a number is a **square root** of that number.
If $A = s^2$, then s is a square root of A. Every positive number has two
square roots.

> **Example**
>
> Find the square roots of 400.
>
> **Sample Response**
>
> Since $(20)^2 = 400$ and $(-20)^2 = 400$, the square roots of 400 are 20 and −20.

The **principal square root** of a *positive* number, indicated by $\sqrt{}$, is the
positive square root. A number is a **perfect square** if its principal square
root is a whole number.

> **Example**
>
> **a.** $\sqrt{625} = 25$, so 625 is a perfect square, and 25 is the principal square root of 625.
>
> **b.** $\sqrt{114} \approx 10.58$, so 114 is not a perfect square. The approximation 10.58 is the
> principal square root of 114.

Exploration 2: Surface Areas of Prisms

Prisms and Surface Area

A **prism** is a space figure that has flat surfaces or **faces** shaped like
polygons. Two of the faces, the **bases**, are parallel and congruent.
The other faces are parallelograms. Pairs of faces meet in segments
called **edges**, and the edges meet in points called **vertices**.

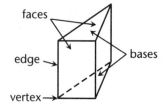

MODULE 6 SECTION 2   **STUDY GUIDE**

The **surface area** of a prism is the sum of the areas of all its faces.
You can use a net to help find the surface area of a prism.

Example

a. Name the prism at the right. Tell how many faces,
how many vertices, and how many edges it has.

b. Draw a net for the prism and use it to find the surface area.

1 cm
1 cm
3 cm

Sample Response

a. This is a right rectangular prism. It has 6 faces, 8 vertices, and 12 edges.

b.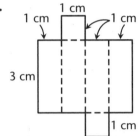

Each square has an area of 1 cm^2.
Each rectangle has an area of 3 cm^2.
$1 + 1 + 3 + 3 + 3 + 3 = 14$

The surface area of the prism is 14 cm^2.

Exploration 3: Area of a Circle

The area, A, of a circle is equal to πr^2, where r is the radius of the circle.
Recall that the radius of a circle is half its diameter and that π is a constant
approximated by 3.14.

Example

Find the area of a circle with diameter 2.4 cm.

Sample Response

Since the diameter of the circle is 2.4 cm, the radius is $\frac{1}{2}(2.4)$, or 1.2 cm.

$$A = \pi r^2$$
$$= \pi (1.2)^2$$
$$= 1.44\pi$$

The exact area of the circle is 1.44π cm^2.

To find a numerical approximation for the area, substitute 3.14 for π or use the π key.

$$A \approx 3.14 \cdot 1.44 = 4.5216$$

An approximate area of the circle is 4.52 cm^2.

Name _____   Date _____

Exploration 1

Find each square root. If the square root is not a whole number, find the two consecutive integers it is between.

1. $\sqrt{121}$ **2.** $\sqrt{81}$ **3.** $-\sqrt{36}$ **4.** $\sqrt{150}$

Estimate each square root to the nearest tenth.

5. $\sqrt{7}$ **6.** $\sqrt{43}$ **7.** $\sqrt{20}$ **8.** $\sqrt{155}$

Exploration 2

For Exercises 9 and 10, use the prism shown at the right.

9. What kind of prism is this?

10. How many faces, vertices, and edges does this prism have?

11. Use the right rectangular prism shown.

    a. Sketch a net for the prism.

    b. Find the area of each face.

    c. Find the surface area of the prism.

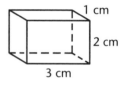

1 cm
2 cm
3 cm

Exploration 3

Use π to write an expression for the exact area of each circle. Then use 3.14 or the π key on a calculator to find the approximate area.

12. radius: 4 mm   **13.** diameter: 5.4 ft   **14.** radius: 3.1 cm

Spiral Review

Write an inequality to represent each statement. (Module 6, p. 388)

15. x is greater than or equal to 6.   **16.** r is less than 8.

Use division to write each fraction as a decimal. (Module 4, p. 256)

17. $\frac{3}{8}$ **18.** $\frac{4}{5}$ **19.** $\frac{9}{20}$ **20.** $\frac{21}{32}$

Write each fraction in lowest terms. (Module 3, p. 170)

21. $\frac{6}{8}$ **22.** $\frac{6}{16}$ **23.** $\frac{20}{25}$ **24.** $\frac{15}{55}$

Name _____   Date _____

Barnstorming   Triangles and Similarity

GOAL   **LEARN HOW TO:** • identify similar and congruent polygons
• find the scale of a drawing or model
• classify triangles by the measures of their angles
• find unknown measures of similar figures

AS YOU: • learn about the Curtiss Jenny airplane used by barnstormers
• use scale drawings of a Curtiss Jenny

Exploration 1: Scale Drawings and Similarity

Similar and Congruent Figures

Similar figures have the same shape but not necessarily the same size. Parts on similar figures that match are called **corresponding parts**. In similar polygons, the measures of the corresponding angles are equal and the ratios of the lengths of the corresponding sides are equal.

Example

In the figure at the right, $\triangle ABC$ is similar to $\triangle DEF$.

a. $\overline{AB}$ corresponds to $\overline{DE}$. What segments correspond to $\overline{BC}$ and $\overline{AC}$?

b. Find the measures of $\angle D$, $\angle E$, and $\angle F$, and the lengths of $\overline{EF}$ and $\overline{DF}$.

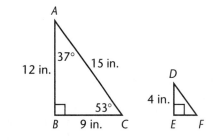

Sample Response

a. $\overline{EF}$ corresponds to $\overline{BC}$, and $\overline{DF}$ corresponds to $\overline{AC}$.

b. $m\angle D = 37°$, $m\angle E = 90°$, and $m\angle F = 53°$

Since $\dfrac{AB}{DE} = \dfrac{12}{4} = 3$, each side of $\triangle ABC$ is 3 times as long as the corresponding side of $\triangle DEF$.

So, $DE = 9 \div 3$, or 3 in., and $DF = 15 \div 3$, or 5 in.

Similar figures that have the same shape and the same size are *congruent*. The lengths of corresponding sides and the measures of corresponding angles of congruent polygons are equal.

Name _____ Date _____

The **scale of a model or drawing** is the ratio of a length on the model or drawing to the length of the corresponding part on the actual object.

Example

An architect has built a model of a new office building she has designed. The model was built using a scale of 1 in. = 15 ft. If the height of the model is 6.25 in., what will be the height of the actual building?

Sample Response

Use a proportion.

$$\frac{1 \text{ in.}}{15 \text{ ft}} = \frac{6.25 \text{ in.}}{x \text{ ft}}$$

$$x = 6.25(15)$$

$$= 93.75$$

The building will be 93.75 ft tall.

Exploration 2: Unknown Measures in Similar Figures

Classifying Triangles

Triangles can be classified by the measures of their angles. A triangle that has only acute angles is an **acute triangle**. An **obtuse triangle** has one obtuse angle. A **right triangle** has one right angle.

Example

Classify each triangle as *acute*, *obtuse*, or *right*.

a. 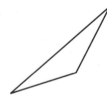   **b.**   **c.**

Sample Response

a. obtuse   **b.** acute   **c.** right

Name _____   Date _____

Exploration 1

Trapezoid *ABDC* is similar to trapezoid *EFHG*.

1. $\overline{AB}$ corresponds to $\overline{EF}$. Which segments correspond to $\overline{BC}$, $\overline{CD}$, and $\overline{AC}$, respectively?

2. Find the measures of $\angle A$, $\angle B$, $\angle C$, and $\angle D$.

3. Find the lengths of $\overline{BC}$, $\overline{CD}$, and $\overline{AD}$.

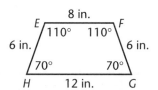

The amount of magnification under a microscope is given. For each scale, how long does a 2 mm long cell appear to be when seen through a microscope?

4. $15 : 1$ | 5. $100 : 1$ | 6. $200 : 1$

Exploration 2

Classify each triangle as *acute*, *obtuse*, or *right*.

7.    8.    9.

Spiral Review

Find the surface area of each prism. (Module 6, p. 404)

10.   11.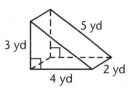

Find each difference. (Module 3, p. 183)

12. $4\frac{3}{8} - 2\frac{3}{4}$ 13. $6\frac{4}{5} - 3\frac{4}{5}$ 14. $2\frac{1}{2} - 1\frac{1}{3}$

For each angle, find the measure of a supplementary angle.
(Module 2, p. 83)

15. $36°$ 16. $45°$ 17. $125°$ 18. $179°$

Math Thematics, Book 2 **6-89**

MODULE 6 SECTION 4   **STUDY GUIDE**

Winging It   Parallel Lines and Angles of Polygons

GOAL   **LEARN HOW TO:** • find relationships among angles formed
by parallel lines and a transversal
• find the sum of the measures of the angles
of triangles and quadrilaterals

     AS YOU: • make a model wing
• experiment with ways to make your wing more rigid

Exploration 1: Angles Formed by a Transversal

Parallel Lines and Transversals

A line that intersects two lines is a **transversal**. When a transversal
intersects two parallel lines, the measures of the eight angles formed are
related. Four of the angles are **exterior angles** because they are outside of
the parallel lines. The other four angles are called **interior angles** because
they are on the inside of, or between, the parallel lines.

A pair of nonadjacent exterior angles found on opposite sides of the
transversal are called **alternate exterior angles**. Nonadjacent pairs of
interior angles found on opposite sides of the transversal are called
alternate interior angles. Angles that have the same position on the two
lines cut by a transversal are called **corresponding angles**. There are also
four pairs of **vertical angles** formed by the intersecting lines. These angle
pairs are directly opposite each other at the intersection of the transversal
and one of the other two lines.

When the two lines intersected by the transversal are parallel, each of the
angle pairs mentioned above is congruent. Recall that congruent angles
have the same measure.

Example

In the figure at the right, line *l* intersects parallel lines
m and *n*. Name all the congruent pairs of angles and
tell why they are congruent.

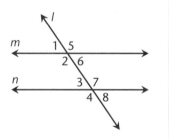

MODULE 6 SECTION 4   **STUDY GUIDE**

Sample Response

$\angle 1 \cong \angle 3$ since corresponding angles are congruent.
$\angle 1 \cong \angle 6$ since vertical angles are congruent.
$\angle 1 \cong \angle 8$ since alternate exterior angles are congruent.
$\angle 2 \cong \angle 4$ since corresponding angles are congruent.
$\angle 2 \cong \angle 5$ since vertical angles are congruent.
$\angle 2 \cong \angle 7$ since alternate interior angles are congruent.
$\angle 3 \cong \angle 6$ since alternate interior angles are congruent.
$\angle 3 \cong \angle 8$ since vertical angles are congruent.
$\angle 4 \cong \angle 5$ since alternate exterior angles are congruent.
$\angle 4 \cong \angle 7$ since vertical angles are congruent.
$\angle 5 \cong \angle 7$ since corresponding angles are congruent.
$\angle 6 \cong \angle 8$ since corresponding angles are congruent.

Exploration 2: Angles of Triangles and Quadrilaterals

Sum of the Angles of a Triangle and of a Quadrilateral

The sum of the measures of the angles of a triangle is 180°.

The sum of the measures of the angles of a quadrilateral is 360°.

A **diagonal** of a polygon is a segment whose endpoints are two non-consecutive vertices of the polygon.

Example

Use the figure at the right.

a. Find the measure of $\angle ABC$ in $\triangle ABC$.

b. Find the measure of $\angle CDE$ in quadrilateral *ACDE*.

c. Name a diagonal of polygon *ABCDE*.

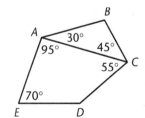

Sample Response

a. Since the sum of the measures of the angles of a triangle is 180°,

$$m\angle ABC = 180° - (30° + 45°) = 180° - 75° = 105°$$

b. Since the sum of the measures of the angles of a quadrilateral is 360°,

$$m\angle CDE = 360° - (70° + 95° + 55°) = 360° - 220° = 140°$$

c. $\overline{AC}$ is a diagonal of polygon *ABCDE*.

Name _____ Date _____

Exploration 1

The figure at the right shows two parallel lines, *s* and *t*, intersected by transversal *r*. Use this diagram for Exercises 1–12.

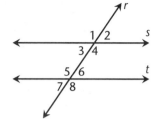

Name the angles or pairs of angles that fit each description.

  1. four interior angles   **2.** four exterior angles

  3. two pairs of alternate interior angles   **4.** four pairs of vertical angles

  5. two pairs of alternate exterior angles   **6.** four pairs of corresponding angles

Find the measure of each angle if the measure of ∠3 is 52°.

  7. ∠1   **8.** ∠2   **9.** ∠4

10. ∠5   **11.** ∠6   **12.** ∠7

Exploration 2

Find the unknown measure in each triangle or quadrilateral.

13.   **14.** 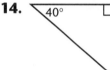   **15.**

Spiral Review

Classify each triangle as *acute*, *obtuse*, or *right*. (Module 6, p. 417)

16.   **17.**   **18.**

Solve each equation. Check each solution. (Module 4, p. 300)

19. $3 + 4x = 7$ **20.** $5n - 6 = 4$ **21.** $\frac{t}{3} - 1 = 9$

Find the volume of a cube with each side length. (Module 1, p. 21)

22. 5 mm   **23.** 3 ft   **24.** 9 cm   **25.** 6 in.

MODULE 6 SECTION 5   **STUDY GUIDE**

A Whale of a Problem   Volume of a Prism and Metric Relationships

GOAL   **LEARN HOW TO:** • find the volume of a prism
 • use the relationships among metric units of volume, capacity, and mass
 • use networks

AS YOU: • compare the sizes of Keiko's old and new pools
 • investigate how Keiko was shipped
 • analyze delivery routes

Exploration 1: Volume of a Prism

The volume V of a prism is the product of the area of a base B and the height h.

Example

Find the volume of this right triangular prism.

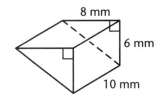

Sample Response

Since the bases are triangles, use the area formula for a triangle.

$$\text{area of base} = \frac{1}{2} \times \text{base} \times \text{height}$$

$$= \frac{1}{2} \cdot 6 \cdot 8$$

$$= 24$$

$$\text{volume} = \text{area of base} \times \text{height}$$
$$= 24 \cdot 10$$
$$= 240$$

The volume of the prism is 240 mm^3.

Name _____ Date _____

Exploration 2: Relationships Among Metric Units

Mass, Capacity, and Volume

A container's **capacity** is the amount of fluid it can hold. In the metric system, mass, capacity, and volume are related as follows:

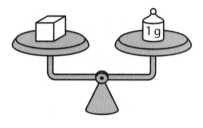

The volume of one **cubic centimeter (cm³)** is equal to ...

the capacity of one **milliliter (mL)** which is equal to ...

the **mass** of one **gram (g)** of water.

One **liter (L)** of liquid will fill a cube measuring 10 cm on each side. There are 1000 mL in 1 L. The mass of 1 L of water is 1 **kilogram (kg)**. One kg is equivalent to 1000 g.

Exploration 3: Weighted Networks

Networks

A **network** is a figure made up of points called **vertices** that are connected by segments or curves called **arcs**. A network in which the arcs are labeled with numbers representing such things as distances or times is a **weighted network**.

> **Example**
>
> Find the length of the two shortest paths from vertex A to vertex E in the network shown at the right.
>
>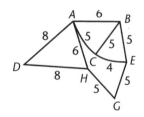
>
> **Sample Response**
>
> The path A–C–E has a length of $5 + 4$, or 9.
>
> The path A–B–E has a length of $6 + 5$, or 11.
>
> The lengths of all the other possible paths from A to E are greater than 11.

Name _____ Date _____

MODULE 6 SECTION 5 | PRACTICE & APPLICATION EXERCISES | STUDY GUIDE

Exploration 1

Find the volume of each prism.

1.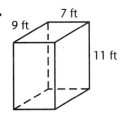

2.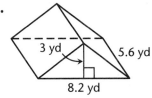

Exploration 2

Replace each ___?___ with the number that makes the statement true.

3. $155 \text{ cm}^3 = $ ___?___ mL

4. $2.1 \text{ L} = $ ___?___ cm^3

5. $18 \text{ L} = $ ___?___ mL

Exploration 3

Use the network at the right to answer Exercises 6 and 7.

6. Find the length of the shortest path from *A* to *C*.

7. Find the length of the path *A-B-D-E*.

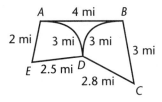

Spiral Review

Find each unknown angle measure. (Module 6, p. 429)

8.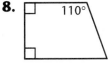

9.

10.

Use the box-and-whisker plots shown. (Module 5, p. 337)

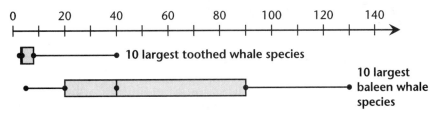

11. How is the smallest baleen whale represented on the box plot?

12. Estimate the median of both data sets.

Find the area of a circle with each radius. Use 3.14 for π.
(Module 6, p. 405)

13. 1.2 mm

14. 8 mm

15. 5 ft

16. 2.15 cm

Name _____ Date _____

For Use with Sections 1 and 2

You can use the programming capability of a graphing calculator to solve problems involving area of polygons.

The screen on the left (below) shows a program for the TI-80. You can use the program to find the area of a triangle. Input the length of the base and the height of the triangle, and the calculator will calculate and display the area. For example, if you input 10 as the value of B and 8 as the value of H, the calculator will use those values in the formula 0.5*B*H and display the message "AREA OF TRI IS" and the number 40. You see this result in the screen on the right (below).

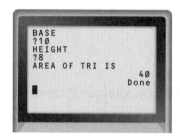

1. If you input 12 for B and 14 for H, what number will the calculator display for the area of the triangle? _____

2. The first screen (below) shows a program you can use to calculate the height of a triangle if you know the area of the triangle and the length of the base.

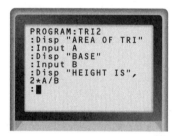

a. What formula does the program use to calculate the height? _____

b. For the screen on the right (above), what input value was used for A? _____ for B? _____

What is the height of the triangle? _____

MODULE 6

3. The program on the screen on the left (below) computes the base of a parallelogram, given the area and height of the parallelogram.

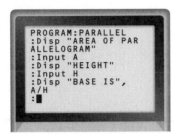 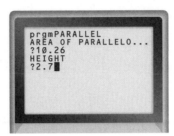

a. What values for A and H are used for the screen on the right?

_____

b. If the area of a parallelogram is 10.26 cm² the height is 2.7 cm, what is the length of the base? _____

4. The program below computes the radius and diameter of a circle, given the area of the circle.

a. What formula is used to calculate the radius?

_____

b. What formula is used to calculate the diameter?

_____

c. If the area of a circle is 113.10 square units,
what is the radius? _____
the diameter? _____

Name _____ Date _____

1. George has at least $240 but no more than $275 in his checking account. Write and graph an inequality to represent this situation.

For Exercises 2–4, refer to the figure at the right.

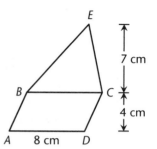

2. What is the area of the parallelogram *ABCD*?

3. What is the area of triangle *BEC*?

4. What is the probability that a small object dropped on the figure will land on the triangle?

Find each square root. If the square root is not an integer, estimate it to the nearest tenth.

5. $\sqrt{900}$ **6.** $\sqrt{33}$ **7.** $\sqrt{441}$ **8.** $\sqrt{140}$

Use the prism shown at the right.

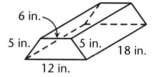

9. What kind of prism is this?

10. How many faces, edges, and vertices does the prism have?

11. Sketch a net for the prism.

12. If each base has an area of 36 in.^{2}, what is the surface area of the prism?

Use π to write an expression for the exact area of each circle. Then use the [π] key on a calculator or 3.14 for π to find the approximate area. Round each answer to the nearest tenth.

13.   **14.**   **15.**

Find the radius of a circle with each area. Round each answer to the nearest tenth.

16. $A = 9\pi$ in.^{2} **17.** $A = 120$ cm^2 **18.** $A = 40$ ft^2

Use the similar polygons shown for Exercises 21–24.

19. What angle corresponds to ∠*C* and what is its measure?

20. Find the measures of ∠*E* and ∠*H*.

21. What segment corresponds to $\overline{CD}$? What is its length?

22. Find the lengths of $\overline{FG}$ and $\overline{EH}$.

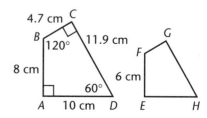

Name _____ Date _____

For Exercises 1 and 2, write and graph an inequality to represent each situation.

1. A cruise ship has a maximum capacity of 360 passengers, but the company will cancel a cruise unless 200 people have made reservations.

2. Sara practices the piano at least 40 minutes each day.

3. Find the area of the triangle at the right.

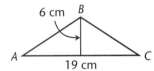

4. Find the probability that a small object dropped onto the figure shown at the right will land on the shaded part of the figure.

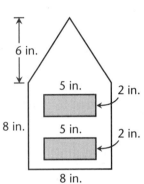

Find each square root. If the square root is not an integer, estimate it to the nearest tenth.

5. $\sqrt{180}$ 6. $\sqrt{484}$ 7. $\sqrt{45}$

Use the triangular prism for Exercises 8 and 9.

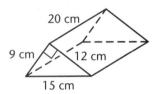

8. Find the surface area of the prism.

9. Sketch a net for the prism. Label the dimensions of each face.

Find the exact area of each circle. Then use the [π] **key on a calculator or 3.14 for π to find the approximate area. Round each answer to the nearest tenth.**

10.
     11.
     12.

13. A model of the original Boeing 747 "Jumbo Jet" is $19\frac{1}{2}$ in. long. The actual length of the aircraft is about 232 ft.

   a. What is the scale of the model?

   b. If the wingspan of the model is $16\frac{1}{3}$ in., estimate the actual wingspan.

14. Quadrilateral *ABCD* is similar to quadrilateral *PLMN*. Find the measures of all the unlabeled segments. If you know the angle measures of *ABCD*, what can you say about the angles in *PLMN*?

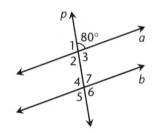

15. Lines *a* and *b* are parallel. Find the measures of angles 1, 2, 3, 4, 5, 6, and 7.

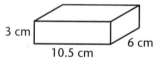

In Exercises 16–18, the measures of two of the angles of a triangle are given. Find the measure of the third angle of each triangle and tell whether the triangle is *acute*, *obtuse*, or *right*.

16. 42° and 37°   **17.** 81° and 25°   **18.** 61° and 29°

Use the rectangular prism for Exercises 19 and 20.

19. What is the volume of the prism?

20. What is the capacity of the prism in milliliters? in liters?

Replace each __?__ with the number that makes the statement true.

21. 4200 mL = __?__ L   **22.** 6.1 L = __?__ cm³   **23.** 18 kL = __?__ L

For Exercises 24–26, use the network, which shows distances in miles between six towns.

24. Which towns shown are connected directly to town *D*?

25. How long is the route from town *A* to town *D* to town *F*?

26. Find a route from town *A* to town *F* that is shorter than the route in Exercise 25.

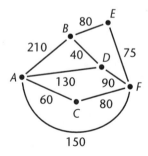

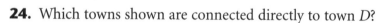

Name _____   Date _____

For Exercises 1 and 2, write and graph an inequality to represent each situation.

1. The maximum load on the elevator is 3000 lb.

2. A wild elephant eats between 500 and 600 lb of food per day.

3. Find the area of the parallelogram at the right.

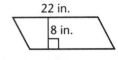

4. Find the probability that a small object dropped onto the figure shown at the right will land on the shaded part of the figure.

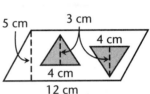

Find each square root. If the square root is not an integer, estimate it to the nearest tenth.

5. $\sqrt{60}$ **6.** $\sqrt{676}$ **7.** $\sqrt{5}$

Use the rectangular prism for Exercises 8 and 9.

8. Find the surface area of the prism.

9. Sketch a net for the prism. Label the dimensions of each face.

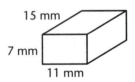

Find the exact area of each circle. Then use the $\boxed{\pi}$ key on a calculator or 3.14 for π to find the approximate area. Round each answer to the nearest tenth.

10.   **11.**   **12.**

13. A model of the smallest biplane ever flown is 26.5 cm long. Its actual length is 8 ft 10 in.

    a. What is the scale of the model?

    b. If the wingspan of the model is 16.5 cm, estimate the actual wingspan.

MODULE 6 TEST   FORM **B**

14. Quadrilateral *ABCD* is similar to quadrilateral *XZYW*. Find the measures of all the unlabeled segments. If you know the angle measures of *ABCD*, what can you say about the angles in *XZYW*?

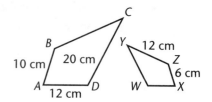

15. Lines *p* and *q* are parallel. Find the measures of angles 1, 2, 3, 4, 5, 6, and 7.

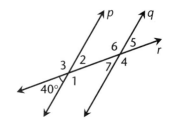

In Exercises 16–18, the measures of two of the angles of a triangle are given. Find the measure of the third angle of each triangle and tell whether the triangle is *acute*, *obtuse*, or *right*.

16. 68° and 19°   **17.** 42° and 48°   **18.** 51° and 66°

Use the triangular prism for Exercises 19 and 20.

19. What is the volume of the prism?

20. What is the capacity of the prism in milliliters? in liters?

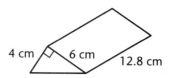

Replace each __?__ with the number that makes the statement true.

21. 5600 cm³ = __?__ L   **22.** 75 mL = __?__ L   **23.** 89 L = __?__ kL

For Exercises 24–26, use the network below, which shows distances in miles between six towns.

24. Which towns shown are connected directly to town *B*?

25. How long is the route from town *A* to town *B* to town *E*?

26. Find a route from town *A* to town *E* that is shorter than the route in Exercise 25.

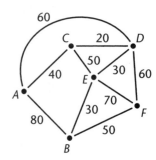

MODULE 6   **STANDARDIZED ASSESSMENT**

1. Which is represented by the graph?

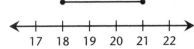

  17 18 19 20 21 22

  a. Sue has no more than $21 in the bank.

  b. Only students between the ages of 18 and 21 should apply.

  c. Each of the 21 snakes is at least 18 inches long.

  d. The baby weighs at least 18 lb but less than 21 lb.

2. What is the area of the parallelogram?

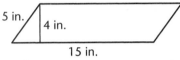

5 in.   4 in.   15 in.

  a. 30 in.^{2} **b.** 40 in.^{2}

  c. 60 in.^{2} **d.** 75 in.^{2}

3. Estimate $\sqrt{14}$ to the nearest tenth.

  a. 3.6   **b.** 3.7

  c. 3.8   **d.** 3.9

4. Find the surface area.

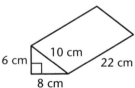

10 cm   6 cm   22 cm   8 cm

  a. 10,560 cm^2 **b.** 624 cm^2

  c. 576 cm^2 **d.** 528 cm^2

5. The longest suspension bridge in the world, the Humber Estuary Bridge in England, is 4626 ft long. A model of it is 18 in. long with towers 2.07 in. tall. To the nearest foot, what is the actual height of the towers?

  a. 532 ft   **b.** 549 ft

  c. 586 ft   **d.** 624 ft

6. Use the network below to find the shortest path from *A* to *F*. (Distances are in miles.)

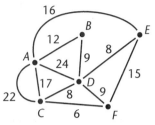

  a. 21 mi   **b.** 23 mi

  c. 28 mi   **d.** 30 mi

7. Find the area of this circle.

12 in.

  a. 12π in.^{2} **b.** 36π in.^{2}

  c. 60π in.^{2} **d.** 144π in.^{2}

8. What is the volume of a rectangular prism with base 4 ft by 6.3 ft and height 5.8 ft?

  a. 16.1 ft^3 **b.** 23.2 ft^3

  c. 104.92 ft^3 **d.** 146.16 ft^3

9. If $\triangle ABC \sim \triangle MNL$, find *NL*.

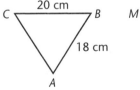

20 cm   18 cm   8

  a. 7.2 cm   **b.** 7.8 cm

  c. 8.3 cm   **d.** 8.8̄ cm

10. If lines *p* and *q* are parallel, what is $m\angle 6$?

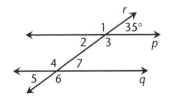

35°

  a. 35°   **b.** 70°

  c. 145°   **d.** 155°

MODULE 6   **MODULE PERFORMANCE ASSESSMENT**

Three sisters, Anastasia, Beulah, and Chrysilla, had lived for many years in different parts of the world. Anastasia had settled in Switzerland, where she lived in a blue and white A-frame chateau high in the Swiss Alps. Beulah lived in Mexico in a traditional flat-roofed adobe hacienda. Chrysilla lived in Kansas in a simple farm house with a peaked roof.

Now, after many years apart, the sisters have decided to buy some land in Delaware. They plan to build a house large enough for all of them to live in together. But each sister wants the house to look like the one in which she has lived.

The three sisters decide to solve the problem by choosing the design which is most efficient at holding heat. They have reasoned that the house with the smallest surface-area-to-volume ratio will be the one with the most heat-efficient design. So, they want to find the surface area and volume of each house design, and then calculate the surface-area-to-volume ratio.

1. Use the dimensions, given in feet, of the house plans shown below to calculate the surface area, volume, and surface-area-to-volume ratio of each house.

Anastasia's Plan

Beulah's Plan

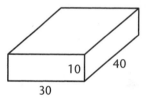

Chrysilla's Plan

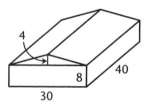

2. Which house should they build?

3. Chrysilla decides that they should build a bigger house, regardless of the plan they use. She wants the width of the base to be 45 ft instead of 30 ft. The remaining dimensions should be in the same scale as the original structure. Re-draw each house design, and calculate the new dimensions for each house.

4. Beulah says they will need to calculate the surface-area-to-volume ratio all over again, because the ratio changes when the dimensions change. Is Beulah right?

Answers

PRACTICE AND APPLICATIONS

Module 6, Section 1
1. a. $x < 5$ **b.** $b \geq 7$ **c.** $6 < h \leq 14$ **d.** $2 < p < 9$
e. $a > 3$ **f.** $k \leq 6$ **g.** $2 < r < 5$ **h.** $4 < s < 17$
i. $4 < t \leq 16$ **j.** $8 < b \leq 10$
2. a. about 5 in. **b.** about 9.5 in.
3. a. No; the quadrilateral has only one pair of opposite sides parallel, and a parallelogram has two such pairs. **b.** Yes. **c.** Yes.
4. a. concave **b.** convex **c.** concave
5. Sample response:

6. a. $\frac{9}{64}$, or about 14% **b.** $\frac{4}{45}$, or about 9% **c.** $\frac{9}{16}$, or about 56% **d.** $\frac{2}{3}$, or about 67% **e.** $\frac{8}{25}$, or 32%
f. $\frac{1}{2}$, or 50%
7. a. $\frac{1}{4}$ **b.** 48 m^2
8. a. Board B **b.** Board A

Module 6, Section 2
1. a. $49 = 7 \cdot 7 = 7^2$ **b.** $900 = 30 \cdot 30 = 30^2$
c. $225 = 15 \cdot 15 = 15^2$
2. a. 12 **b.** 6 **c.** 0 **d.** 13 **e.** –4 **f.** –10 **g.** 20
h. –11 **i.** –9 **j.** –14 **k.** 18 **l.** –16 **m.** 17 **n.** –5
o. –1 **p.** 8 **q.** 0 **r.** 19
3. a. 4 and 5; 4.2 **b.** 6 and 7; 6.8 **c.** 10 and 11; 10.7
d. 5 and 6; 5.5 **e.** 2 and 3; 2.6 **f.** 11 and 12; 11.8
4. a. 8.5 **b.** 12.6 **c.** 5.3 **d.** 15.2 **e.** 7.5 **f.** 20.4
g. 8.9 **h.** 6.2 **i.** 15.8 **j.** 7.1 **k.** 11.4 **l.** 16.1 **m.** 4.5
n. 10.5 **o.** 7.8 **p.** 11.7 **q.** 14.5 **r.** 6.5
5. 28 ft
6. a. pentagonal prism **b.** 7 faces, 10 vertices, 15 edges
7. a. octagonal prism **b.** 10 faces, 16 vertices, 24 edges
8. a. Sample Response:

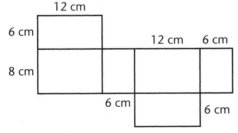

b. 432 cm2
9. 100 in.^{2}

10, 11. Approximate answers were calculated by using 3.14 for π.
10. a. 529π in.^{2}; 1661.06 in.^{2} **b.** 17.64π cm^2; 55.39 cm^2 **c.** 36π m^2; 113.04 m^2 **d.** 225π m^2; 706.5 m^2 **e.** 268.9π cm^2; 844.5 cm^2 **f.** 156.25π ft^2; 490.63 ft^2
11. about 254.34 in.^{2}

Module 6, Section 3
1. a. congruent; Sample Response: $ABC \cong FED$
b. similar; Sample Response: $ABCDEF \sim MNOPQR$
c. neither **d.** similar; Sample Response: $JKLM \sim ABCD$
2. a. 5.4 m **b.** 0.6 m **c.** 4.8 m
3. a. 12 mm **b.** 30 mm **c.** 60 mm **d.** 90 mm
e. 108 mm **f.** 120 mm
4. 210 mi
5. a. acute **b.** right **c.** acute **d.** right **e.** obtuse
6. a. $\overline{PQ}$, $\overline{QR}$ **b.** 104°, 29°, 47° **c.** 4.5 cm, 6.75 cm
7. a. $\angle ZWX$, 90° **b.** 126°, 65.5°, 78.5° **c.** CD, 20 ft
d. 36 ft, 48 ft
8. 9 cm

Module 6, Section 4
1. a. $\angle 3, \angle 4, \angle 5, \angle 6$ **b.** $\angle 1, \angle 2, \angle 7, \angle 8$ **c.** $\angle 3$ and $\angle 5$, $\angle 4$ and $\angle 6$ **d.** $\angle 1$ and $\angle 7$, $\angle 2$ and $\angle 8$ **e.** Any two of the following pairs: $\angle 1$ and $\angle 3$, $\angle 2$ and $\angle 4$, $\angle 5$ and $\angle 7$, $\angle 6$ and $\angle 8$ **f.** Any two of the following pairs: $\angle 1$ and $\angle 5$, $\angle 3$ and $\angle 7$, $\angle 2$ and $\angle 6$, $\angle 4$ and $\angle 8$
2. a. 127° **b.** 53° **c.** 127° **d.** 53° **e.** 127° **f.** 53°
3. a. True. **b.** True. **c.** False. **d.** True. **e.** False.
f. True. **g.** False. **h.** True. **i.** True. **j.** True. **k.** True.
l. False.
4. a. 47° **b.** 33° **c.** 158° **d.** 118° **e.** 83° **f.** 107°
g. 121° **h.** 82° **i.** 60° **j.** 68° **k.** 80° **l.** 132°
5. a. 100°; obtuse **b.** 84°; acute **c.** 65°; acute
d. 21°; obtuse **e.** 82°; acute **f.** 90°; right **g.** 128°; obtuse **h.** 94°; obtuse **i.** 79°; right **j.** 78°; acute
k. 123°; obtuse **l.** 71°; acute
6. 74°

Module 6, Section 5
1. a. 22.5 cm^3 **b.** 756 ft^3 **c.** 45.92 m^3 **d.** 72 m^3
e. 143 in.^{3} **f.** 324 cm^3 **g.** 20.16 cm^3 **h.** 384 m^3
i. 300 in.^{3}
2. a. 72 in.^{3} **b.** 15 pedestals
3. a. 6 cm **b.** 16 cm^2 **c.** 4 cm
4. a. 24,000 **b.** 55 **c.** 2.8 **d.** 3.5 **e.** 6400 **f.** 0.283
g. 4710 **h.** 800 **i.** 600 **j.** 19,000 **k.** 4,300,000
l. 31 **m.** 63,000 **n.** 0.059 **o.** 0.085
5. a. 10.2 m^3 **b.** 10,200 L **c.** 10,200 kg
6. 197 g

7. a. 986 mi **b.** 746 mi **c.** 4 mi **d.** No, the path Hearst–Cochrane–Montreal looks much shorter than the path Hearst–Cochrane–North Bay–Ottawa–Montreal.

Module 6, Sections 1–5

1. a. No; the quadrilateral has no pairs of opposite sides parallel, and a parallelogram has two such pairs. **b.** Yes. **c.** Yes.
2. a. convex **b.** concave **c.** convex
3. Approximate answers were calculated by using 3.14 for π. **a.** 30.25π in.^{2}; 94.99 in.^{2} **b.** 68.89π cm^2; 216.31 cm^2 **c.** 441π m^2; 1384.74 m^2
4. a. similar; $CDAB \sim WXYZ$ **b.** neither
5. 300 mi
6. 15 mm or 1.5 cm
7. a. 71°, 83°, 60° **b.** 11 ft, 18 ft, 12 ft
8. a. 42° **b.** 42° **c.** 138° **d.** 138° **e.** 42° **f.** 138°
9. a. 1580 mi **b.** 2627 mi **c.** San Francisco–Salt Lake City–NY **d.** Seattle–San Francisco–Phoenix–Atlanta

STUDY GUIDE

Module 6, Section 1

1. $w > 5$
2. $j \leq 13$
3. $1 < y < 4$
4. $3 < r \leq 7$

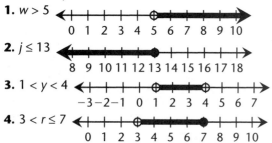

5. Yes.
6. No; there is only one pair of parallel sides.
7. concave
8. convex
9. $\frac{2}{8} = \frac{1}{4}$, or 25%
10. $\frac{32}{96} = \frac{1}{3}$, or $33\frac{1}{3}$%
11. about 45%
12. about 80%
13. about 50%
14. 30%
15. $2 \cdot 2 \cdot 5$
16. $3 \cdot 3 \cdot 5$
17. $2 \cdot 5 \cdot 5$
18. $2 \cdot 5 \cdot 13$
19. 9
20. 16
21. 49
22. 64

Module 6, Section 2

1. 11
2. 9
3. –6
4. 12 and 13
5–8. Sample Responses are given.
5. 2.6
6. 6.6
7. 4.5
8. 12.4
9. a triangular prism
10. 5 faces, 6 vertices, and 9 edges
11. a.

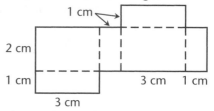

b. 3 cm^2, 3 cm^2, 2 cm^2, 2 cm^2, 6 cm^2, 6 cm^2
c. 22 cm^2
12. 16π mm^2; Sample Responses: 50.24 mm^2 or 50.27 mm^2
13. 7.29π ft^2; Sample Responses: 22.89 ft^2 or 22.90 ft^2
14. 9.61π cm^2; Sample Responses: 30.18 cm^2 or 30.19 cm^2
15. $x \geq 6$
16. $r < 8$
17. 0.375
18. 0.8
19. 0.45
20. 0.65625
21. $\frac{3}{4}$
22. $\frac{3}{8}$
23. $\frac{4}{5}$
24. $\frac{3}{11}$

Module 6, Section 3

1. $\overline{FG}$; $\overline{GH}$; $\overline{EH}$
2. 110°; 110°; 70°; 70°
3. $1\frac{1}{2}$ in.; 3 in.; $1\frac{1}{2}$ in.
4. 30 mm
5. 200 mm
6. 400 mm
7. right
8. obtuse
9. acute
10. 96 ft^2
11. 36 yd^2
12. $1\frac{5}{8}$
13. 3
14. $1\frac{1}{6}$

15. 144°
16. 135°
17. 55°
18. 1°

Module 6, Section 4
1. ∠3, ∠4, ∠5, and ∠6
2. ∠1, ∠2, ∠7, and ∠8
3. ∠3 and ∠6, ∠4 and ∠5
4. ∠1 and ∠4, ∠2 and ∠3, ∠5 and ∠8, ∠6 and ∠7
5. ∠1 and ∠8, ∠2 and ∠7
6. ∠1 and ∠5; ∠2 and ∠6; ∠3 and ∠7; ∠4 and ∠8
7. 128°
8. 52°
9. 128°
10. 128°
11. 52°
12. 52°
13. 90°
14. 50°
15. 60°
16. acute
17. right
18. obtuse
19. $x = 1$
20. $n = 2$
21. $t = 30$
22. 125 mm^3
23. 27 ft^3
24. 729 cm^3
25. 216 in.^{3}

Module 6, Section 5
1. 693 ft^3
2. 68.88 yd^3
3. 155
4. 2100
5. 18,000
6. 5.8 mi (A–D–C)
7. 9.5 mi
8. 70°
9. 70°
10. 90°
11. by the end point of the left-hand whisker in the lower box plot
12. upper: about 3000 kg; lower: about 40,000 kg
13. 4.5216 mm^2
14. 200.96 m^2
15. 78.5 ft^2
16. about 14.51 cm^2

TECHNOLOGY

Module 6
1. 84
2. a. 2*A/B **b.** 36; 4; 18
3. a. 10.26 for A, 2.7 for H **b.** 3.8 cm
4. a. $\sqrt{(A/\pi)}$ **b.** $2*\sqrt{(A/\pi)}$ **c.** about 6 cm; about 12 cm

ASSESSMENT

Mid-Module 6 Quiz
1. $240 \leq c \leq 275$, where c is the amount in his checking account

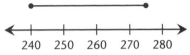

2. 32 cm^2
3. 28 cm^2
4. $\frac{7}{15}$
5. 30
6. 5.7
7. 21
8. 11.8
9. trapezoidal prism
10. 6, 12, 8
11.

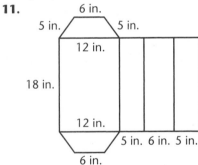

12. 576 in.^{2}
13. 225π mm^2; 706.9 mm^2
14. 36π in.^{2}; 113.1 in.^{2}
15. 17.64π ft^2; 55.4 ft^2
16. 3 in.
17. 6.2 cm
18. 3.6 ft
19. ∠G, 90°
20. 90°, 60°
21. GH; about 8.9 cm
22. about 3.5 cm, 7.5 cm

Module 6 Test (Form A)

1. $200 \le n \le 360$, where n is the number of passengers on the cruise

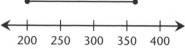

2. $p \ge 40$, where p is the number of minutes Sara practices on a given day

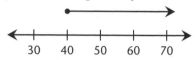

3. 57 cm²
4. 22.7%
5. 13.4
6. 22
7. 6.7
8. 828 cm²
9.

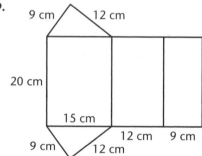

10–12. Answers were calculated by using the calculator value of π.
10. 210.25π ft²; about 660.5 ft²
11. 900π mm²; about 2827.4 mm²
12. 16π^3 in.²; about 496.1 in.²
13. a. 1 in. : 12 ft **b.** 196 ft
14. $BC = 18\frac{2}{3}$ cm, $CD = 5\frac{1}{3}$ cm, $PN = 7\frac{1}{2}$ cm; corresponding pairs of angles are congruent, that is, $m\angle A = m\angle P$, $m\angle B = m\angle L$, $m\angle C = m\angle M$, and $m\angle D = m\angle N$.
15. $m\angle 2 = m\angle 5 = m\angle 7 = 80°$, $m\angle 1 = m\angle 3 = m\angle 4 = m\angle 6 = 100°$
16. 101°, obtuse
17. 74°, acute
18. 90°, right
19. 189 cm³
20. 189 mL, 0.189 L
21. 4.2
22. 6100
23. 18,000
24. A, B, and F
25. 220 mi
26. A to C to F is 140 mi.

Module 6 Test (Form B)

1. $l \le 3000$, where l is the permissible load for the elevator

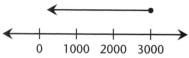

2. $500 \le f \le 600$, where f is the number of pounds of food eaten by an elephant on a given day

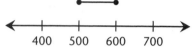

3. 176 in.²
4. $\frac{1}{5}$, or 20%
5. 7.7
6. 26
7. 2.2
8. 694 mm²
9.

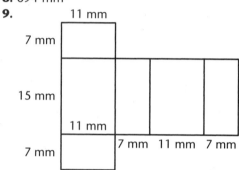

10–12. Answers were calculated by using the calculator value of π.
10. 25π^3 ft²; about 775.2 ft²
11. 331.24π cm²; about 1040.6 cm²
12. 5184π in.²; about 16,286 in.²
13. a. 1 cm : 4 in. $\left(\text{or } 1 \text{ cm} : \frac{1}{3} \text{ ft}\right)$ **b.** $5\frac{1}{2}$ ft
14. $WX = 7.2$ cm, $WY = 12$ cm, $BC = 20$ cm; corresponding pairs of angles are congruent, that is, $m\angle A = m\angle X$, $m\angle B = m\angle Z$, $m\angle C = m\angle Y$, and $m\angle D = m\angle W$.
15. $m\angle 2 = m\angle 5 = m\angle 7 = 40°$, $m\angle 1 = m\angle 3 = m\angle 4 = m\angle 6 = 140°$
16. 93°, obtuse
17. 90°, right
18. 63°, acute
19. 153.6 cm³
20. 153.6 mL, 0.1536 L
21. 5.6
22. 0.075
23. 0.089
24. A, E, and F
25. 110 mi
26. any three of the following routes: A to C to D to E, A to D to E, A to C to E

STANDARDIZED TEST

Module 6

1. b
2. c
3. b
4. c
5. c
6. a
7. d
8. b
9. c
10. d

MODULE PERFORMANCE ASSESSMENT

Module 6

1. Anastasia's Plan   Beulah's Plan   Chrysilla's Plan
    $S.A. = 3800$ ft^2 $S.A. = 3800$ ft^2 $S.A. \approx 3680$ ft^2
    $V = 12,000$ ft^3 $V = 12,000$ ft^3 $V = 12,000$ ft^3
    $\frac{S.A.}{V} \approx 0.32$ $\frac{S.A.}{V} \approx 0.32$ $\frac{S.A.}{V} \approx 0.31$

2. They should build Chrysilla's house, because it has the lowest surface area to volume ratio.

3. **Anastasia's New Plan** $S.A. = 8550$ ft^2
    $V = 40,500$ ft^3
    $\frac{S.A.}{V} \approx 0.21$

30   60

45

Beulah's New Plan $S.A. = 8550$ ft^2
    $V = 40,500$ ft^3
    $\frac{S.A.}{V} \approx \approx 0.21$

15   60

45

Chrysilla's New Plan $S.A. = 8286$ ft^2
    $V = 40,500$ ft^3
    $\frac{S.A.}{V} \approx \approx 0.20$

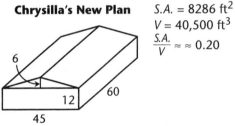

6

12   60

45

4. Beulah is correct. The ratios change as the dimensions increase.

Name _____   Date _____

MODULES 5 AND 6 TEST   CUMULATIVE

Write each rate as a unit rate.

1. $\dfrac{\$8.64}{2.4\,\text{lb}}$

2. $\dfrac{14°}{3\,\text{h}}$

3. $\dfrac{446.4\,\text{mi}}{18\,\text{gal}}$

4. $\dfrac{22\,\text{in.}}{4\,\text{h}}$

5. Make a stem-and-leaf plot for the following data. Then find the range, the mean, the median, and the mode.

Games Won by American League Baseball Teams, 1997

Baltimore	98	Cleveland	86	Seattle	90
New York	96	Chicago	80	Anaheim	84
Detroit	79	Milwaukee	78	Texas	77
Boston	78	Minnesota	68	Oakland	65
Toronto	76	Kansas City	67		

Use the histogram for Exercises 6 and 7.

6. How many Nobel prize winners for 1997 were less than 60 years old?

7. Which of the following information can you get from this histogram: the median of the data, the range of the data, the mean of the data, or the mode of the data? Explain.

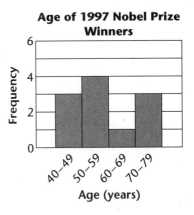

Age of 1997 Nobel Prize Winners

Solve each proportion.

8. $\dfrac{x}{18} = \dfrac{21}{40}$

9. $\dfrac{6}{11} = \dfrac{150}{y}$

10. $\dfrac{15}{28} = \dfrac{z}{210}$

11. Use the box-and-whisker plot to estimate the median number of countries who have participated in the Winter Olympics. What fraction of the Winter Olympics have had more than 43 countries participating?

Number of Countries Participating in Winter Olympics, 1924–1994

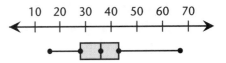

Find each unknown number.

12. 18% of a number is 9.

13. A number is 72% of 400.

14. A bag contains 2 white marbles and 3 blue marbles. Marbles are drawn out of the bag one at a time and the color recorded; the selected marbles are replaced into the bag after each draw. What is the theoretical probability that a blue marble is drawn first, followed by two whites? Express your answer as a fraction, a decimal, and a percent.

MODULES 5 AND 6 TEST **CUMULATIVE**

15. Write an example of a situation that could be represented by this graph, and then write the inequality.

21   65

16. Find the probability that a small object dropped onto this right triangle will land on the shaded part of the figure.

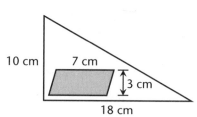

10 cm   7 cm   3 cm   18 cm

Find each square root. If the square root is not an integer, estimate it to the nearest tenth.

17. $\sqrt{49}$

18. $\sqrt{115}$

19. $\sqrt{900}$

20. Find the surface area and volume of this triangular prism.

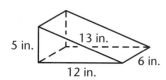

5 in.   13 in.   6 in.   12 in.

Find the exact area of the circles described. Then use the $\boxed{\pi}$ **key on a calculator or 3.14 for π to find the approximate area.**

21. a circle with diameter 14 m

22. a circle with radius 2.7 in.

23. △*ABC* is similar to △*JKL*. Find the measures of all the unlabeled segments.

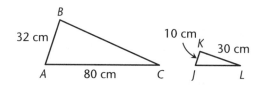

B   32 cm   10 cm   K   30 cm   A   80 cm   C   J   L

The measures of two of the angles of a triangle are given. Find the measure of the third angle of each triangle and tell whether the triangle is *acute*, *obtuse*, or *right*.

24. 19° and 110°

25. 45° and 50°

26. 32° and 58°

27. What is the capacity in mL of a rectangular prism that has base 8 cm by 12 cm and height 4.5 cm?

28. Use the network to find the shortest route from *A* to *D*. (Distances are in miles.)

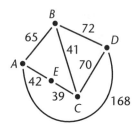

B   72   65   D   41   A   70   E   42   39   C   168

Answers

CUMULATIVE TEST

Modules 5 and 6

1. $3.60/1 lb

2. 4.7°/1 h

3. 24.8 mi/1 gal

4. 5.5 in./1 h

5. Games Won by American League Baseball Teams in 1997

```
6 | 5  7  8
7 | 6  7  8  8  9
8 | 0  4  6
9 | 0  6  8
```

     6 | 5 represents 65 games

range = 33, mean = 80.1, median = 78.5, mode = 78

6. 7 Nobel prize winners

7. None of this information is available from the histogram because the data are given only in intervals.

8. 9.45

9. 275

10. 112.5

11. 36, $\frac{1}{4}$

12. 50

13. 288

14. $\frac{12}{125}$, 0.096, 9.6%

15. I expect to have to work from the time I am 21 years old until I am 65; $21 \leq x \leq 65$.

16. $\frac{7}{30}$

17. 7

18. 10.7

19. 30

20. 240 in.^{2}, 180 in.^{3}

21. 49π m^2; about 153.9 m^2

22. 7.29π in.^{2}; about 22.9 in.^{2}

23. JL = 25 cm, BC = 96 cm

24. 51°, obtuse

25. 85°, acute

26. 90°, right

27. 432 mL

28. 137 mi